The Praeger Handbook of Education and Psychology

Volume 2

Edited by JOE L. KINCHELOE AND
RAYMOND A. HORN Jr.

Shirley R. Steinberg, *Associate Editor*

Westport, Connecticut
London

Library of Congress Cataloging-in-Publication Data

The Praeger handbook of education and psychology / edited by Joe L. Kincheloe and
Raymond A. Horn Jr.
     v. cm.
    Includes bibliographical references and index.
    ISBN 0–313–33122–7 (set : alk. paper)—ISBN 0–313–33123–5 (vol 1 : alk. paper)—
    ISBN 0–313–33124–3 (vol 2 : alk. paper)—ISBN 0–313–34056–0 (vol 3 : alk. paper)—
    ISBN 0–313–34057–9 (vol 4 : alk. paper)   1. Educational psychology—Handbooks, manuals, etc.
    I. Kincheloe, Joe L.   II. Horn, R. A. (Raymond A.)
  LB1051.P635   2007
  371.4–dc22   2006031061

British Library Cataloguing in Publication Data is available.

Library of Congress Catalog Card Number: 2006031061
ISBN: 0–313–33122–7 (set)
      0–313–33123–5 (vol. 1)
      0–313–33124–3 (vol. 2)
      0–313–34056–0 (vol. 3)
      0–313–34057–9 (vol. 4)

First published in 2007

Praeger Publishers, 88 Post Road West, Westport, CT 06881
An imprint of Greenwood Publishing Group, Inc.
www.praeger.com

Printed in the United States of America

The paper used in this book complies with the
Permanent Paper Standard issued by the National
Information Standards Organization (Z39.48–1984).

10 9 8 7 6 5 4 3 2 1

Contents

VOLUME 2

PART III   ISSUES IN EDUCATION AND PSYCHOLOGY

Constructivism

VOLUME 4

Situated Cognition

Teaching

PART III

Issues in Education and Psychology

Constructivism

CHAPTER 37

Constructivism and Educational Psychology

MONTSERRAT CASTELLÓ AND LUIS BOTELLA

CONSTRUCTIVIST METATHEORY

As we discussed in previous works, essentially the prefix *meta-* indicates a reflexive loop. In this sense, a metatheory should be a theory that deals with the nature of theories, that is, with the nature of epistemic and paradigmatic assumptions implicit in theory construction. Such a definition is closely related to the use of the term *paradigm* to refer to a set of basic beliefs. Metatheories are superordinate to the content of any particular theory, and include at least two basic sets of assumptions: (a) *the nature of knowledge*, and (b) *epistemic values*.

As for the nature of knowledge, constructivist metatheory assumes that knowledge is a human construction, not the neutral discovery of an objective truth. Thus, it departs from the traditional objectivist conception of knowledge as an internalized representation of an external and objective reality.

Epistemic values are criteria employed to choose among competing explanations. Questions on epistemic values rarely arise in objectivist metatheory, since knowledge is viewed as a representation of reality and, consequently, explanations are chosen according to their truth value—that is, their correspondence with the external reality they represent. The objectivist conception of knowledge and truth are thus closely linked and imbued with science—with the reliance on *facts* to justify a given knowledge claim.

Constructivism cannot rely on the original/copy correspondence metaphor, since it departs from a representational conception of knowledge. Justification by means of the authority of truth is then regarded as an illusion. This nonjustificationist position leaves constructivist metatheory facing the task of articulating an alternative set of epistemic values, taking into account that values are, by definition, subjective preferences.

Although constructivist epistemic values vary according to different constructivist theories, all of them can be viewed as alternatives to the justificationist position. Two of the most pervasive sets of epistemic values in constructivist metatheory, however, correspond to (a) the pragmatic value of knowledge claims (i.e., their predictive efficiency, viability, and fertility) and (b) the coherence of knowledge claims (i.e., their internal and external consistency and unifying power).

A series of corollaries can be derived from these two basic epistemic assumptions of constructivist metatheory. In fact, different constructivist theories emphasize different possible corollaries. This differential emphasis led to the proliferation of different forms of constructivism. The next section of our work presents a brief discussion of six of such varieties (radical constructivism, social constructionism, narrative psychology, developmental constructivism, assimilation theory, and personal construct psychology) plus our own integrative proposal (relational constructivism).

CONSTRUCTIVIST THEORIES: UNITY AND DIVERSITY

Radical constructivism as discussed by authors such as Maturana and Varela, von Foerster, and von Glaserfeld rejects the possibility of objective knowledge, since all knowledge depends upon the structure of the knower. Thus, subject and object are constructions (or operations) of the observer, and not independently existing entities. Even if there is an ontological reality, we can only know it by assessing how well our knowledge fits with it. Thus, radical constructivism views knowledge as a construction—versus an internalized representation of an externally independent reality.

According to Maturana and Varela, living beings are autopoietic (self-creating or self-producing) systems in the sense that they are capable of maintaining "their own organization, the organization which is developed and maintained being identical with that which performs the development and maintenance." The notion of autopoiesis is supported by von Foerster's contention that the central nervous system operates as a closed system organized to produce a stable reality.

Organisms interact by means of structural coupling, that is, by codrifting and setting up the mutual conditions for effective action. Maturana and Varela equated effective action with survival. Consciousness and language emerge through the experience of structural coupling and effective action. By equating knowledge with effective action, or with viability, radical constructivism subscribes to the second theme in the definition of constructivist metatheory—the rejection of epistemic justificationism.

Social constructionism (as proposed chiefly by Kenneth Gergen) focuses explicitly on the role of social processes in the construction of meaning. Consequently, Gergen rejected both exogenic and endogenic epistemologies. Endogenic epistemologies are those that emphasize the role of the individual mind in the construction of meaning, while exogenic epistemologies emphasize the role of external reality. Social constructionism places knowledge neither within individual minds nor outside them, but between people. In other words, according to social constructionism, knowledge is generated by people interacting and collectively negotiating a set of shared meanings. By rejecting the objectivist conception of knowledge as an internal representation, social constructionism shares the view of knowledge as a construction—a social construction in this case.

The question of how to choose among knowledge claims has evolved in the work of social constructionists but, in any case, the criteria proposed by social constructionists can generally be seen as instances of the social and political uses of knowledge, and share the constructivist rejection of justificationism.

While both radical constructivists and social constructionists share the critique to representation and justificationism, the latter prefers the term *constructionism* to emphasize their mutual differences. Some reviewers have noted that while radical constructivism tends to promote an image of the nervous system as a closed unity, social constructionism sees knowledge as arising in social interchange, and mediated through language.

Narrative psychology proposes narrative emplotment as the organizing principle in the proactive construction of meaning. According to the seminal work of Theodore R. Sarbin, human beings make sense of otherwise unrelated events by imposing a narrative structure on them. Thus, for instance, when presented two or three pictures, we tend to construe the plot of a story that relates them to each other in some way and helps us predict how will it likely evolve. Narrative emplotment, then, equates knowledge with the anticipatory construction of narrative meaning.

Both Sarbin and Donald P. Spence proposed narrative smoothing as the criterion according to which knowledge claims are tacitly chosen. In his approach to self-deception, Sarbin noted how some people maintain self-narratives that are apparently counterfactual, a phenomenon traditionally explained by means of such mechanistic constructs as repression or dissociation. When narrative smoothing is used as an explanatory principle, however, such constructs are redundant. Narrative psychology proposes that people tacitly edit their self-narratives (by spelling out inconsistent information) so that the self as a narrative figure is protected, defended, or enhanced. Thus, narrative psychology shares the constructivist critique of knowledge justification by means of its correspondence with objective reality.

Developmental constructivism as originally discussed by Jean Piaget and further elaborated by researchers of postformal development also views knowledge as a proactive construction of the knowing organism. According to developmental constructivism (particularly Piaget's version of it), knowledge is an active construction of the knowing subject, triggered by the quest for equilibrium, that is, by the cognitive system's need for order and stability. Piaget's rejection of the empiricist conception of knowledge, for example, is founded on the constructivist notion that knowledge cannot be viewed as a copy of the external world.

Developmental constructivism also departs from the objectivist conception of truth as correspondence between mental representations and reality. According to most organismic perspectives, including the Piagetian approach, knowledge systems develop by means of recurrent qualitative shifts in the direction of increased complexity. Thus, knowledge can never be considered an accurate depiction of reality, since each new refinement will require justification at a newer and higher level. Developmental and organismic constructivism, then, equates useful knowledge with dialectically adaptive action, that is, the ability to adapt one's knowledge structures to the environment and to adapt the environment to one's knowledge structures.

Piagetian constructivism, however, is controversial in two ways. First, it limited its focus of convenience to the development of logico-mathematical reasoning from birth to adolescence. Second—and related—it equated adult cognition with the construction of a world that has been described as constituted by closed systems. The attempt to extend Piagetian thinking beyond formal operations has generated a growing body of research on adult cognition from metatheoretical positions even closer to constructivism than Piaget's initial one.

Assimilation theory as originally proposed by Ausubel represents an alternative constructivist approach to Piagetian ideas in educational psychology. Assimilation theory equates meaningful learning with the learner's deliberate effort to relate new knowledge to concepts he or she already possesses. Thus, learning is equated with meaning making instead of information processing, thereby emphasizing the proactive role of the learner's construction processes in the creation of new knowledge.

In assimilation theory terms, the usefulness of a new concept depends on its being relatable to other concepts in the subject's knowledge system—that is, its being assimilated. Propositions linking concepts are not necessarily right or wrong, true or false, but accepted or unaccepted by a community of learners. Thus, epistemic values can be viewed as a composite of social consensus (as proposed by social constructionism) and increasing complexity (as proposed by developmental constructivism).

Personal construct psychology (PCP) as originally proposed by George A. Kelly can be defined as a constructivist theory to the extent that one accepts the characterization of constructivist metatheory discussed above. Kelly's theory of personal constructs was the first attempt to devise a theory of personality based on a formal model of the organization of human knowledge. Kelly's philosophy of constructive alternativism asserts that reality is subject to many alternative constructions, since it does not reveal to us directly but through the templates that we create and then attempt to fit over the world.

The constructivist conception of knowledge as an anticipatory construction is explicit in PCP's fundamental postulate: a person's processes are psychologically channelized by the ways in which he or she anticipates events. PCP also shares the constructivist notion of predictive efficiency as an epistemic value.

Finally, what we call *relational constructivism* constitutes our attempt to press the dialogue between constructivism and social constructionism further and to enrich it with the voice of narrative and postmodern approaches. It is based upon the following nine interrelated propositions, all of them sharing the aforementioned set of constructivist metatheoretical principles:

1. Being human entails construing meaning.
2. Meaning is an interpretative and linguistic achievement.
3. Language and interpretations are relational achievements.
4. Relationships are conversational.
5. Conversations are constitutive of subject positions.
6. Subject positions are expressed as voices.
7. Voices expressed along a time dimension constitute narratives.
8. Identity is both the product and the process of self-narrative construction.
9. Psychological processes are embedded in the process of construing narratives of identity.

Even this sketchy discussion of different constructivist theories shows some features of the contemporary constructivist scene that we will focus on in the next pages.

First, not all of the constructivist approaches have the same theoretical status. Some of them constitute formal theoretical systems (e.g., PCP, Piaget's theory), while others are younger and, therefore, less developed.

Second, while all of the approaches mentioned broadly share a common conception of knowledge as a construction and nonjustificationist epistemic values, their mutual compatibility at subordinate levels is sometimes controversial. For instance, social constructionism and PCP differ in their relative emphasis on the social versus personal origin of construing. However, some PCP theorists have recently tried to reconcile both approaches by proposing a social constructivist psychology. Such reconciliation is also the explicit intention of our own efforts to articulate a *relational constructivist* framework in the realm of psychotherapy and a *socio-constructivist* one in the realm of educational psychology.

Similarly, some authors who even suggested that Piaget's philosophical assumptions are not constructivist (since the assimilation/accommodation process means that we can experience *outer reality* and distinguish it from our *inner world*) have questioned the compatibility between Piaget's approach and PCP. However, Piaget's approach has been included in our discussion because it has been explicitly characterized as constructivist by some other authors and is one of the most influential authors to first consider children as meaning makers. Thus, we are not suggesting that all constructivist theories constitute a unified whole, but that they share a superordinate core of metatheoretical assumptions. This shared metatheoretical core allows the ongoing exploration of cross-fertilizations between different constructivist approaches, the final goal being not an overarching unification but the increasing complexity of constructivist thought.

CONSTRUCTIVIST APPROACHES TO EDUCATIONAL PSYCHOLOGY

Before proceeding to specify the characteristics of the main constructivist approaches to educational psychology we need to locate it within the framework of constructivist epistemology.

Our aim in doing so is to approach educational psychology as a specific applied discipline that is both psychological and educational in itself.

From its very origins, discussions about the object of study of educational psychology have maintained two antagonistic positions: (a) regarding educational psychology as an *applied field of study of general psychology* and (b) regarding it as an *applied discipline* bridging the gap between psychology and education. The latter ultimately involves overcoming the psychological reductionism that is typical of the former, since it requires assuming that there are disciplines other than psychology that contribute to explaining and improving the teaching and learning processes. This vision leads to substantial changes in traditional approaches to educational psychology, which can be summarized as follows:

i. Fields of study should be prioritized taking into account the problems and issues experienced by practitioners;

ii. Instead of promoting an excessively specialized and technical discourse to explain and approach the problems generated by practice, it should be shared with practitioners in the educational field;

iii. The outcomes of educational psychology should be approached as means to improve educational practice;

iv. Educational psychology should accept the fact that its contributions are partial—although valuable—and they must thus be contrasted and combined with those coming from other disciplines also dealing with educational phenomena;

v. Educational psychologists should try to analyze the situated and implicit knowledge that professionals within the field of education have of their own practice, so as to be able to enrich it instead of trying to replace it with disciplinary and scientific knowledge;

vi. Finally, educational psychologists should take a stand in the ideological and ethical debates that characterize any educational option. Also, they should accept that contributing to the improvement of education necessarily entails taking part in the social debates dealing with core educational issues.

Having said that, the goal of educational psychology can be equated (in the words of César Coll) to the study of change processes taking place in people as a consequence of their participation in educational activities. Such a definition locates disciplinary knowledge halfway between a strictly psychological and an educational one. At the same time it incorporates the study of personal change processes (psychological knowledge), avoids reductionism, and fosters interdisciplinary approaches by placing such change processes within the broader framework of educational practices.

As an applied discipline—and in collaboration with the rest of educational disciplines— educational psychology is committed to elaborating a comprehensive scientifically based educational theory as well as to guiding a series of practices that are coherent with such a theoretical development. This provides a threefold dimension to educational psychology as a (a) theoretical, (b) technological, and (c) practical discipline.

Having thus defined the object of study of educational psychology, we will now focus our analysis on the varieties of constructivist approaches to educational psychology from a conceptual and epistemological point of view.

Educational psychology as a field is a subject of diverging theoretical and epistemological positions. In the last decades, authors from different conceptual traditions highlighted some common threads among such divergences:

i. The existence of an individual mind or, rather, the usefulness and need of studying intrapsychic processes *versus* the relevance of concepts such as "distributed mind" or "shared cognition."

ii. The existence and functionality of individual mental representations, the nature of these representations, and their relation to social processes.

iii. The validity of the units of analysis adopted according to the answer given to several previous questions. In this respect, the discussion focuses on the viability and validity of using units of analysis that can bring together both mind and culture.

We will devote the next paragraphs in our paper to discuss the different answers that may be given to the above questions by grounding the constructivist option in which we position ourselves.

Regarding the first question, it may be fruitful to focus the debate not so much on whether intrapsychic processes exist or not, but on the question of what can such processes add to our understanding of the learning process. For instance, if we adopt a broader approach to the concept of *mind*, the question could be, how does such a broadening affect our understanding of the processes taking place in the classroom?

The answer, at least taking into account what we presently know, cannot be a simple one. As Salomon argues in his compilation on distributed cognition, we may consider different entities in different contexts. Thus, in certain educational contexts cognition is likely to be a collective process, depending above all on the organization of such cultural contexts. A good example is classrooms which are organized as learning communities, that is, classrooms in which learning benefits from the social interaction among equals. However, not all contexts are organized in this way and, in some cases, they function as individual contexts as well. Thus, contexts where we think with others and contexts where we think on our own with the help of other cultural artifacts can coexist.

This point leads us to the second question suggested: the existence and/or functionality of the notion of individual mental representations. The connection between individual representations and social activities is difficult to ignore, but it is also obvious that it is not an isomorphic one, and that it is not always a smooth one. Salomon defines it as a "spiral of effects" that mutually influence each other.

Moreover, research results from studies on conceptual and representational change consistently question the existence of schematic representations that are stable and relatively independent from their context. As a result, among other things, of the persistence of implicit theories, the coexistence of contradictory knowledge, and the nonactivation of certain schemata in certain contexts, a new representational model has been proposed from cognitive psychology which is more in line with the social approach to learning and cognition, and more congruent with a view of cognitive functioning characterized by flexibility and adaptation to context.

Such a new model, as we have already pointed out in previous works, includes the existence of intermediate levels of representation between schemata and action—levels of a potentially explicit nature and highly context-dependent—called *mental models* (Liesa & Castelló, in press). We believe that this new representational model constitutes a potentially significant cornerstone for the construction of a new integrative paradigm in which individual representations as well as a cultural approach to teaching and learning processes can find room.

Finally, regarding the third of the threads suggested above and following the previous line of thought, we believe that it is not only possible but also highly desirable to broaden the unit of analysis of educational psychology to the social and cultural, that is, to action, activity, interaction, or interactivity. This is particularly the case if we assume that educational situations must be studied in context and that teaching and learning processes in school settings are always socially and culturally situated.

However, this does not solve the problem of the complexity of devising and conducting educational research studies in culturally situated contexts—quite the contrary. Even if an interactive unit of analysis facilitates the understanding of social action taking place in the classroom, it does not allow us to grasp the relationship between such an action and the different levels of representation as defined above. In this respect, even if options depend on the kind of research conducted and on the goals we want to accomplish, the most valid option is likely to be one that includes different complementary units of analysis capable of explaining both action and representation.

From what we have just discussed, it can be inferred that our positioning in constructivist educational psychology is neither a radically cognitivist nor an extremely social and cultural one. As we highlighted in previous works, we believe that the adoption of a *socio-constructivist* perspective is currently the most comprehensive and coherent option so as to respond to the challenges faced both by research and intervention in educational psychology.

CURRENT ISSUES IN EDUCATIONAL PSYCHOLOGY: A SOCIO-CONSTRUCTIVIST PERSPECTIVE

We would like to begin our analysis of the current state of the art in educational psychology by reflecting upon the implications of *research on specific content teaching and learning* in educational psychology. The tendency to study supposedly content-free psychological processes, highly criticized in the 70s, seems to have been finally abandoned to the extent that, in the next few years, the epistemology of disciplinary knowledge acquisition is likely to become one of the emergent areas in educational psychology.

We still don't know much about the processes of knowledge construction in specific content areas and, even if this is a field to be studied in collaboration with other disciplines, it is also an unavoidable one to face if educational psychology is to progress along these lines.

Regarding the line of interest dealing with the *teaching process*, advances in the understanding of the processes of new knowledge acquisition are clearer and more substantial than the ones focusing on the elucidation of educational influence or on criteria for enhancing teaching processes. This should be one of the future research lines in educational psychology, hence incorporating the results of studies conducted following social and cultural approaches and, particularly, relating these results to the ones on knowledge acquisition processes.

In terms of the dichotomy *descriptive versus experimental research* it should be noted that the development of educational psychology research in the last twenty years reveals an increasing tendency to design experimental research studies in contrast to descriptive studies. However, given the significant shortages and gaps in our understanding of such relevant elements as teaching processes, the relationship between explicit representations and implicit knowledge, or between representations in general and performance, and if we are to progress toward the integration of different theoretical perspectives, we will have to admit that it will be advisable to incorporate research strategies more focused on descriptive and interpretative studies.

Regarding the *relationship between the classroom and other educational settings*, we would like to point out that, as noted by other authors, considering the classroom as a privileged environment for the study of teaching and learning processes is a recent and increasingly significant trend. However, and concerning the research agenda, it would be necessary to also bear in mind the relationship between the classroom subsystem and other subsystems which are part of the educational context—institution, community, etc.—as well as the different levels in which the classroom is embedded—transcultural, national, and institutional.

Another relevant issue within educational psychology deals with the *relation between educational practices in school and in other contexts*. In this respect educational psychology research has historically focused on the study of educational practices in school. However, it will be necessary to incorporate the study of other educational practices in the future decades, especially taking into account that a great deal of career development thus require it, and that this kind of knowledge would redound in a better understanding of educational change. Emergent research about learning communities may accomplish this function.

Finally, we would like to briefly discuss the integration of different theoretical perspectives in emergent paradigms. Following other authors' considerations, we have already argued that we are witnessing the emergence of a new paradigm characterized by a necessary integration of cognitive and social assumptions which allows us to account both for the construction of individual representations and for the social situations where teaching and learning processes take place.

We believe that a large part of the research studies taking place in the next decades should decisively contribute to the articulation of this new integrative conceptual framework. In order for this to be possible, researchers must be sensitive to the present status of knowledge in educational psychology, and must also be capable of devising complex research studies addressing both the cognitive and the interactive aspects of instructional contexts.

FURTHER READING

Biddle, B. J., Good, T. L., and Goodson, I. F. (1997). *International Handbook of Teachers and Teaching.* Dordrecht, NL: Kluwer.

Claxton, G., and Wells, G. (Eds.). (2002). *Learning for Life in the 21st Century: Sociocultural Perspectives on the Future of Education.* Oxford, U.K.: Blackwell.

CHAPTER 38

Reconsidering Teacher Professional Development Through Constructivist Principles

KATHRYN KINNUCAN-WELSCH

The literature on the professional development of teachers through the decade of the 1990s and into the twenty-first century has highlighted one common theme: substantive professional development opportunities for teachers are sorely lacking. Many have pointed to the scarce resources dedicated to professional development; many have suggested that a focus on standards, curriculum, and student assessment has obscured the relationship between teacher learning and student learning; many have commented that the prevailing culture of schools and schooling poses barriers to teacher engagement in quality professional development. However one chooses to cast the current state of professional development for practicing teachers, it is clear that teachers are under closer public scrutiny than ever before, without any radical changes in support for improving classroom practice. It is in this context that I share a portrait of professional development for teachers that is grounded in constructivist principles. This portrait has evolved from over fifteen years of working with teachers, principals, curriculum directors, and teacher educators in designing professional development experiences that have deepened teachers' understandings of what and how children learn, and scaffolding those understandings to improved practice.

Constructivism has been discussed from multiple perspectives, including philosophical, psychological, social, and educational. These perspectives, of course, overlap when we shape what we do in the day-to-day realities of teaching and learning. The perspective that I bring to this chapter describing the professional development of teachers is that constructivism is a theory of learning that suggests that individuals make meaning of the world through an ongoing interaction between what they already know and believe and what they experience. In other words, learners actively construct knowledge through interactions in the environment as individuals and as members of groups. It is from this understanding of constructivism that I describe how professional development of teachers can be guided by constructivist principles of learning. It is worth noting here that the literature on constructivism has predominantly addressed students in PK-12 settings. An understanding of how teachers learn is critical to substantive and ongoing improvement of instruction in schools. It is with that premise in mind that I offer the following vignettes and related thoughts on the professional development of teachers through a constructivist lens.

TEACHERS CONSTRUCT THEIR OWN UNDERSTANDING THROUGH EXPERIENCES

The underlying principle of constructivism as a theory of learning is that the learner constructs meaning and deep understanding through experience. One might ask why constructing meaning and deep understanding is important. Teachers have available to them an abundance of ready-made lesson plans and scripted materials to guide them through the instructional day. Unfortunately, these ready-made materials do not support teachers in making those in-the-moment instructional moves that scaffold children to deep understanding and insights. Children come to any instructional setting and learning goal at very different places. Teachers must be able to craft instruction through varied pathways that brings every learner into the instructional conversation. This requires both knowledge of content and of related pedagogy. One way to accomplish this is to provide teachers with experiences that provide them with opportunities to explore the relationships between content knowledge and pedagogy.

Immersion and Distancing

One of the cornerstones of professional development initiatives that I have found to be successful is the notion of providing experiences for teachers through *immersion and distancing*. This simply means that when designing professional development, cofacilitators and I plan experiences that engage, or immerse, participants in some active learning connected to the goals of the professional development initiative. After that immersion, all the participants, including those facilitating the group, step back from the experience, or distance from it, and reflect on how the experience challenged their beliefs and practices. The reflection can be written in a journal and/or shared orally with group members. It is through the process of connecting the experience to currently held beliefs and practices that often leads to a dissonance, or space of discomfort. If teachers feel safe to experience this dissonance, then the way is open for new understandings about content and pedagogy. Let me share a few examples from my professional development work with teachers.

I cofacilitated groups of teachers in rural Southwest Michigan from 1994 to 1996, the Cadre for Authentic Education, who were interested in bringing constructivist principles to their teaching, particularly in the area of math and science. One of the first challenges we had as facilitators was to help the teachers construct an understanding of constructivist pedagogy. We designed a two-week summer immersion experience in which the teachers engaged in exploring the principles of constructivism in the morning and applied their emerging understandings with groups of children enrolled in a math and science summer camp during the morning of the second week. The schedule for this immersion is presented in Table 38.1.

We followed this two-week immersion with monthly meetings and site visits throughout the subsequent school year. We were committed to a professional development design that acknowledged that deep understanding and shifts in teaching can best be accomplished through ongoing immersion within the local context of teaching.

Our summer immersion activities followed principles of constructivist pedagogy by including learning through many modalities: reading and discussing books and articles, viewing videos, presentations by experts in the field, and group learning activities. During the second week, the teachers were immersed through pedagogy. Children from the surrounding school districts came during the morning to participate in learning activities that were planned by the teachers on the basis of the content and pedagogy that was being explored.

Each day of the two-week immersion allowed for ample time for distancing through dialogue, reflection, and journaling. The commitment to distancing was a departure from the prevailing professional development. Teachers often experience a "sit and get" scenario for staff development

Table 38.1
Schedule for *Cadre for Authentic Education* Two-Week Summer Immersion

	Monday	Tuesday	Wednesday	Thursday	Friday
		Cadre for Authentic Education Week of July 18			
8:00 a.m.	Overview	Opening (Administrator's Day #1) Sharon Hobson: "Constructing A Learning Community Through Communication"	Opening Judy Sprague: Lunar Activity	Opening Math Video: "Conceptual Change" Featuring Deb Ball	Assessment Issues Video: "Private Universe"
9:15 a.m.–9:25 a.m.	Break	Break	Break	Break	Break
9:30 a.m.	Action Learning Activity "Link Activities Forward" Reading: "Immersion and Distancing: The Ins and Outs of Inservice Education"	Sharon (Cont.) Links Forward	Reflection: Self-Assessment and Group Assessment "Identifying Content As it Relates to Core Curriculum"	Feedback: Balloon Activity (Assessment Criteria)	
11:30 a.m.	Lunch	Lunch	Lunch	Lunch	Lunch
12:00 p.m.	"Journaling—A Reflective Practice"	Judy Ball: "Cooperative Learning Groups: Establishing Standards"	Jeff Crowe: "Dynamics of Assessing Group Work"	Discussion/ planning—Options for Week II: Transference Models, Posing of Questions, Issues	Discussion/ planning
View Write: 3 areas: Talk–write Read–write Talk 5 minutes Write	Reading: "The Need for School-based Teacher Reflection"				

Table 38.1
(continued)

	Monday	Tuesday	Wednesday	Thursday	Friday
1:00 p.m.–1:15 p.m.	Break	Break	Break	Break	Break
1:15 p.m.	Constructivism: "Bridges and Transition"	"Problem Posing–Problem Solving: Building Common Understanding"	Reflection: Lunar Activity Assessment	Discussion/Planning	Discussion/Planning
2:15 p.m.	Days Review	Journaling	Journaling	Journaling	Journaling Wrap-up/Evaluation

2:30 p.m.–3:00 p.m. Resource "Library" open for inspection (Optional Activity)

Cadre for Authentic Education Week of July 25

	Monday	Tuesday	Wednesday	Thursday	Friday
8:00 a.m.	Opening			Administrators Day # 2	

Student Activities (Menu Choices)

	Monday	Tuesday	Wednesday	Thursday	Friday
Students Attend	Leaders: Judy Sprague Lunar-Based Activity	Leaders: Judy Ball Drew Isola Science Options Activities	Leaders: Judy Sprague Judy Ball Drew Isola Math/Science Option Activities	Leaders: Judy Ball Drew Isola Science Optionactivities	
11:30 a.m.	Lunch	Lunch	Lunch	Lunch	Lunch
12:00 p.m.	Discussion/Reflection/ Planning	Discussion/Reflection/ Planning	Deb Ball	Discuss Class Videos with Administrators/ Advocacy Planning with Administrators	Discussion/ Reflection/ Planning/ Evaluation (off site)
2:30 p.m.	Journaling	Journaling	Assessment Issues	Sharon reviews planning with teachers and administrators	Finalize first 1994–1995 follow-up meeting Journaling

that has little opportunity for lasting impact in the classroom. Immersion and distancing was an element of our design we were committed to and carried into our meetings with the teachers during the school year following the summer experience.

We asked the participants to create tangible artifacts of their active construction of meaning about constructivist pedagogy in the follow-up sessions during the school year. In one of the structured activities, the facilitators asked participants to share a problematic issue of experience with a peer, discuss how that problematic experience might be addressed, and articulate initial thoughts about an action. This engagement in active construction of meaning about constructivist pedagogy was particularly powerful for the teachers because it acknowledged that shifts in pedagogy are not simple. Teaching is a complex activity that is often structured around deeply embedded routines and practices. Our goal was to bring those routines to the surface, examine them, and reconstruct through dialogue with a trusted peer. Selected examples from the teachers are presented in Table 38.2.

The examples are clear indication that the teachers were grappling with the day-to-day conflicts of existing structures and expectations and their emerging understanding of constructivist pedagogy. The teachers were questioning not only the external demands such as mandated curriculum and assessment, but also their own struggles as they saw teaching and learning from a different perspective than they had in the past.

It is this struggle, perhaps, that best characterizes constructivist professional development. Teachers must be supported and encouraged through meaningful experiences to question their own beliefs and practices. Current professional development does very little to encourage this examination and reflection. As professional development for teachers continues to be closely scrutinized in this era of accountability, perhaps we will see a commitment from school districts and external professional development providers to learning though experience, *immersion*, and reflecting on how that experience should influence practice, *distancing*, as a necessary element of quality professional development.

Constructing Metaphorical Representations

It has frequently been said that teachers teach as they have been taught. Teachers come to the profession with deeply embedded mental models of classroom practice that have been shaped over many years as students in schools that have not changed much over time. As a facilitator of teacher learning, I have found it useful to engage teachers in uncovering their tacit, or embedded, belief systems. Teachers must realize what they believe and how those beliefs shape practice. Furthermore, within any professional development initiative that is directed toward changing practice, those embedded belief systems must be altered if enduring changes are to occur.

One of the ways that I have supported teachers in examining their belief systems is by asking them to think about their beliefs and practice through metaphor. Metaphors, expressed through language or physical artifacts, become a medium through which belief systems are challenged and opened to new ways of thinking about how teaching and learning should be. I will illustrate how I have used metaphors in two very different professional development initiatives.

The first example is taken from the Cadre for Authentic Education initiative described in the previous section. Teachers participated in this initiative as a way of bringing a more constructivist orientation to their pedagogy. As part of the two-week summer immersion experience, the teachers constructed mobiles of learning that represented classroom practice as it currently existed in their classroom and also, in contrast, practice from a constructivist perspective. The physical construction from each group was very different, but each mobile clearly represented teaching and learning from two very different sets of principles about classroom organization, curriculum, and instruction. For example, one group represented the traditional classroom as three primary colors;

Table 38.2
Selected Responses From Follow-Up Meeting Activity.
Cadre '94 For Authentic Education,
Allegan County InterMediate School District,
October 11, 1995

Reflections on Constuctivist Teaching/Learning: The following is a synthesis of participants' sharings from the activity on selecting a problematic issue of experience, which emerged directly in relationship to changing the teacher "self" and/or their classroom toward a more constructivist orientation. Included are the original problems or issues (in first person) and the shared peer-assisted solutions. In each problem and solution, the underlined areas indicate what each participant identified as constructivist terms, concepts, or language.

Problematic Issues or Experience	**Peer-assisted Solution**
The squelched *creativity* of students is an issue for me. I play a song "Animals Crackers in My Soup," and asked the 5 & 6 year-olds to act it out. Most of them stood around until I finally stood up and did it with them. They then copied my actions. How do I get little ones to think creatively on their own and in groups? They seem to do well in play.	As I watch them at play, I could praise the creative thinking as I perceive it. Later when we have a *group activity*, I could have them *reflect back* to the kind of thinking they were doing during play. By helping them to *become aware of and feel good about their own ideas*, they will be *encouraged* to be more creative.
I have been working on a unit on the solar system. Students are *very interested* in this. They have *willingly researched* the planets and reported on them. They have *created* their own planets, etc. However, the unit has taken too long. I have been told that I should be on rocks and minerals by now. I have to "cover the whole list of outcomes."	I know the students have *internalized* the information covered in this unit and the *ownership* they feel. This attitude is a *reflection* of the "traditional" approach to education. I must gently help those ignorant of *constructivism* become familiar with it. I will invite them in to *experience* the *enthusiasm* of the students and to *interact* with them. I will probably limit the time spent on the next unit, if really necessary, but try to allow some *constructivist* activities as well.
My administrator is "test driven" and very concerned with keeping everyone happy. There are to be no changes with the way things are—status quo is *encouraged*. I find it difficult to be defending my *constructivist approach* on a daily basis only because it causes the administration problems with a few parents. The *children* are happy and *enthusiastic*, I might add but no classroom visits are made. It could be me! A personality conflict, perhaps. (In which case there maybe no hope!!)	I think I might try a 4-part approach. (1) Invite the principal, other staff to visit and help *evaluate often*. (2) Find reasons to have parents in the room—*often*. (3) Once a week give an objective test covering the concepts in the subject that week. (4) Have kids *journal* often about *what I saw, what I learned, how I can use it*—then share as much as possible with principal and peers (yours). Finally, I'd call Cadre members to vent! Oh, I'd also send parents frequent (weekly) notes about what we're doing and why. P.S. Been There!—*Rubrics* (frequent help too. Share rubrics with principal.)
I had 16 groups (4 classes) of kids doing agency. The agency groups had to develop a complete advertising campaign to try to capture a company account. The *scaffolding* included the psychological and secondary needs of man, ad techniques, analyzing ma., TV, radio, and billable adds. When they worked, I allowed *space* for the	Upon reflection, I would supply the superintendent and principal with an outline or some statement of goals and objectives and a *rubric* with respect to assessment techniques—prior to performance. This would indicate to the powers to be that while errors were (will be) made, they were those of the students

Table 38.2
(continued)

groups to take *total ownership*. Finally, when they presented, the technical end was poor, they didn't have the things ready, wasted time locating on the tape, etc. Very bad looking to superintendent and principal. How do I allow ownership, yet have quality control.	(possibly mine, in terms of criteria), the less-than-perfect presentation was a powerful learning tool, and that *we* (as learners) would improve because of them.
I have always struggled with using groups (*cooperative learning*) in my class. Frequently I will find that many of the groups become dysfunctional because of personality clashes and behavioral problems. I have a hard time with the philosophy that all students need to become accepting enough so that they can "get along" with and work with others no matter what. Many times I can't blame students for refusing to work with certain students since I wouldn't want to work with them either given their attitude and behavior.	I think I will begin some *teaming and trust building* so the students will *respect each other*. I can think of situations where once I got to know, really know some people whose behaviors and attitudes were offensive to me that I understand why those behaviors and attitudes were covers for self-protection. If I can create situation(s) that allow this *bonding* to happen then it should carry over in the content groups. I might also work on taking the grading pressure and task pressure off of getting the task done with a good grade. Also, I might take the students aside on a regular basis to talk about why they behave as they do, suggesting some of the possibilities until I find the nerve that triggers the behavior. Once it's out then maybe we can deal with it. Another way might be to look at the number of tasks in the *groups* so all are important and necessary.

within the constructivist classroom the teacher was seen as the artist's hand holding a paintbrush and the student's hand was laid on the artist/teacher's hand. Another group used a jigsaw puzzle as the organizing theme. In the traditional classroom, all the pieces were disconnected; in the constructivist classroom, all pieces were interlocking and labeled with the following characteristics: (1) unlimited possibilities, (2) adaptation to the situation and the needs of the learner, (3) the possibility of an unfinished puzzle, and (4) no specific pattern. A third group constructed an umbrella and depicted the characteristics of constructivism along each spoke. Another group portrayed their past and evolving belief systems as a tapestry, which wove the tenets of constructivism into traditional theory and practice. The materials, natural and irregular such as ivy and wheat, were representative of children's natural curiosity. Cheesecloth was representative of the filtering of new ideas. An electronic cable represented the flow of energy through life. Ivy represented new beginnings. The teachers shared their physical metaphors with each other, and the conversation provided the teachers the opportunity to examine and reflect on beliefs and practice.

A second example of how metaphors can be incorporated into a professional development is taken from an initiative funded by a Michigan Department of Education Goals 2000 professional development grant awarded to a consortium of twenty-five districts in an urban area of Southeast Michigan. The purpose of the initiative, Staff Development 2000, was to examine how study groups can serve as a means for teachers and administrators to continue learning throughout their profession. A second purpose was to examine facilitation as a process within professional development.

As a culminating activity at the end of the eighteen-month initiative, the fifteen teachers and administrators who participated in this initiative gathered for a two-day writing retreat for the purpose of capturing what we had learned from our experiences as members and facilitators of a study group. One of the ways we captured our learning was through written metaphors that addressed the question What is a study group? As in the metaphorical representations of constructivist practice, the participants were encouraged to uncover their belief systems about study groups and represent their construction of meaning through metaphors. An example of the metaphors about study groups is below.

> A study group is the collection of passengers huddled together on the steerage deck of a ship as it steams into New York harbor at the turn of the century. A diverse collection of folks, each bringing a unique set of talents and experiences, coming together for a common purpose. Motivated and willing to do whatever it takes to achieve a common and highly desired goal.

The participants in this initiative had, for the first time, the opportunity to learn in community with others. The metaphor above illustrates how this participant experienced the journey of learning in and about study groups.

In summary, having the opportunity to construct meaning through immersion and distancing and through metaphorical representations of past, present, and evolving belief systems is an important element of professional development grounded in constructivist principles. The second element of constructivist professional development I would like to describe is the importance of learning in community.

TEACHERS LEARN IN COMMUNITIES OF PRACTICE

The recent literature on the professional development of teachers has emphasized the importance of community as a context for learning. From a constructivist perspective, theoretical bases for this assumption can be found in the notions of assisted performance, situated cognition, and communities of practice, as well as many others. Building and sustaining a community of practice as a context for professional development has been one of the most important guiding principles that has influenced my work with teachers.

In a community of practice, teachers come together for a specific purpose that is defined by the community. The specific purpose is typically related to critically examining pedagogy. Communities of practice are characterized by three aspects: (1) mutual engagement, (2) engagement negotiated by members of the community, and (3) development of shared repertoire.

Teachers participate in mutual engagement, or activity, that supports learning. The activity becomes the context in which teachers socially construct emerging understanding about teaching and learning. The activity may include reading books and articles, observing the members of the community teach, and examining student artifacts. The mutual engagement can occur at grade levels, in a building, across an entire district, or beyond district boundaries.

The second aspect of community of practice is that the engagement is negotiated by the members of the community. This is particularly noteworthy given the reality in most districts that teachers participate in district-level mandated professional development that is often disconnected from their practice and needs. In a community of practice, the teachers decide the focus of their learning and how they will structure the engagement to support that learning.

Finally, teachers as members of a community of practice develop a shared repertoire. Teachers engage in conversations about their practice, and each other's practice. They talk about students as also being members of communities of practice. Teachers and students are engaged in the mutually supportive activity recognizable by a shared repertoire.

Teachers have made it very clear to me that learning with others is the most powerful aspect of any given professional development experience, regardless of the content. It is amazing to me that the literature on professional development is so clear on this point, yet policies and practice have not taken this seriously. Teachers for the most part still teach in isolation, with little opportunity for learning from others. There is hope, however, that this is changing. Before I turn to the future, I would like to describe a few ways in which I, and others with whom I have worked, have structured professional development to support the development of authentic communities of practice.

Initial Immersion Experiences

It is critically important to begin any professional development experience with an event that communicates to the participants that they will be engaged as members of a community. If the professional development experience has a clearly demarcated beginning and an end, such as a funded project, then initial and culminating events are appropriate. If the experience is ongoing, such as teachers forming a school community, then the events must be ongoing and authentic.

I have started and ended many grant-funded initiatives with a two-day retreat in a location some distance from where the participants live. A retreat provides the opportunity for intensive immersion and distancing activities, as well as time for conversation and relationship building over meals. From a constructivist perspective, retreat activities must be designed to engage the participants in constructing their initial understanding of the focus of the initiative in the company of and with the assistance of others.

One example of a retreat that was designed from a constructivist perspective was the beginning event for Staff Development 2000, the initiative described above focusing on the exploration of study groups and facilitation. We were fortunate in that the group in this initiative was rather small. Twelve persons joined the group: one principal, two technology coordinators, two staff development coordinators, and seven teachers. My cofacilitators and I wanted to model for the participants ways of facilitation that respected the processes of learning as well as the product. We also wanted to emphasize the importance of trust among group members in a learning community.

Our first activity as an evolving community of learners was a meal, a cornerstone of all community activity. In addition to common mealtime, the retreat activities included generating questions about study groups and facilitation and allowing the participants to address these questions from knowledge and previous experience. Acknowledging where learners are is a foundational principle of a constructivist theory of learning. Posing questions and processing current thinking about those questions provided a starting place for our construction of meaning about study groups and facilitation.

Another powerful activity during the retreat was the Rope Activity, which was designed to build trust and community among the Staff Development 2000 participants. During this activity, the participants were placed in two groups, each with a designated leader. All participants were required to wear blindfolds. Once all had been given blindfolds, the group leaders were taken to another room. The group members were told that they could not speak during the activity, they must hold on with at least one hand to a rope, and they must remain blindfolded throughout the entire activity. The group leaders were also given instructions. They, too, were blindfolded and remained silent throughout. Their task was to guide their respective group members into forming a square while holding onto a rope.

After the groups had accomplished their task of forming a square, everyone removed their blindfolds and shared their thoughts about the experience. Many talked about how they had been uneasy since they could not see and could not talk. Some felt that it was a trick and that others were able to remove their blindfolds. Some were worried they would lose their balance. But, despite the individual feelings of distrust, unease, and discomfort, all responded that the touch of the group leader and the connection to group members through the rope sustained them during the moments of darkness and silence. Many of the participants used the words *trust* and *teamwork* to express the elements of the process. This activity, as well as the entire retreat, was powerful as an initial immersion experience to form community for the SD 2000 participants.

Sustained Engagement of Community Over Time

From a constructivist perspective, the initial forging of community is critical to professional development experiences that will have lasting power for teachers. These initial experiences, however, are useless if they are not followed by sustained engagement. The prevailing professional development venue is a brief, often less than one day, workshop that is unlikely to have any impact on practice. These short workshops are based on a transmission model of learning that suggests if you just give information and tell people what to do, then they will have learned it and applied it as well. As we know, this is not the case for children as learners, nor is it the case for adults as learners. Deep understanding requires deep and sustained engagement. Teachers must have time to grapple with existing belief systems and explore how shifting belief systems translate to practice. *Cadre for Authentic Education* and *Staff Development 2000* both extended over eighteen months and some teachers from both of these initiatives continued to meet beyond the funded initiative. They held regular meetings, either during the day (Cadre) or in the evening (SD 2000) over a school year. In both of these instances, as the year and the initiatives unfolded, the participants identified themselves by a name for their group. The *Cadre for Authentic Education* group came to call themselves simply "Cadre," the *Staff Development 2000* group came to call themselves the "Thursday Night Group" because our meetings throughout the year were held on Thursday nights.

The point I would like to emphasize here is that in both of these instances, educators from different school districts and highly varied experiences forged a learning community over time. These communities were safe places to take a risk, as all learning involves somewhat of a risk. The Cadre participants attempted new ways of teaching that reflected constructivist principles, and they had the opportunity to share their attempts and what they were learning about constructivist pedagogy during facilitated monthly meetings. They continued to explore pedagogy through reading, videos, and team teaching.

The Thursday Night Group also found the engagement over time to be an essential aspect of their professional development. This group began forging their community during a retreat in August and met twice a month following that retreat. During these monthly meetings they explored study groups as a medium for professional learning with the knowledge that they would be facilitating a study group of their own for the final months of the school year. During the culminating retreat at the end of the initiative, one of the participants commented: "I, well, I guess I really feel, that for the most part, there, there's something that happened between us all. That we don't want to lose in some way."

In summary, community is an important feature of professional development from a constructivist perspective. I have found that it is critical to the success of professional development to provide opportunities for the development of communities of practice, including an intensive initial experience and sustained engagement over time. I now turn to the last principle from a constructivist perspective that I have incorporated into professional development design, providing for intentional assistance.

TEACHERS LEARN THROUGH ASSISTED PERFORMANCE

We all learn with the help of others. Young children take their first steps holding onto the hands of another. Cultures across the world provide examples of how members of society are apprenticed into roles. Novices study with accomplished members of professions. These examples demonstrate that humans learn by watching, doing, and receiving feedback. It is sad to note, however, that mechanisms for providing assistance to practicing teachers are weak, at best, and often nonexistent. Yet we know from the literature that competent assistance in the context of authentic tasks provides powerful opportunities to improve teaching.

One promising development in this arena is emerging in schools across the United States. That is, many schools are identifying accomplished teachers and designating a portion of their time, often full day, to coach teachers in improving pedagogy. In some cases, this practice focuses on entry-year teachers as part of statewide mentoring programs for novice teachers. In other cases, districts have placed literacy and mathematics coaches in buildings to support improved pedagogy in literacy and mathematics.

I am currently involved in a State of Ohio professional development initiative, the Literacy Specialist Project, which began in 2000. Faculty from several universities across Ohio work with groups of literacy specialists, or coaches, who, in turn, work with groups of teachers in their buildings or districts. In my work with the coaches I have been very interested in supporting and examining how coaches provide assistance to teachers. One of the ways we have been able to capture and analyze this process is through taped conversations between teachers and coaches in which they systematically analyze a transcript of a lesson that the teacher had previously taught. The coach-teacher dyads analyze the instruction for evidence of instructional features as well as evidence of how the teacher scaffolds the children toward the instructional goal. An excerpt of one such conversation follows. Susan is the coach; Connie is the teacher. They were analyzing a transcript of a lesson Connie had taught in which the instructional focus was on retelling a story.

Susan: I got the sense that they didn't know exactly how to go about retelling a story with puppets. Since I wasn't there, I got the sense that they were doing things with the puppets so they were thinking and therefore engaged at the thinking level with the story, but not at the level you wanted them to be where they actually going to talk . . . the purpose of this lesson to engage them in dialogue.
Connie: Exactly, exactly.
Susan: What do you think? Do you have any ideas about how that might?
Connie: I know that my next story, and I already know what I want to do, will be done differently. As I read it to them, I will engage them in the responses of the little red hen, and so when they say "not I" said the cat, "not I" said the dog, we will already begin rehearsing it before we do the retelling.
Susan: So you're going to use a more predictable book?
Connie: Yes.
Susan: I think that will probably be a good start with them. The other thing I was wondering about is perhaps you might want to consider reading them the story the session before and what do you think about actually modeling the retelling with the stick puppets so they could actually see what a retelling looks like.

In this brief excerpt, we can see that the coach opened with specific feedback and followed with suggestions to the teacher related to what she might do in future lessons to support the children in being more successful in retelling a story.

Transcript analysis is one way in which coaches assist teachers in improving their teaching. Coaches also go into classrooms to model practice, assist teachers in planning lessons incorporating the desired practice, and observe teachers during instruction. This time and labor-intensive professional development is powerful because it is situated in the context of practice. Teachers receive feedback in the moment and can make adjustments in their instruction immediately. The teacher has multiple opportunities to make sense out of the interaction with the coach in nonthreatening and supportive ways.

So, to summarize these thoughts on professional development from a constructivist perspective, I would suggest that the teachers as learners must be central to the design of professional development. We must first acknowledge teachers are learners, and provide ample and meaningful experiences through which they can construct their own understanding of the content of the professional development. Second, building communities of practice is critical for teachers to continue to learn throughout their professional career. Participants in every professional development effort I have facilitated emphasize the importance of learning with others. Finally, opportunity to situate the learning in practice through expert assistance is fundamental. Other professions have recognized this goal and have embedded those opportunities within the career cycle. Why should teachers, who in many respects represent the future in what our children will become, be denied that same opportunity? We know how to create these experiences. The challenge is to structure schools so that they can be.

TERMS FOR READERS

Assisted Performance—What a learner, child or adult, can accomplish with the support of more capable others; of the environment; and of objects, or tools, in the environment. That point at which the learner can successfully accomplish a task, whether it be physical or cognitive, is identified at the zone of proximal development. Assisted performance, then, is teaching within the zone of proximal development.

Community of Practice—Persons who come together for a specific purpose that is defined by mutual engagement. The mutual engagement is what defines the community. For a group of teachers who have come together for professional development, the mutual engagement is learning and professional growth. The second aspect of community of practice is joint engagement negotiated among the members. The third aspect of community of practice is the development of a shared repertoire. (see Wenger (1998) for further descriptions)

Constructivism—A theory of learning that draws from philosophical, psychological, and social origins that posits that persons create (construct) their own understandings of the world through an interaction between what they know and believe and with what they come into contact. Some theorists have emphasized the individual interacting with the environment as the source for knowledge construction. Other theorists have emphasized the importance of those encounters occurring in social settings. The fundamental point of agreement, however, is that the learner is engaged in the active construction of knowledge.

Distancing—Reflecting on an experience for the purpose of making connections to one's context and practice. From a constructivist perspective, distancing from an experience provides the opportunity to actively construct knowledge and shape beliefs through that experience.

Immersion—Deep and substantive engagement in some activity or experience that is connected to a learning goal. Immersion can take many forms: reading a text, viewing a video, teaching a lesson, or constructing a physical representation of classroom practice are but a few examples.

FURTHER READING

Kinnucan-Welsch, K., and Jenlink, P. M. (1998). Challenging assumptions about teaching and learning: Three case studies in constructivist pedagogy. *Teaching and Teacher Education*, 14(4), 413–427.

Lave, J. (1996). Teaching, as learning, in practice. *Mind, Culture, and Activity: An International Journal*, 3, 149–164.

Richardson, V. (Ed.). (1997). *Constructivist Teacher Education: Building a New World of Understandings*. London: The Falmer Press.

Tharp, R. G, and Gallimore, R. (1988). *Rousing Minds to Life: Teaching, Learning, and Schooling In Social Context*. Cambridge, U.K.: Cambridge University Press.

Wenger, E. (1998). *Communities of Practice: Learning, Meaning, and Identity*. Cambridge, U.K.: Cambridge University Press.

CHAPTER 39

Constructivist/Engaged Learning Approaches to Teaching and Learning

CYNTHIA CHEW NATIONS

The author facilitated a class entitled "Inquiry-Based Instruction." The main objective of the class was to transform teacher leadership in instructional planning and implementation of learner-centered pedagogy. This goal was accomplished through reading case studies, employing effective learning experiences in the classroom, in-class activities and discussion, and writing in a reflective journal. This writing includes teachers' voices as expressed in these reflective journals. (Permission was granted by students to use excerpts from their journals; students' names are not disclosed.)

In order to provide our children with the skills they need to function in today's society, constructivist theory and engaged learning practices and approaches have emerged as educators struggle with questions about how to improve teaching and learning. This chapter will describe teachers' experiences and reflections as they examine their own fundamental belief systems about teaching and learning.

Scenario 1: Forty-two *middle school teachers are attending a professional development session centered on changing paradigms in education. In their groups, the teachers are asked to divide a large chart tablet in two columns. On one side they are asked to draw and describe the child of yesterday and discuss how school, learning, the family environment, teachers, the community, and society, were "back then." In the second column, the teachers were asked to draw and describe the child of today—how schools operate, how we learn, family environments and situations, teachers, the community, and our society of today.*

Scenario 2: *A group of fourth-grade teachers are working together to discuss instructional improvement. The question about English Language Learners frequently surfaces, "If research tells us it takes three to ten years to become proficient in reading and writing, why is it there a state mandate for them to take THE TEST in three years? What can we do to help our students?*

Scenario 3: *A group of thirty graduate students are taking a course—"Inquiry-Based Instruction." Their task on the first evening of class is to build a parachute. They are divided into six groups of five. Each group is provided with a set of directions, and materials to build the parachute are provided on a large table in the center of the room. They are to follow the directions, be able to demonstrate how their parachute works, and discuss the creative processes they experienced in their groups. The* *directions provided to each group were different—ranging from specific directions, to some direction, to no direction at all (just build a parachute).*

What do the three scenarios have in common? Teachers experience similar situations as they struggle to examine classroom practices and to improve learning for all students. There are many external political, economic, and social influences that effect education. Teachers work with children in a world different from the world they experienced as a child. Students come to school from different cultures and backgrounds. Students come to school with family problems and differences in first language and English literacy levels. How do we teach students who are marginalized by their background, socioeconomic status, language, lack of academic achievement, and lack of support? How can we best serve these students? Do we really believe "all students can learn?"

CHILDREN OF THE TWENTY-FIRST CENTURY AND CHANGING TEACHING AND LEARNING

It is necessary for educators, society, and families to understand the world in which our children live before we can identify the need to change our pedagogical practices. For children in past generations, knowledge was *finite* and limited. Teachers passed on their own knowledge while students sat, passively listened, and did not have opportunities to explore and expand their learning. In traditional learning environments today, the teacher continues to direct and lead the instruction following structured lesson plans. In traditional lessons, skills are taught sequentially and lower-level skills are "mastered" before students are allowed to participate in activities that involve evaluation, synthesis, or analysis (higher-level activities). Students work individually on specific skills and objectives, and they are evaluated with end-of-chapter and end-of-book tests, six weeks content tests, and other standardized tests that are designed to evaluate the content delivered to them by the teacher.

For children growing up in today's society, knowledge is *infinite*. Our perceptions about what schooling should look like are a mismatch with the reality of today's children. With the need to create effective and engaging pedagogy that addresses the learning needs and styles our students, we look to learning models that provide student-centered instruction, interactive learning environments, and alternative assessment practices. In constructivist and engaged learning student-centered approaches to learning, lessons are less formal and rigid; lessons are more individualized and skills are relevant to students' experience and prior knowledge; students are provided with opportunities to participate in higher- and basic-level skills during the activities; group work is encouraged; and alternative methods of testing and assessment are used. Family and societal support go hand-in-hand with school support as required contexts for necessary changes in teaching and learning.

Classroom learner-centered instructional issues are the focus of school improvement discussions. What is constructivism and engaged learning? Why are these methods difficult to implement in classrooms? How do we assess learning for understanding? How do we focus on learner understanding while preparing them for norm- and criterion-referenced testing that is a requirement in our current accountability systems? Will students be successful? Do we believe all children can learn? What systems need to be in place in order to improve our classroom practices? How do we become transformative teachers?

WHAT IS CONSTRUCTIVISM AND ENGAGED LEARNING?

Constructivism and engaged learning will be used synonymously due to the similarities of the activities utilized in classroom practices. Similar philosophies include: problem-based learning and project-based learning. Engaged learning includes collaborative and cooperative, as well as individualized, activities. When engaged learning experiences are utilized in the classroom, students become independent thinkers and learners who participate in, and extend, their own learning processes. Students develop life-long skills and strategies that help them apply knowledge in situations outside the classroom. Students are actively involved in their own learning.

Journal entry: I have always considered myself to be a good teacher; however, my goal is to be an effective one. I consider myself a life-long learner who attends workshops and reads educational material to improve my craft. Administrators and teachers have always complimented me on my classroom management, and parents would request me for their children because of my structured environment in the classroom. My test scores on the state test were always impressive because I taught what needed to be taught in order for students to be successful on the exam. Now, I realize there are holes in my teaching, gaps between what my students need to learn at the moment and what they need to learn to become life-long learners. I don't want my students to learn something that will benefit them for the moment; I want them to acquire knowledge which they can utilize the rest of their lives.

As instructional issues are discussed and debated in schools today, big differences exist between constructivism, a theory about knowledge and learning in the information age, and traditional practices of teaching and learning. The traditional learning model views the teacher as the source of knowledge and the students as the receptacles of knowledge. While the students listen, the teacher is center stage, following the didactic model of teaching in which content information is provided by the teacher. Students are required to listen and "learn" (memorize) the content. In traditional teaching the previous background and experiences of students are not taken into account. Students sit still and absorb the information presented by the teacher, and students usually work alone. If they do work with others, groups are usually formed placing students of similar abilities together.

This notion of teaching and learning contrasts with the constructivist/engaged learning model (Figure 39.1) that emphasizes the creation of active learning environments promoting learner-centered critical thinking, collaboration, and discovery. The constructivist model of teaching and learning focuses on the student. The teacher designs student-centered lessons and facilitates student learning during the lesson. Students are provided with opportunities to think, problem-solve, investigate, and explore; and they are allowed to individually and collaboratively construct their own understanding of the content. As students collaborate, discuss, and share their prior knowledge and experiences with each other, they learn the content of the lesson.

Journal entry: After the presentation of the history of constructivism, I realized the theory is not new. It has been around for hundreds of years. It's interesting that it's been hundreds of years since constructivist learning was first introduced, and we are still working on ways to implement these strategies. I feel there are several reasons for this. It is very difficult for teachers to let students be responsible for their own learning. It is easier for students to depend on their teachers to "spoon-feed" the information.

In order to provide children with the skills they need to function in today's society, educators are examining different teaching and learning models that differ from traditional approaches used in the past. Constructivist education empowers student learning through the construction of meaning in a learner-centered inquiry environment. Learning in constructivist terms is both the process and the result of questioning, interpreting, and analyzing information; using this information and thinking process to develop, build, and alter our meaning and understanding of concepts and ideas; and integrating current experiences with our past experiences and what we already know about a given subject. Engaged learning and the constructivist learning model

Figure 39.1
Constructing New Knowledge

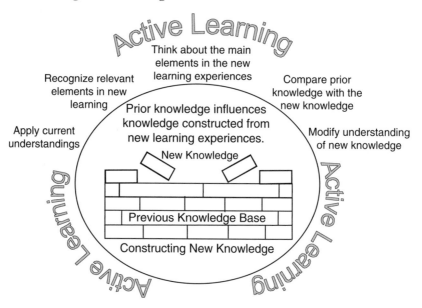

are in direct contrast to traditional methods in which teachers provide students with unchanging knowledge they are to memorize.

Journal entry: I thought I knew what constructivism was, but the more I learn, the less I know. I guess that this is true of most things in life. I think an important word here is disequilibrium. To have to examine and reflect on my practices and beliefs of education has had an unbalancing effect. I guess I thought I had it all together before I discovered constructivist approaches to use in my classroom.

If we are to meet students' needs and help them to be successful now and in the future, classroom planning, instructional practices, and the way we assess will undergo changes. Some recommendations include:

1. recognizing, planning, and creating learning experiences that cover the skills that are to be learned at every grade level *versus* teaching lessons that do not follow the recommended curriculum

2. planning learning experiences that will increase self-directed learning *versus* teacher-directed learning

3. planning for learning that is collaborative and communicative *versus* individual learning

4. the use of different instructional methods and grouping *versus* traditional whole-class instruction

5. instructional planning that recognizes student differences *versus* addressing differences after students have failed

6. using multiple forms of diagnostic assessment (formative and summative) before, during, and after the lesson *versus* summative assessments at the end of the lesson

7. recognizing and believing all students can learn *versus* sorting students out (tracking) to provide them with different learning experiences that might not be at grade level or up to the standard.

Teachers want to improve classroom practices, but have doubts about utilizing learner-centered approaches in their classrooms.

Journal entry: I do believe that many of us have tried to implement this kind of classroom environment where the students work on hands-on projects and develop their critical thinking skills while conducting their own research and investigations. I find it very rewarding to see the students' anticipation and excitement when I present them with the next unit of study in which they will be engaged. I have really tried to empower them to construct their own learning, and I've seen a difference even in the students that don't usually seem excited about doing schoolwork. I believe that half the battle is won when a teacher manages to engage and excite the students about learning.

WHY ARE ENGAGED LEARNING METHODS DIFFICULT TO IMPLEMENT?

In spite of a growing body of evidence that supports constructivism and engaged learning methods, teachers and students do not adjust easily to different ways of learning and teaching. A dichotomy exists between traditional (directed/didactic) approaches to learning and teaching and constructivist and engaged learning approaches. The way we learn and teach has shifted from a purest, cognitive traditional approach that has been present since the Industrial Age to more problem- and inquiry-based, learner-centered, constructivist approaches.

Constructivist and engaged learning practices represent a significant departure from teachers' established teaching philosophies, their own experience in school, and the way teaching was modeled for them in their student teaching experience. Also, in many instances, support and understanding from administration, school boards, parents, the community, and other teachers do not convey support for implementation.

Journal entry: I believe that all of us want to achieve these goals, but due to outside influences such as time management, reluctant administrators, and an uncooperative staff, we are constantly discouraged and thrown off our paths.

Journal entry: It is difficult to implement new ways of teaching and learning because of several major changes that have taken place at our school. One is that we are working very closely with our colleagues at school. I believed it would be a welcome change to work with individuals who felt as I did, but this is simply not the case. We are learning about progressive education and critical pedagogy, and these concepts are really difficult since everything we read points to the fact that education is not an isolated action that takes place in the classroom. It has been disheartening that not all teachers recognize and agree with this while some of us do.

Change is slow, and one recommendation for implementation is for teachers to "ease" in to experimenting with different approaches. In the traditional model of learning and teaching, students' experiences, background knowledge, and practical knowledge of the content is not considered when designing classroom learning activities. Students are required to learn book knowledge that is often unrelated to the practical knowledge they experience in their own lives. When teachers acquire knowledge about engaged learning and constructivist approaches to lesson design, they are often willing to try new approaches. It is important not to dive in to the water at warp speed! Rather, wading into the waters gradually would be a better beginning and will lead to sustained practice. When designing lessons, teachers can include constructivist/engaged learning activities and assessments in their lessons to see how the process works. Reflection is encouraged:

1. Were the students successful?
2. Did students know about the content to be learned, how they were going to learn it, and how they would be assessed?

Figure 39.2
Learning Together

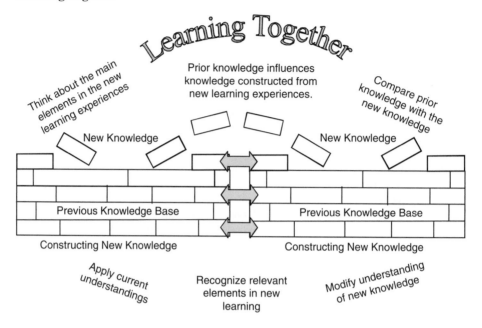

3. How did I feel about trying out new approaches?
4. Did I "let go" and allow students to explore the content and think for themselves?
5. Were students allowed to work collaboratively and share their own knowledge of the content with each other?
6. Did I assess in different ways before, during, and after the lesson?

How can a teacher start designing lessons that will engage learners? Learning experiences are designed to provide students with opportunities to explore and investigate. In constructivist/engaged learning lesson designs, the responsibility for learning is shifted to the learner. Materials and resources, in addition to the textbook, are provided. Students are allowed to explore and find answers on the Internet in addition to texts and resources found in the classroom. Using hands-on, manipulative materials facilitates the investigative and discovery process for students. The teacher designs and models learning experiences that provide students with opportunities to evaluate, analyze, predict, discover, and create in collaborative groups or individually (Figure 39.2). Students are encouraged to provide explanations and reasons for their learning, and constant dialogue is encouraged.

Teachers have found that trying new approaches can open new doors to the way they plan and assess lessons.

Journal entry: (Written before developing, writing, and facilitating an engaged learning unit in a mathematics class) I want my students to be independent and have the desire to learn more. I want to feel confident that after they have left my classroom, I have made an impact. I am often called the "cool teacher" or the "fun teacher," but I have rarely had the compliment of, "I learned so much in your class." My students are doing the minimum, because that is all that is required.

Journal entry: (Written after describing a 3-week unit on the structure and properties of cubes and rectangular prisms) Looking back on the activity, I am pleased. Sure, we experienced some difficulties during the lesson, but I think the students learned a lot and will retain more of the information because of it. Perhaps some of the difficulties came from the fact that this was out of character for me. The students were actually having fun, and learning something meaningful as well. All year long, I dictated the learning...I'm inspired and up to the challenge of "thinking outside the box."

HOW DO WE ASSESS LEARNING FOR UNDERSTANDING?

How do we focus on learner understanding while preparing for norm- and criterion-referenced testing that is a requirement in accountability systems?

A dichotomy between traditional and constructivist/engaged learning assessment practices and methods also exists in current learning and teaching practices. In a traditional environment, assessment of student learning is separate from learning experiences and is usually provided in the form of tests given at the end of the lesson. Traditional tests of student learning and knowledge usually cover the "basics." In addition to the basics, today's students need to be able to think critically, to predict, analyze, and make inferences about the content. Changes in the way students are assessed are necessary in order to help our students develop these skills.

Constructivist and engaged learning environments call for the use of authentic assessment practices before, during, and after the learning experience(s). Teachers ask the question, "If I use engaged learning and constructivist approaches in my classroom, will students meet accountability requirements as measured by state testing?"

Journal entry: As a teacher I am conflicted about the best teaching practices to use. I'm hoping I will learn and use effective teaching strategies to incorporate in my classroom. I also realize that I am accountable to the state test, which, in my opinion, contradicts learner-centered instruction.

Assessment in traditional approaches includes grading daily student work, end of chapter/unit tests, six weeks tests, semester tests, etc. These are all summative assessments—assessments that take place at the end of the learning experience. Ideally, assessment practices in constructivism and engaged learning environments would eliminate grades and standardized testing; however, this is not the reality of accountability systems in schools.

How do we combine accountability systems with constructivism and engaged learning approaches? School accountability systems are required to measure student learning. Currently, standardized tests are a part of every accountability system. There are ways to look at results to help improve instruction for children. If the test is aligned with the standards set at each grade level, teachers can use the results to examine areas in which students excel and areas in which students are not successful. Teachers can look at each objective, see how individual students performed, and adjust instruction accordingly. Teachers can then use this knowledge to make improvements when planning teaching, learning, and assessment activities.

Journal entry: In our grade level we have analyzed the results of last year's tests. In mathematics, for example, we know the objectives in which students need more help. We teach these concepts more, and we design our lessons so students will gain deeper understanding of the content. We also teach these concepts using different approaches. After they understand the concept, we show them what it might look like on a test. Understanding the concept first has really helped our students' performance on the test. It takes a little longer for us to develop and prepare the lessons, but we have worked together to save time and energy, and our students have shown improvement.

Standardized testing is a reality of assessment practices in schools. Standardized testing procedures have followed teach-and-test models, and testing formats require specific answers in multiple-choice formats. Practicing teach and test models over and over during the school year provides gains in achievement scores in some schools. When examining teach and test models, important questions should be asked: (1) Are we providing children with the critical thinking and problem-solving skills needed to be successful in life? (2) Are students really understanding the content, and will they be able to apply the knowledge gained from the content in life situations? There is a need to look further than test results to know what our students understand.

Performance-based assessments that address national and state standards provide a way educators can design and utilize more balanced assessment practices. Assessments that include not only the summative forms of assessment (norm-and criterion-referenced tests, end of chapter tests, daily quizzes, etc.), but also include formative assessments, provide balance in evaluation practices. It is important for students to be involved in formative assessment practices that include: student journals, student portfolios, the use of higher cognitive demand questioning strategies, student inquiry and investigation projects, activities in which students design a product, debates, science projects, video and technology productions, etc.

Journal entry: Using higher cognitive demand questioning strategies develops and fosters critical thinking, evaluation, and knowledge. I would like to learn more so I will be able to further develop this strategy in my classroom. As we were discussing questioning strategies, I shared how I have my students develop their own questions while they read. The students become the teacher as they share their questions with the rest of the students. They normally work in groups of two and help each other develop the questions. There is a sense of pride when they ask the question. We avoid the yes/no answers.

Students remember these learning and assessment activities, and these activities help them practice critical thinking habits and become lifelong learners.

Journal entry: Every morning of each school day, my students have to solve a mathematics "Problem of the Day." The problem consists of a challenging word problem in mathematics. One strategy I recommend is for students to ask themselves questions about the problem. These questions include: What is the question asking me? What information do I know? What information do I need? By utilizing this strategy for each problem, student success increases. The answer is much more meaningful when these questions are asked. This strategy has become an incredible learning tool.

The role the student plays in his or her own understanding of the content is an important part of assessment. If teachers ensure students know the objectives and goals of the lesson from the beginning, they will be able to see the direction of the lesson and will be able to tie the content to the goals through practical and engaging learning experiences.

Journal entry: Learner autonomy can be equated to independence, self- motivation, and an intrinsic desire to learn. Instilling the value of autonomy in the learner comes in many shapes and sizes. It is a result and a process, exposing students to a different way of acquiring knowledge, and being held accountable for the newly acquired knowledge. I do not believe it means independent work all the time. I believe the focus should be on accountability (the responsibility) to learn.

The goals and objectives are the roadmap of the lesson, and if everyone knows the direction, they can help each other arrive at the destination.

WILL STUDENTS BE SUCCESSFUL?

Constructivism and engaged learning practices emphasize leaner-centered instruction. The focus is not on what teachers teach, but on what learners learn. The focus is on the individual learning experiences. The teachers know their students and plan a safe, nurturing environment for learning. This caring learning environment sets the stage for not only the content that will be taught on that day, but also for future motivation to learn. In this process the teacher provides opportunities and time to listen to students. Students talk about what they want to learn, how they are learning, how they work with their peers, questions they have about the content, and questions they have formulated as the result of their learning.

Journal entry: The reading and discussions this week really drove home the importance of encouraging students to construct their own learning based on their own background and experiences. I realize it's "easier" to plan traditional lessons and have the students work on a series of isolated tasks that go from one content area to the next, but it's much more interesting and exciting, not only for the students, but for the teacher as well, to develop a well-rounded unit surrounding one major theme that the students can dig their teeth into. Their level of interest soars, as does their reading, writing and, yes, research abilities, when they are faced with open-ended questions that they must research and analyze. The theory of constructivism works very well because the students really become responsible for their own learning.

Students do not come to school knowing how to think critically, evaluate, ask good questions, work with their peers, conduct investigations, and think logically. In engaged learning environments, teachers model these processes for students. A gradual shift occurs from teacher-centered to student-centered practices. Teachers work to plan lessons centered around the content knowledge and skills students are to learn and the best way to facilitate the learning process so each student will be successful.

DO WE BELIEVE ALL CHILDREN CAN LEARN?

Included in many school mission statements is the phrase, "all children can learn." Do we believe all children can learn? Individual teachers and administrators have different perspectives and beliefs about children concerning the nature of intelligence, socioeconomic status and learning, English language proficiency levels and learning, minorities and learning, gender equity and learning, and special needs and learning. Ability tracking systems, the way we serve our special needs students, our remedial programs, our gifted and advance placement programs, and gender biases, are evidence of belief systems in schools.

Journal entry: Tonight's class was very uplifting. I made the comment about our AP (Advanced Placement) curriculum, and my thinking was challenged by the professor. She's right. We should give all our students the same opportunities. I will have to work on this idea and be more aware as we continue to write the curriculum map for the non-AP students. I will also try to be more thoughtful and positive (as a life-long pessimist who is having a hard time taking a walk on the constructivist side)!

No matter how effective current practices are in some classrooms, schools, and districts, there is always room for improvement. In order to believe all children can learn, teachers study and learn about different learning paradigms, try different approaches in their classroom, examine their own belief systems about teaching and learning, and recognize their own shift in instructional practices. An important part of this shift in the teaching and learning paradigm is for teachers to establish a partnership in learning with their students. Students are given a "voice" in planning and extending learning; their voice, opinions, and ideas are valued in the learning process.

WHAT SYSTEMS NEED TO BE IN PLACE IN ORDER TO IMPROVE OUR CLASSROOM PRACTICES?

Districts require teachers to attend professional development days during the school year. Traditionally, these days consist of "sitting and listening," "making and taking" (activities for the classroom), learning to implement a program, or trying a few new instructional strategies that make no connections to the content. Rarely do teachers have opportunities to learn new approaches to teaching and learning; try new strategies in their classrooms related to content; and, think, reflect, discuss, and continuously make instructional improvements. Without continuous support and dialogue, teachers do not change classroom practices. If teaching practices are to change, systems are in place for teachers to have strong content knowledge of their subject matter, opportunities to discuss and observe new practices, and experiment with them in their own classrooms.

Journal entry: The greatest benefit to this different approach to learning is that I, too, am becoming an autonomous learner. As I have begun to engage in the reflective practices of my craft, teaching, I have been able to see my areas of strength, as well as areas of teaching that I need to learn more about, need to improve on and refocus on. I have the end in mind when I apply a new concept to my teaching. Sometimes, I can return to school after a night of reflection with colleagues and make immediate changes to benefit the children. Other times, I need to put a notation in my journal and realize, next year I will be better. I am a life-long learner and would like my students to feel this fulfillment one day.

Having the desire to create understanding of the content for all students and provide a caring environment where students are not afraid to discuss their thoughts about their learning, will help to enhance and improve instructional practices.

Journal entry: How will I keep learners engaged in my classroom? I think I have already started the process thanks to these classes and sharing experiences with my peers. I am using author studies, genre studies, rubrics, readers/writers workshops, and developing my own inquiry-based lessons. What I have learned is how to reflect as the facilitator in this way of learning. I feel I have become a better "reflector." I have the students reflect on their learning, and usually I write myself notes on what has worked and what hasn't, and I have learned to begin to ask myself some "harder" questions about my teaching. Questions that help me reflect on my beliefs and best practices. The "why" of what I am doing, not just the "what" and the "how." I have learned to "inquire" and dig below the "What went wrong?" or "What went well?" questions. Now I dig deep into "WHY I even attempted the lesson, unit, and different instructional approach."

In most areas, beginning or intern teachers have a mentor who assists them by modeling lessons by helping them know about the different programs in the school, by observing them teach, and by showing them how to do the required paperwork. In many cases, the mentor teacher does not have enough time to spend with the intern teacher.

Journal entry: It is my responsibility to create a caring environment for those I mentor. Collaborative learning among teachers is one of the ideas I would like to bring to our school. I would like to provide a more caring environment for our in-service teacher candidates. The first day of internship, the fear and apprehension is very evident in the intern's eyes. Putting them at ease and providing them with a sense of belonging is our obligation as teachers. They come with fresh ideas and high expectations only to be crushed by some of us who have forgotten that we too were new to the profession at one time. The environment we provide is probably the most important beginning for the intern's career. Collaborating by sharing the new and the seasoned ideas creates a strong and successful partnership.

If mentor teachers were trained to be good mentors, if they were provided with some time to work with the intern, and if they could focus on sharing ways to effectively teach the content, these teachers-in-training would enter the teaching profession better equipped to implement better instructional practices in the classroom.

How will we improve instructional practices for a diverse student population? Teachers are involved in learning about diversity through university classes, professional development programs, and other courses. Information concerning social, racial, ethnic, religion, gender, and language diversity is provided. While the teachers are provided with the information, the focus is not on looking at every child individually and treating all children equally.

Journal entry: I cultivate diversity in my classroom by having the children work in small groups so they will mingle with all their classmates and not just with their friends. We mix the English language learners with the English speakers and they work on projects together. As I reflect on my teaching, I ask myself the following questions: Do I model the very virtue I am teaching my students? Are they accepting their classmates and their individuality? Are my students setting high expectations for themselves? Do my students feel a sense of family in our classroom?

When addressing diversity, teachers understand every student and consider his or her needs. Students are treated equally, they share ideas, they are engaged with the content, and they participate in the content lessons that are designed for all students.

HOW DO WE BECOME TRANSFORMATIVE TEACHERS?

There has been a shift in the understanding of constructivist and engaged learning approaches in schools. More teachers realize we have only been minimally successful in the way we approach instructional improvement. We are trying these new approaches, and we are reflecting on our practices and participating in more conversations with our peers about teaching and learning. There is nothing easy about becoming a transformative teacher.

Journal entry: The idea of becoming a transformative teacher is a daunting one for me. I am definitely committed to my own journey of professional growth, and I always try to collaborate with my colleagues in group studies, etc., but I honestly have never really engaged in school reform. My personality is reserved and I find it quite difficult at times to speak publicly, even though I know I have something valuable to say.

Journal entry: So far we have looked at ourselves and reflected on our teaching practices. I never really thought about taking this philosophy and sharing it with the school community. I realize we are covering a lot of material concerning inquiry and change will take time. I see the transformative teacher as one who has spent a considerable amount of time reflecting on teaching practices and really has a sound base in best teaching practices. Also, a transformational teacher is very confident in who she/he is and truly believes reform will be a positive step in the professional lives of her/his colleagues.

We are faced with the challenge of understanding the best way to go about the business of teaching and learning. In classrooms, teachers and students work together to make meaning of content and to make sense of our world in a variety of ways. We use cognitive strategies; we are social in our learning; we reflect on our learning and form our own ideas and opinions about content; and we communicate and share with others as we are learning. Understanding the balance between traditional practices and the many dimensions of constructivism and engaged learning practices will assist us as we face this challenge. As this work is accomplished, it is important to keep in mind our joint goal—providing the best education that fulfills the needs of all children.

TERMS FOR READERS

Constructivism—A philosophy of learning in which we construct our own understanding of the world we live in through reflection on our experiences and sharing and building ideas with others.

Content Standards—The themes, big ideas, and content objectives related to and important to the content to be studied.

Engaged Learning—Classroom practices that focus on making connections and creating new understandings; extensive student-student dialogue; open-ended inquiry; focus on making the student process of analyzing, interpreting, predicting, and synthesizing visible; learning is collaborative; tasks of learning are challenging and authentic; teacher is the facilitator of learning.

Formative Assessment—Assessment that takes place before, during, and after the lesson; assessment is part of the learning process; students take part in their own assessment and know the goals of the standards; assessment is performance-based.

Pedagogy—The principles and method of instruction; the activities of educating or instructing or teaching; activities that impart knowledge or skill to learners.

Problem-based Learning—A learning experience in which students work together to solve problems that are meaningful to them. Students work collaboratively by testing possible solutions to the problem, and they look for answers from different resources.

Project-based Learning—A learning experience in which a big, important, real-world question is posed, and students work collaboratively to explore, investigate, and collect data in order to draw conclusions concerning possible answers to the question.

Summative Assessment—The test given at the end of a chapter, a final exam, a quiz, a standardized test, etc.

FURTHER READING

Bruner, J. (1966). *Toward a Theory of Instruction*. Cambridge, MA: Harvard University Press.

Gruber, H. E., and Voneche, J. J. (Eds.). (1995). *The Essential Piaget: An Interpretive Reference and Guide*. Northvale, N J: Jason Aronson Publishers.

Henderson, J. G. (2001). *Reflective Teaching: Professional Artistry through Inquiry* (3rd ed.). Upper Saddle River, NJ: Merrill Prentice Hall.

Kohn, A. (1999). *The Schools Our Children Deserve: Moving Beyond Traditional Classrooms and Tougher Standards*. Boston, MA: Houghton Mifflin Company.

Marlowe, B., and Page, M. (1998). *Creating and Sustaining the Constructivist Classroom*. Thousand Oaks, CA: Corwin Press, Inc.

Vygotsky, L. (1978). *Mind in Society*. Cambridge, MA: MIT Press.

CHAPTER 40

Creative Problem Solving

JULIA ELLIS

It is interesting to listen to how people talk about creativity or "being creative." Often, people will say that they are not creative because they do not write poetry, paint pictures, or engage in the performing arts. In so doing, they dismiss the creative ideas they generate to improvise solutions to everyday problems such as revising a recipe, making a child's costume out of too little of the needed materials, or planning an event that will accommodate the diverse needs and interests of a group of people. Creativity has been the focus of much research and debate. People have argued about whether the word, "creative," should be awarded to the person or the process, or reserved for the product. Maybe some people are creative only some time. And maybe some people are creative but never accomplish anything of broad social significance. Nevertheless, through all the research and debates we have come to better appreciate the nature of the creative process and the attributes, habits and processes of people who are capable of generating a creative response to the challenging events of life or work. Through this work we have become more attuned to the conditions that make creative responses more possible or likely. In this chapter I hope to share a few ideas about how we can support students in classrooms in being creative throughout their lives. I will begin with an autobiographical reflection highlighting key events in my own journey with creativity and creative problem solving. Then I will present some specific suggestions for how to engage students in creative problem solving in the classroom. Finally, I will highlight some of the happy side effects of using such practices in the classroom.

MY JOURNEY WITH "CREATIVITY"

Although I didn't yet have the word, creativity, in my vocabulary, my appreciation of it first emerged when I realized how much I enjoyed companions who made me laugh. Laughter makes you feel wonderful and connects you to the people you laugh with. The friends we laughed with when we were ten are still so easy to relate to forty years later. The conceptual playfulness that gives rise to wit and humor are manifestations of the creative process.

Still without the word, creativity, as a focus, I found in English literature courses in my undergraduate program. I wondered most about the authors of the pieces we read. How could they do it? What was the process? How had they become the process?

At the end of my undergraduate program, I took a drama course in which the majority of the time was spent doing dramatic improvisations. Through our weekly exercises I found myself inducted into a new way of being. In the dramatic improvisations, a person had only one task: pursue one's assigned objective—for example, sell brushes—as resourcefully as possible. To be resourceful, one had to make sense of what everyone else in the improvisation was trying to do. If straightforward attempts at pursuing your objective were not successful, it was expected that your strategies might become more and more bizarre. We were all Mr Beans in the making. The experience in this class made me a more hopeful person. I finally realized that in any challenging situation in life, I had only to assign myself an objective and pursue it resourcefully. I also realized that I could complicate my objective to ensure acceptable consequences or conditions—for example, "I want to sell brushes, but in a way that doesn't involve annoying people and doesn't require too much of my time."

In my teacher education program I took a course on gifted education and then became involved as a researcher working with the classes of gifted grade 4 and 5 students who were using creative problem solving as an enrichment approach. The teachers used the *Covington Crutchfield Productive Thinking Program* for language arts and thereby introduced students to a broad range of strategies and meta-cognitive skills for creative problem solving. The program was based on a story about two children who were set problems by their uncle who was a detective. They learned to use strategies to explore all possibilities in order to eliminate all possible hypotheses except for the one right answer in "whodunit" fashion. Each week, a fellow graduate student and I visited the classes and invited the students to use group creative problem solving approaches with playful, everyday life problems. In this way, we endeavored to support their work with developing creative products or plans with open-ended problems as opposed to only "one right answer" problems.

During my doctoral work with creative problem solving in the early 1980s, I read a broad range of literature about creativity and creative problem solving. I learned that creativity was understood as an important aspect of mental health and had consequences for physical health as one aged. This is not surprising given its association with characteristics such as flexibility, tolerance for ambiguity, being able to delay closure, openness to inner and outer experience, humor, being nonjudgmental, playfulness, intuitiveness, optimism, being self-accepting, and being willing to take risks.

Through reading research on the processes used by adults who were recognized as being creative problem solvers in their work, I learned that they had an awareness of process and could monitor their own steps to ensure the opportunity to develop creative solutions. The literature was also replete with stories about how people access the rhythm of creative thinking when needed in their everyday lives. A key dynamic seemed to be preparation and then incubation. Preparation typically involved gathering all the information and related ideas pertaining to the problem and clarifying the attributes of a solution that would satisfy. It was important to refrain from attempting to develop solutions until preparation was completed.

Once preparation was completed, one had to know how to enable and access one's incubation processes. Incubation usually involves some form of relaxation, becoming quiet, and refraining from trying to solve the problem consciously. We have all heard stories about the ideas that come when one is in the bathtub, in bed, or driving. Even the 10-year-old children in my doctoral study were able to tell me about the process. As one boy said, "I think and I think as hard as I can. And then if I can't think of anything I just wait for the idea to come." Many of the children specifically mentioned breathing and relaxation and having a special place where they sit quietly and relax while they wait for their ideas.

When ideas start to come, it's very important to refrain from considering the ideas with skepticism. It's as though there's a little man in the back of your head who has figured it all out while you've been sleeping. He has made an answer, is trying to offer it, but will freeze up or run away if he meets with suspicion. When the ideas come you have to start scribbling them down and just keep scribbling, trusting that the whole package will be there. Relaxation, openness, and optimism are absolutely necessary. The ideas may seem silly or strange at first appearance, so a playful, exploratory attitude is particularly important when getting started with the scribbling down. Evaluation and tweaking come into play much later.

In the creativity literature I also read about people who, having worked their way up to middle management, were dismayed to find that after years of doing things exactly the way others wanted them done, they could no longer generate creative ideas. They attended creativity workshops hoping to reclaim the creative capacities they recalled having when they were ten. Preschoolers typically have no difficulty using their imagination to invent ideas. As they draw from the materials of their experience to make games, stories, or scripts for make-believe, they keep the door open to the "little man in the back of one's head," their preconscious processes. With encouragement and emotional support, young children can maintain their access to the creative process. A ten-year-old girl in my doctoral study reported that her father still insisted on sitting with her and coaxing her to make up a story for him.

Sadly, by the age of seven, many children lose their capacity to create new ideas. As their life experience becomes more concerned with learning "how things are" and less with imagining "how things might be" they can lose their access to the creative process. In my doctoral research I worked with twelve grade 5 classrooms. As one of the activities in each class, I asked students to individually develop original plans for a party they could put on for another class in the school. I displayed an idea tree showing lists of well-known party games, food, decorations, and so forth. In the warm-up or introduction to the notion of developing "unusual activities" for a party, we practiced forcing connections between party themes and favorite party activities. For example, if a student liked the Halloween activity of bobbing for apples but wanted to have a Western theme for the party, how might one modify the apple bobbing activity to have it fit in with a Western theme? Or, if one wanted to serve ice cream at a party with a Dracula theme, how could that activity be modified or elaborated? We worked through several examples like these and in most classes only three or four students were able to offer ideas. All the children were eager to interact with me and I felt compelled to keep offering basic knowledge questions about "how things are" in order to give more students a chance to put their hands up. In one class, where there were in fact seven students who offered ideas during the warm-up, I expressed my delight to the teacher. She, however, expressed her disappointment that it was always only the same seven students who offered ideas in her activities with them.

I wondered whether classrooms at all grade levels could somehow support students' opportunities for engaging in creative thinking. I taught twelve courses on gifted and enrichment programming with groups of practicing teachers in communities throughout British Columbia, Yukon, and Alberta. In each of these courses I introduced creative problem solving strategies and invited teachers to use them with regular curriculum content. Many teachers used some of the strategies and came back each week to show us what the students had done and to confer about where to take the activities from there. In the second section of this chapter, I present a number of the strategies and discuss some of the ways they might be used in the classroom.

Later, I worked with 150 pre-service teachers each year for four years at the University of Toronto, in a one-year after degree teacher education program. Each year I asked the students to use creative assignments and creative problem solving strategies with their practicum classrooms. I also asked them to systematically study the students' products or performances and to give a report on these in class. These written and oral reports alerted me to many of the unanticipated positive benefits of such activities. I will relate and discuss a number of these in the third section of this chapter.

CREATIVE PROBLEM SOLVING IN THE CLASSROOM

In this section I present some strategies for creative problem solving and discuss ways to incorporate these in classroom life. Using such strategies and activities would give students the following opportunities:

- Develop their fluency and flexibility in generating ideas.
- Practice being conceptually playful with ideas.
- Develop their analytic abilities.
- Deepen their awareness of and confidence with the creative process.
- Organize the content of curriculum units and intensify their work with this content.
- Develop meta-cognitive strategies that will support their autonomous work.

A number of the strategies entail using "trees" or charts to organize ideas or information. Creative thoughts result from the reorganization of existing knowledge (i.e., principles, ideas, information, images, etc.) In order for such knowledge to be reorganized, it must be brought into focus, activated, and made available throughout the problem solving stages. To be truly available for manipulation or recombination, all elements of a problem must be free of any constraining conditions arising from previous contexts (Blank, 1982). The visual organizers discussed in this section help to make knowledge visually available and the procedures discussed provide structure and focus for recombination.

Some of the strategies or sample activities outlined in this section are intended to set up a good opportunity for incubation to work well. As mentioned briefly in the first section of this chapter, preparation—identifying all information and pertinent ideas—should be completed before any attempts are made to generate a creative product or plan. After preparation, students should try to solve the problem in more than one way. Then they should be prepared to "leave it alone" but with confident expectation that an even better idea will come to them either spontaneously or the next time they sit down with this work (Parnes et al., 1977).

BRAINSTORMING "HOW THINGS MIGHT BE"

I can still remember the first time I invited a class to engage in brainstorming in my practicum at a secondary school. First I established the following ground rules:

1. Produce lots of ideas.
2. No criticism of others' ideas.
3. It's okay to piggyback on other people's ideas.
4. It's okay to offer silly or playful ideas.

I was new at this so I fumbled a bit, but they did not. They were excited and were clearly enjoying giving me all their ideas and seeing them recorded on the chalkboard. When one student offered an idea that made me realize he misunderstand the topic for the brainstorming I wanted to interject and clarify this for him. The class, however, stopped me and reminded me of the rule about "No criticism." They got it! They knew this would interrupt the flow.

Teachers often ask a class to brainstorm what they know about "how things are." This typically takes place at the beginning of a unit as teachers ask students to brainstorm everything they already know about the new topic of study. This is very different from brainstorming for ideas about "how things might be." Some students cannot participate if they don't have a lot of knowledge about the topic. There is also an awareness that some contributions might be incorrect.

When we have students brainstorm ideas about "how things might be," we can also use this activity to teach them a strategy for generating more ideas. We can call this strategy, *Brainstorm-Categorize-Brainstorm*, and the product that results can be called an *Idea Tree*.

MAKING AN IDEA TREE

To introduce the procedures for making an Idea Tree, it is good to use a topic for which students are likely to have many ideas. Let's say for example, that a teacher is anticipating having the students write stories about a horse that becomes a hero. The teacher could begin by having the class brainstorm ideas for names for horses. This would be the process.

1. *Brainstorm*. The teacher asks the class to tell her all the different names that people might give to a horse. All the names offered are recorded on the chalkboard. Maybe these would be the first names offered:

Silver	Black Beauty	Daisy
Star	Princess	Spend-a-Buck
Flash	Sam	Spot
Pegasus	Thunder	Lightning

2. *Categorize*. After several contributions, the teacher pauses, draws circles around two or three of the names, and asks the class how those names are similar to each other, for example, "How are Lightning and Star and Thunder the same? Where do those names come from, or what are those names about?" After getting a "category" from students, the class would be asked to identify other pairs or groups of names that could belong together in categories. All the categories and associated horse names would be transferred to an Idea Tree. The students would be told that it is okay for the same name to belong to more than one branch or category.

3. *Brainstorm*. After all the initial horse names had been categorized and transferred to the Idea Tree as shown in Figure 40.1, the students would be asked to brainstorm both additional categories and more examples of possible names in each category.

Before students began work on writing their stories about how a horse became a hero, the teacher could have them use any of a number of different strategies for generating ideas about how a horse might become a hero. The first one we will look at here is called an *Analogies Chart*.

MAKING AND USING AN ANALOGIES CHART

The teacher could let the class know that she expected that they could all write very different stories about how a horse became a hero. To support them in coming up with a large number of ideas they would use an *Analogies Chart*. To complete a chart such as that shown in Table 40.1, the teacher would supply the left column and have the students do research and/or pool their knowledge to complete the right-hand column. Once the chart was completed, the teacher would have students practice *Forcing Connections*.

FORCING CONNECTIONS

To practice forcing connections, students would randomly select ideas from the right hand column of the Analogies Chart and try to use these in story prompt questions. For example:

How could a horse become a hero in a way that involved *carrying messages*?

How could a horse become a hero in a way that involved *having magic powers*?

How could a horse become a hero in a way that involved having *unusual skills*?

Figure 40.1
Idea Tree for Names of Horses

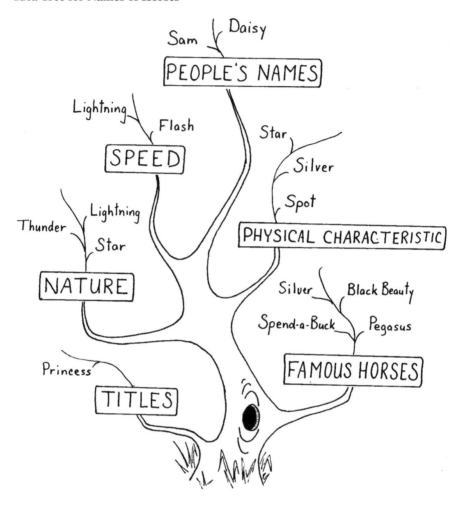

The teacher would invite the whole class to offer ideas in response to each of these story prompts. Then students would work in small groups or individually with three more randomly selected ideas from the chart. The teacher would talk to the students about *incubation* and tell them to expect to have an even better idea occur before they started working on the stories the next day.

ONE, TWO, THREE, GO!

It is important for students to learn to develop at least two or three alternate approaches or big ideas for their project or product. If they make themselves think of at least two or three possibilities, then "the little man in the back of their heads" will keep asking "Yes, and what else could be?" If students stop with their first idea and try to develop that, the "little man" shuts down. Students can then find themselves stuck if that idea doesn't work out well. Similarly, incubation

Table 40.1
Analogies Chart for How a Horse could Become a Hero

Kinds of Heroes	How They Became Heroes
People	Saved lives
	Invented things
	Broke records
	Explorers/discoverers
	Artistic excellence
	Athletic excellence
	Changed the world
	Took risks
	Winning in the Olympics
	Helped people
Animals	Carried messages
	Found their way home
	Performed difficult tasks
	Loyalty
	Carried/served important people
	Won prizes
Fairy tale characters	Granted wishes
	Cast spells
	Had magic powers
	Were very big
	Were very clever
	Saved someone
	Tricked someone
Fictional characters	Have super powers
	Have unusual skills
	Always win

will also work better if the students have first consciously entertained multiple possibilities for how to do their projects.

ATTRIBUTES TREE

As an additional or alternate strategy for generating ideas for the "horse-as-hero stories," the teacher could have the class make and use an *Attributes Tree* as shown in Figure 40.2. To make the tree, the teacher would begin by asking students:

"What are all the ways that horses can be the same or different from each other?"

Students' answers might look like these:

How fast they run

What color they are

Figure 40.2
Attributes Tree for Horses

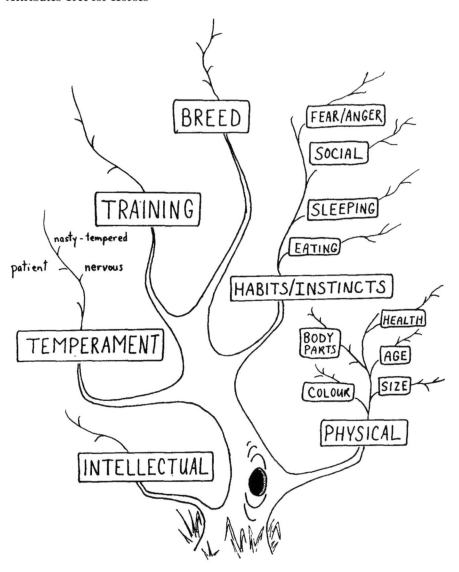

If it's a pony

If they're mean

The teacher would work with these kinds of initial responses to move the students to an awareness of general attributes through comments such as:

Yes, some horses are mean and some are calm or friendly. What do we call that part or that aspect of horses?

Table 40.2
Attributes—Implications Chart for Horses as Heroes

Characteristics of My Horse	Implications for How it Might Become a Hero
Nasty-tempered	
White in color	
Likes to eat apples	

Once general attributes were identified and labeled on an Attributes Tree, examples of possible values for each attribute would be added to the branches as "twigs."

FORCING CONNECTIONS

Once the Attributes Tree was completed, the teacher would have students practice forcing connections by randomly selecting "twigs" from the Attributes Tree to form story prompt questions such as these:

How could *being a pony* enable the horse to become a hero?

How could *being nasty-tempered* enable the horse to become a hero?

How could *being gray in color* enable the horse to become a hero?

The teacher would ask for three different possibilities in response to each question. Then students would practice the same process with additional randomly selected twigs in small groups. They could use an *Attributes – Implications Chart*, such as that shown in Table 40.2, to record their ideas. They would be reminded about incubation and be told to expect an even better idea to come to them before or when they started work on the stories on another day.

IMPOSING CONSTRAINTS OR ASSIGNING A CENTRAL FEATURE

Sometimes the challenge for students is not a lack of ideas but a surplus. For example, it might be difficult to get started on the assignment, "Write a poem about nature," because there are too many possibilities. Similarly, students might have so many ideas for "horse-as-hero" stories that it might be difficult to find a focus and get started. That's when it might be helpful to use the strategy called *Imposing Constraints*. Here are two examples of what Imposing Constraints could look like.

In the "write poem about nature" assignment, the teacher might say that each line in the poem has to start with the same letter and that she would arbitrarily assign a letter to each student.

In the horse stories assignment, the teacher might assign each group of students a different location or setting for the story as an imposed constraint: an island, in the mountains, on a desert, in our neighborhood/town/city, in a park.

An arbitrarily imposed constraint helps students to get started because it eliminates many possible ideas but is at the same time a source of ideas. In group work, a stimulating imposed constraint can help the group to focus and get started. If an imposed constraint is to ignite novel ideas, it is important that it *not* be logically related to the problem. The locations for "horse-as-hero stories," for example, did not include sites such as farms, ranches, or racetracks.

Table 40.3
Future Projection Chart for a Lost Horse in the Neighborhood

When	What Could Be Going Right?	What Could Be Going Wrong?
After one hour		
After one month		
After one year		

FUTURE PROJECTION

Another idea generation strategy is called *Future Projection*. Let's imagine that a teacher simply wanted to have students write stories about what might happen if a lost horse was found in their own neighborhood. To develop possible ideas for the story, the teacher could have the students work in small groups to brainstorm entries for the *Future Projection Chart* shown in Table 40.3. The teacher would insist that the students try to generate three ideas for each cell in the chart.

"WHAT IF . . ." ASSIGNMENTS

Sometimes teachers may wish to give students the opportunity to engage in playful, imaginative thinking and the production of ideas without taking time to use any of the strategies presented above. This can work well and be valuable if the assignment is well chosen for the students' interests and knowledge base. Here are some examples of "What if . . ." assignments.

What if the power went out in our city? Prepare a news report highlighting many of the things that would happen.

What if the story/novel we have just read took place in a different location? Pick a location, imagine how the story would be different, and draw and color a picture to show a key scene in the story.

What if you could have your own studio apartment? Draw a diagram or picture of the apartment, showing how everything in it would reflect who you are, your interests, values, and so forth.

What if the Teddy Bears could have a party? Work together to make a mural to show everything that would happen at the party.

What if a monster lived in its own house? What would the house be like? Make a three-dimensional construction of the house to show your ideas.

What if there were special celebrations for Ground Hog Day in a French speaking community? What songs would they sing, what dances or games? Make some up and teach them to rest of the class. (In the context of a second language class, i.e., French)

What if you could make your own fort in the woods? Draw a picture or labeled diagram of what you would construct. Write a description of how you would build it.

These kinds of activities keep students using imaginative thinking, drawing upon the materials of their experience, and enjoying showing others their ideas. When students produce their own ideas in these kinds of activities and products they are motivated to write and speak about their ideas. When these playful "What if . . ." assignments are group activities, they serve to enhance relationships among students. These benefits and others will be discussed further in the third section of this chapter.

Figure 40.3
Idea Trees for Witches' Farms

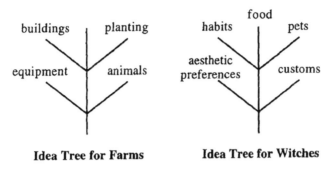

Idea Tree for Farms   Idea Tree for Witches

USING CREATIVE PROBLEM SOLVING STRATEGIES IN CURRICULUM UNITS

Teachers can offer students creative assignments or have them use creative problem solving strategies in a variety of ways in curriculum units. A number of examples are shown in Table 40.4. In this subsection I will discuss ways of using these in culminating assignments, at the beginning of units or topics, or in other subject areas.

Culminating Assignments. If teachers use a creative assignment—a playful or fanciful activity—as a culminating project for a unit, this can create a purposeful context for reviewing and organizing a great deal of the material from the unit. It can also give the class a shared knowledge base with which to be conceptually playful. Here are three examples:

> In an accounting class, the teacher asked students to imagine that they won a $1,000,000 in a lottery. They were to brainstorm a list of ideas for how they would want to use the winnings. Then they were to prepare financial statements to show all transactions and summaries one year later. The students were asked to complete Future Projection Charts to generate ideas for entries in their statements.

> In a word-processing course, students were asked to develop application forms/templates for potential life partners to complete.

> In a grade 2 or 3 classroom, as Halloween approached and the class was concluding a unit on farms, the teacher had students work in groups to make floor murals of witches' farms. To produce ideas for their witches' farms, the teacher had the class force connections between an Idea Tree about farms and an Idea Tree about witches. Figure 40.3 shows such trees with only the main branches labeled.

The culminating assignments do not always have to be extensive or time-consuming. It is mainly important that students find them engaging and that they provide a reason for reviewing the material in the unit and using strategies to generate conceptually playful ideas. For example,

> After a unit on Halloween safety rules, the teacher might ask the students to each make a poster that uses a Halloween character to teach a safety rule. Each student makes only one poster to advertise one rule, but in the process of doing so considers all the safety rules there are to choose from. The students' posters collectively reiterate all the safety rules as well.

Playful or fanciful activities can take the form of creating games, dramatic performances, murals or three-dimensional constructions, posters, news reports, story plot lines. Being aware of themes, preoccupations, or activities of high interest to students can help teachers to imagine suitable creative assignments.

At the Beginning of Units or Topics. There can be many benefits to having students make Idea Trees or Attributes trees at the beginning of a unit. Here are two examples:

Table 40.4
Examples of Using Creative Problem-Solving Strategies in Curriculum Units

Context	Examples
At the beginning of a topic	Have students work in groups to make an Attributes Tree showing all the ways that the topic of study—*animals/cities/plants/geographic regions*—can be same or different from each other. All groups contribute to a master *Attributes Tree* the teacher makes for the whole class. The tree is used by students as an organizer for researching specific animals/cities, etc.
	Before starting a new topic in *grammar*, the teacher of the target language has the class work together to make an *Idea Tree* showing everything they already know about grammar in the language being learned.
	Prior to *reading a story* about a student who moves to a new school, the teacher has students complete *Future Projection Charts* to imagine all the things that could go right or wrong when moving to a new school.
As conceptually playful assignments in other subject areas	Imagine that you are a sports commentator for your favorite sport. Using as many words as you can from our unit on *weather*, report what happened in a game or pretend to describe a few minutes of play.
	Use the terminology we learned in our unit on *electricity* to explain the "circuitry" of friendships.
As culminating creative projects to conclude units	We have studied the five *geographic regions* of our province or state. Your group will be assigned one of these geographic regions. Imagine that, on a family trip, the family pet gets lost while in this region. Develop a storyboard outlining all the adventures the pet might have while lost there for three days.
	We have studied three popular models of *science fair projects*: experimental, descriptive/analytic, and active demonstration or working model. Before starting on your own favorite idea for a project, please generate two ideas for each model. Each idea should somehow be related to the idea of "beauty" (imposed constraint).
	We have just finished reading a particular *play/story/novel*. Pretend that this is a true story. Plan a television documentary program about these dramatic events (e.g., interviews with characters, witnesses, and "experts"; show footage of reenacted key moments.)
	Design a game that will give players the opportunity to practice their *addition and subtraction skills*. The game must use empty milk cartons (imposed constraint) in a central way.
	Using activities and objects we have been working with in our *gymnastics* unit, plan presentations for the school assembly. You can use music and costumes. We will brainstorm possible themes and pick one.
	To conclude our unit on *ecology*, work in a group to design an imaginary settlement in a bubble submerged in the ocean (imposed constraint). Show your ideas on a large mural.

To begin a unit on nutrition, a teacher leads the class in making an Idea Tree about everything that comes to mind when they think of the word, "food."

To begin a unit on fractions, the teacher has the class make an Idea Tree about all the activities and objects in their lives that involve fractions.

Through such activities, the teacher can learn what is already salient to students with regards to the topic. Students share their knowledge and ideas with each other. The class has an opportunity to create shared meaning for some of the important concepts pertaining to the topic. What the teacher learns about the students' related interests and experience can be a source of ideas for activities within the unit. The teacher can show students where the unit of study will fit in with the bigger picture of the Idea or Attributes Tree they have created. If Attributes Trees are produced, students can then use these as meaningful organizers for individual research within the unit. And best of all, students find it very motivating to brainstorm their ideas in such activities.

"What if..." assignments can also be used to advantage at the beginning of a unit. When students produce something imaginative, their assumptions and preconceptions slip out sideways. Thus the assignment can invite the use of imagination, get students thinking about the new topic of study, and also reveal students' misconceptions, gaps in knowledge, or related concerns. For example:

Design a James Bond type briefcase containing special gadgets that would help the mayor with his or her job. (This would be at the beginning of a unit on municipal government.)

Imagine that you were the President/Prime Minister. What would you try to do in the first year of office? (This would be at the beginning of a unit on federal government.)

In Other Subject Areas. Sometimes teachers can use the knowledge students have been acquiring in one curriculum unit as a base for a conceptually playful activity in another subject area. Teachers might draw from current topics in science, social studies, or even math to design "What if...?" assignments in language arts or art. Here are two examples:

What if you had to make a picture of a flower (or an automobile) using only two randomly selected shapes? (Students have been studying shapes in geometry in math class.)

Work in a group to design an imaginary machine (diagram or three-dimensional construction) that would somehow help with pollution problems. Have each member of the group participate in an oral presentation to explain the design. (The students are studying pollution problems in science. Each group would be assigned a different imposed constraint. "Your group's machine must be small enough to fit in your pocket/use lots and lots of hose/have lots of blue ribbons/make a very loud or high-pitched noise/make a ticking sound/have a smiley face as a central feature.")

Activities such as these keep students interacting purposefully with the material from the unit of study while also encouraging conceptual playfulness. Students are usually excited about the ideas they have produced and are motivated to communicate these through speaking, writing, or other forms of representation.

This section has presented a number of strategies and suggestions for using creative problem solving in the classroom. The conceptual playfulness of the activities can enable students to extend their capacities for generating ideas and accessing preconscious processes for creative thought. By having creative assignments linked to curriculum content, students have an inviting and purposeful context for revisiting and working with material in a curriculum topic or unit. As students acquire experience with using the visual organizers and procedures from creative problem solving, they also become more autonomous and self-directed with topics of personal interest. In the next section of this chapter, I discuss a number of additional benefits of using creative assignments and creative problem solving strategies in the classroom.

BENEFITS OF USING CREATIVE PROBLEM SOLVING IN THE CLASSROOM

Over a four-year period, 450 preservice teachers were invited to use creative assignments and creative problem solving strategies in their practicum classrooms. They studied their students' processes and products and gave oral and written reports in our classes on campus. Through their reports, it was learned how such activities contribute to the quality of life and learning in the classroom.

RELATIONSHIPS

"Creative assignment" activities quickly and easily warmed up or ignited relationships among students or between students and student teachers. Student teachers were thrilled that students at all grade levels were so eager to approach them to show their work with these activities. They noticed with interest that students who didn't usually interact with each other eagerly shared and compared their products. And they were happy and relieved to see that once "loners" worked in a group on "creative assignment," they began to hang out with the same students at recess and at assemblies.

Engagement, Pride in Work, and Social Competence

Although the "creative assignments" may seem playful or fanciful, they have the wonderful effect of evoking the most serious work from students. Students at all grade levels were serious about their work on these projects and took the work of other students seriously. They shared scarce materials, negotiated diplomatically, and collaborated and cooperated with ease. Their greatest concerns were to have opportunities to continue working on their projects and to "finish them right." Both student teachers and cooperating teachers were delighted to observe that when students worked on creative assignments, there were no avoidance strategies or "behavior problems."

Writing and Speaking

Student teachers were surprised and pleased to witness the richness of oral language and the skillful writing that resulted from work on "creative assignments." When students worked in groups to make murals or other constructions to show their ideas, every member of a group was able and eager to give an oral presentation explaining all the ideas in the project. When students were asked to give written explanations or stories about their projects, the quality of the writing was much better than usual. Often, through the use of brief "What if. . ." activities, student teachers were able to help students discover preoccupations or ideas they would be motivated to write about.

Talents, Recognition, and Belonging

Because many of the creative assignments are open-ended and complex, they create space for students to draw upon diverse skills, talents, or knowledge to contribute to a project. Even in kindergarten, children quickly divided up various aspects of group projects according to each child's skills and interests. Sometimes, within group projects, students who lacked strength in the subject area but had leadership ability had the opportunity to experience their classmates' and teachers' appreciation. Because the creative assignments often entail a visual presentation or performance, they provide excellent opportunities for students to have their contributions recognized.

Students' Interests, Concerns, and Preoccupations

Student teachers got to know their students so much better through the creative assignments. Through listening to the students while they worked or through studying their completed products, they learned what students know, believe, and care about. Many student teachers were able to incorporate students' interests and concerns in the remainder of their practicum planning.

My experience with practicing teachers and student teachers using creative problem solving in the classroom has clarified for me the many benefits of structuring students' curriculum work within the context of imagining "how things might be." Teachers are energized by seeing students' "unconventional" or non-adult ideas about how to understand and approach problems and possibilities. Students show that they can "contain" themselves very well when they are freed to use everything they know and can imagine to produce and share ideas. Creative assignments give students a safe and supportive place to remain engaged with generating ideas. Creative problem solving strategies help all students to push themselves further and to see how to work creatively with curriculum content. I hope that more teachers may entertain the use of these strategies and assignments. I believe they can help students and teachers to experience the classroom as a more welcoming and spirited place for being engaged with positive possibilities.

This chapter suggests that regular opportunities for creative work be built into the curriculum of all students rather than being treated as "different" methods of instruction for "different" populations. It makes no sense to say that creatively talented students prefer open-ended methods of instruction and to imply that closed-structure learning experiences that emphasize products rather process and teacher-oriented assignments are fine for everyone else. If classroom experiences were reconceptualized to make open-ended, creative activities for students commonplace, all children would have on-going opportunities to both find their creative selves and to bring everything they know from their out of classroom experience—culture, lifestyle, interests, hobbies, talents—into their classroom work. Critical and creative higher-order thinking skills have traditionally been a concern of programs for gifted and talented students. Even there, they are often treated in isolation as skills that can be modeled and taught through joyless exercises. Students can develop higher order thinking skills more spontaneously in the context of meaningful activities such as those discussed in this chapter. Programs for gifted students also need to be reconsidered for their role in either supporting or impeding students' creativity. While such programs typically provide for some acceleration, enrichment, and advanced topics they do not always provide regular opportunities for students to develop and present original ideas. Instead programs for gifted often cultivate pressured, competitive, grade-conscious climates in which ambiguous assignments would only be a source of anxiety. This chapter on creative problem solving is intended to invite consideration about educators' responsibilities to more holistically support students' growth and learning and to cultivate classroom climates in which students can experience each other as a source of support and affirmation.

REFERENCES

Blank, S. (1982). *The Challenge: Encouraging Creative Thinking and Problem Solving in the Gifted.* San Diego: San Diego Unified School District.

Parnes, S., Noller, R., and Biondi, A. (1977). *Guide to Creative Action.* New York: Charles Scribner's Sons.

CHAPTER 41

Creativity

JANE PIIRTO

Creativity is fashionable these days. Everyone uses the word. Yet creativity is confusing. By late 2003, the term was used in over 16,500 references to titles of scholarly books and articles. Topics included creativity in business, creativity in psychology, creativity for parents, creativity and spirituality, creativity and teaching, creativity and aging, creativity and the arts, creativity and the sciences, creativity and mathematics, creativity and problem solving, creativity and problem finding.

This phenomenon of interest in creativity is a truly postmodern perplexity, for little is tangible, all is one, one is many, everything is true, and nothing is true. However, few can get an authoritative and comprehensive handle on creativity. The terms *chaos*, *fracture*, and *split*, fit the creativity enterprise well. Yet the plethora of purported experts on creativity suggests that creativity is slippery, porous, and resistant to definition, quantification, and access. Just when one thinks one knows everything about it, one realizes that one cannot possess it.

By 1999, creativity had been so imbued into the psychological, educational, and business culture that a two-volume *Encyclopedia of Creativity* was published. Topics ranged from the esoteric (Perceptgenesis, Matthew Effects) to the idiosyncratic (Fernando Pessoa, Robert Schumann). Each was written by a scholar in the field. I myself wrote two entries, one on Poetry, and one on Synchronicity. The encyclopedia's two volumes are the latest and most comprehensive summary of creativity research and thought.

CREATIVITY AND PSYCHOLOGY

Creativity has been a topic of discussion and of research in the field of psychology for approximately fifty years. Psychology, the scientific study of mental operations and behavior, asks, What makes people creative? How can creativity be measured? How can creativity be enhanced? What can we learn from creative adults that will help us raise more creative children? Is creativity an aptitude? Is creativity an ability? Is creativity a domain? Is creativity acquired? Is creativity innate? What happens in the mind while a person is creating? What are the conditions for creative production? What inhibits creative production? What does the social setting contribute to creativity? Is creativity a solitary or community activity? All these, and more, are questions psychologists have sought to study with regard to creativity.

The idea of domain and field is pertinent here. A domain is part of a field with special organization, rules of practice, and body of knowledge. Mathematics is a field, but algebra, geometry, number theory, are domains. Literature is a field, but poetry is a domain. Education is a field, but educational research is a domain. Educational psychology is a hybrid domain that crosses two fields, education and psychology. Each domain has ways of knowing and representation that are unique to it. This is done through symbol systems special to the domain, including a special vocabulary and special technologies used only within that domain. A field is transformed through individual creators pushing the boundaries of their domains. People working within the domain, and connoisseurs of the domain decide what creative products are to be valued. In order to transform a field, the creator, must have mastery of the theory, the rules, the ways of knowing of that field, and also of the domain that is being used to transform it.

Psychology has several threads of research into creativity. *Psychometricians* (Guilford, Torrance), *developmentalists* (Feldman, Gardner, Csikszentmihalyi); *social psychologists* (Simonton, Amabile); *personality psychologists* (Barron, MacKinnon, Gough, and the other researchers at the famous Institute of Personality Assessment and Research); *humanistic psychologists* (Rogers, Maslow, May) *cognitive psychologists* (Sternberg , Ward, Perkins); *psychoanalysts* (Freud, Jung, Panter, Rothenberg, Weisberg); *domain psychologists* (Benbow, Bloom, Piirto) have all contributed work to psychological research on creativity. Educational psychology, however, has, to its detriment, concentrated on the psychometric approach to understanding creativity, to the exclusion of the others listed above.

PSYCHOMETRIC APPROACHES TO CREATIVITY

In 1950, J. P. Guilford, who was then President of the American Psychological Association, gave a speech that is often called the beginning of the modern interest in creativity as a measurable phenomenon. Guilford was the developer of a theory called The Structure of Intellect, where he theorized that there are 120 kinds of measurable intelligence factored across five operations, four contents, and six products. One of the five operations was divergent intellect.

J. P. Guilford differentiated between "convergent" and "divergent" intellect. "Convergent" intellect is a way of thinking that emphasized remembering what is known, being able to learn what exists, and being able to save that information in one's brain. "Divergent" intellect is a mode of cognition that emphasized the revision of what was already known, of exploring what would be known, and of building new information. People who prefer the "convergent" mode of intellect supposedly tend to do what is expected of them, while those who prefer the "divergent" mode of intellect supposedly tend to take risks and to speculate. Here are Guilford's original psychometric terms: (1) Fluency, (2) Novelty, (3) Flexibility (4) Synthesizing ability, (5) Analyzing ability. (6) Reorganization or redefinition of already existing ideas (7) Degree of complexity, and (8) Evaluation. He developed ways to measure each of these, and called them *divergent production*. Divergent production has been confused with creativity. Whole industries of exercise books, curricula, assessment systems, and suggestions have been based on the psychometrically measured Guilfordian "operation" of divergent production.

Taking up Guilford's call, researchers at the University of Chicago did several studies in the 1960s. Among the most frequently cited were those by Getzels, Jackson, Wallach, and Kogan. They were trying to quantify creativity, to make tests of divergent production. These studies were widely interpreted to mean that those with high creative potential need a certain *threshold* of *intelligence*, about one standard deviation above the mean, but not necessarily the highest intelligence (two or more standard deviations above the mean). This separation of creativity and intelligence has led to much confusion. However, by the early 1970s, Wallach said that the most fruitful researches would probably be into the areas of creativity within domains. Bloom, in the 1980s, was one of the first psychologists to study creativity in domains. He and his colleagues explored the patterns in the lives of research neurologists, pianists, sculptors, mathematicians, and tennis players. Likewise, a multitude of studies done at the Study for Mathematically Precocious Youth (SMPY) by Benbow, Brody, and Stanley have exposed the paths that lead to high mathematical creativity and its cousin, scientific creativity.

Another educational psychologist, E. P. Torrance, set out to create and validate tests that would identify creative potential. His Torrance Tests of Creative Thinking (TTCT) have been used in schools, to select students. These tests were similar to the Guilford tests of divergent production, and tested the ability to be fluent, flexible, and the like. The higher the score, the more potentially creative the child was. The logical fallacy was engaged. Scoring high on a *divergent production* test meant that a student was called *creative*. Torrance and his colleagues continued, until his death in 2003, to publish follow-up studies and refinements on his tests. He also invented many activities and exercises meant to help people be more creative (again, a logical fallacy, for they were mostly exercises in divergent production, which may be a part of creativity, but which was taken for creativity).

Two other psychologists have influenced the education enterprise. Educational psychologist Joseph Renzulli came up with a definition of giftedness, which said that a gifted person had three characteristics: above average intelligence, creativity, and task commitment. Renzulli insists that the gifted person must have "creativity," and not simply a high IQ. Renzulli and his colleagues developed a widely used creativity checklist used to identify creative children. The checklist has three of eleven items that feature the presence of a sense of humor. For schools to say that "creative potential" is *measurably* separate from having academic ability or high academic achievement has produced identification systems for creative thinking, based on a threshold of intelligence test scores and using divergent production tests or creativity checklists.

Cognitive psychologist Howard Gardner's theory of multiple intelligences and creativity was explicated in a book (1993) illustrating that creativity is possible within each of his first seven intelligences (he has since added an eighth), and he explicated this using case examples of a famous writer (T. S. Eliot), painter (Pablo Picasso), social reformer (Gandhi), scientist (Darwin), dancer (Martha Graham), composer (Stravinsky), and psychoanalyst (Freud). Gardner's intelligences are abstractions that have to meet eight criteria, including being psychometrically measurable. These intelligences are not domains of creativity. For example, bodily kinesthetic intelligence is related to the domain of dance, but it is not dance. However, a dancer needs other types of Gardner's intelligences, for example, spatial intelligence. None of the intelligences exists in a pure form in human creators.

Educational Psychology and Creativity

Domain-based creativity emphasizes that the domain itself (literature, visual arts, science, mathematics, music, theater, dance, and the like) defines what products are creative and what people are creative. The creative person is creative in *something*, not just generally creative. Creativity in domains is task specific, idiosyncratic to the domain. Creativity enhancement programs must modify their tasks to be specific to the domain. For example, brainstorming is a common divergent production fluency technique, but it should be used to enhance creativity within the domain. People in business can brainstorm about business-related problems; people writing a comedy show can brainstorm about ideas for the next episode; people in a dance troupe can brainstorm with their bodies, ideas for new dances.

Successful creators have similar patterns of education and familial influence, depending on the *domain* in which the creativity is practiced. Domain-based creativity is featured in a recent book (Kaufman and Baer, 2004). The researchers have studied persons by domain of creativity rather than by general creativity aptitude, with a view to how their life paths can inform the educational process. Studies of creative people within domains of achievement have led to some of the best evidence of what behaviors and situations predict the likelihood of creative productivity in adulthood. Each domain has its own rules of accomplishment and paths to achievement.

CREATIVITY AS CREATORS IN DOMAINS PRACTICE IT

Many books of exercises in fluency, flexibility, elaboration, and the like, exist. A popular technique taught in creativity enhancement classes is SCAMPER (Substitute, Combine, Alter, Modify, Put to another use, Eliminate, Reverse). They are based on the Guilfordian psychometric model, and they do not go far enough in describing the creative process as practiced by real creators in the domains. Real creators in real domains, as demonstrated in their memoirs, biographies, and interviews, do not talk about fluency, flexibility, elaboration, or SCAMPER. In their creative process, they seem to demonstrate several core attitudes (Piirto, 2004). These are an attitude of naiveté, of self-discipline, of risk-taking, and of group trust if in collaboration.

Core Attitude of Naiveté

Naiveté means openness, and refers to the fact that creative people pay attention to the small things, and are able to view their fields and domains by seeing the old as if it were new. Naiveté is an attitude of acceptance and curiosity about the odd and strange. Naiveté includes the ability to notice and to remark differences in details. Igor Stravinsky called it "the gift of observation." He said, "The true creator may be recognized by his ability always to find about him, in the commonest and humblest thing, items worthy of note."

Core Attitude of Self-Discipline

When one studies the lives of creators, one often finds they have created many, many works, even though they are only known for one, two, or a few. This self-discipline leads to the great productivity of creators. Van Gogh wrote to Theo, "I am daily working on drawing figures. I shall make a hundred of them before I paint them." Choreographer Agnes de Mille, noted that "all artists—indeed all great careerists—submit themselves, as well as their friends, to lifelong, relentless discipline, largely self-imposed and never for any reason relinquished." Most well-known creators are known for only a few of their voluminous numbers of creative works, produced through great self-discipline over a period of years. Expertise research says that one cannot contribute anything new to a domain unless one has been working in the domain for at least ten years.

Core Attitude of Risk-Taking

Risk-taking in creative people has been noticed since creativity began to be studied at the Institute of Personality Assessment and Research in the 1950s. Risk-taking enables one to try new things. While introverted and shy creators may eschew physical risk-taking, professional risk-taking in creators may be manifested in trying new forms, styles, or subjects. The kind of courage they have is the courage to stumble, fail, and, after rejection, to try again. Creative courage is finding the new, providing the vanguard's warning of what is about to happen in the culture, showing in image and symbol, through their imaginations, what is possible. The creative artists and scientists threaten what is. That is why, in repressive societies, those creators who speak out in image and in symbol are jailed or exiled. This requires courage in the presence of censure and rejection.

Core Attitude of Group Trust

In collaborative creativity, which is the kind used in team efforts, the group must have some modicum of trust. The comedy writing team, the business innovation team, need to create in a climate where the unorthodox, the unusual, the zany, the unconventional, are valued and not put down or ridiculed. Group trust is also important in dance, and in the theater. Working in a group creates an interdependency, as each member has a role to play, and a job to do, and they cannot be egotistical or selfish, or the whole project will suffer. One person cannot dominate; everyone must play and experience together. Trust is necessary among the members of the group.

THE SEVEN *I*'S

Here are some further aspects of the creative process as really practiced by real creators in the arts, sciences, and business (Piirto, 2004).

Inspiration

All creators talk about inspiration. Literally, inspiration is a taking in of breath. In terms of creativity, inspiration provides the motivation to create. Inspiration is a breathing or infusion into the mind or soul of an exaltation. Several types of inspiration are discussed by creators in domains.

The Visitation of the Muse: The Inspiration of Love.   Being inspired by regard for another has been called the visitation of the muse. Muse originally meant "reminder." Today, when we speak of the muse, we speak of the inspiration of love, or Erato, the muse of love. Inspiration often comes in response to a feeling for someone, quite possibly a sexual feeling, certainly an emotional identification. Everyone has written a secret love poem whether the love is requited or unrequited. Poets write love poems, as Elizabeth Barrett Browning did with her sonnet, "How do I love thee? Let me count the ways." Choreographers make ballets for their muses, as Balanchine did for Suzanne Farrell, Maria Tallchief, and his other ballerina wives. Visual artists paint nudes, as Picasso did for each of his many muses (and then he painted them as monsters after the relationships ended). Many of these works are efforts to express eroticism within the boundaries of the medium within which the artists are working. The creator longs for the muse, and in the process of longing, creates a song, a play, a poem, a theorem. Many creators throughout history have claimed they take dictation from a muse and claim no relationship between their own selves and the selves they create on paper. The muse possesses the creator.

Creators often speak as if what they write was sent from something within but afar. Inspirations "come." Some creators feel as if they are go-betweens, mediums. Some mysterious force impels them, works through their hands, wiggles through them, shoots from them. This type of inspiration also applies in theater. For example, some actors speak of being receptacles for their characters' souls, of being possessed. Today actors talk about "getting into" the character. Athletes talk of putting on their "game face." They often have preperformance rituals for entering the state of mind necessary. This might include putting on their makeup, meditating, or being alone for a period of time.

Einstein envisioned the theory of relativity kinesthetically, through his muscles; Tesla saw the design of the alternating current generator in a vision; Gauss could calculate complex formulas instantly; the uneducated mathematical genius, Ramanujan said that his genius came in dreams from a goddess named Namagiri. Brahms said that the inspiration for his music flowed into him from God, and that he could see them in his mind's eye. The inspirations arrived in the following.

The Inspiration of Nature.   The inspiration of nature, of trees, brooks, skies, birds, and other flora and fauna is a well-known venue for breathtaking writing. The poets of the T'Ang Dynasty of eighth century China influenced countless modern poets with their natural scene setting. The English romantics used nature as inspiration, and decried the industrial revolution as in Wordsworth's sonnet, "The world is too much with us; late and soon, / Getting and spending, we lay waste our powers; / Little we see in nature that is ours."

To grow dizzy from contemplation and in-taking of natural glories is so commonplace in the creative process that it almost goes unnoticed. What causes youngsters to want to become scientists, especially biologists? The inspiration of nature. What inspires Sunday painters to stand by the seashore dabbing away? The inspiration of nature. Surely nature inspired the art of Audubon, the books of Roger Tory Peterson, and the musical compositions of Jean Sibelius.

Inspiration through Substances.   The use of substances—alcohol, drugs, herbs—has a long and respectable reputation within the literature on the creative process in writers, artists, and others. Aldous Huxley wrote about the influence of mescaline; Samuel Taylor Coleridge about the influence of opium; Jack Kerouac about amphetamines; Edgar Allen Poe about absinthe; the seventh-century Chinese Zen poet Li Po about wine; Fyodor Dostoevsky about whiskey; Allen Ginsberg about LSD; Michael McClure about mushrooms, peyote, and also about heroin and cocaine.

The list of substances used could go on and on. The altered mental state brought about by substances has been thought to enhance creativity—to a certain extent. The partaker must have enough wits about self to descend into the abyss to reap what is learned there, but to also be able to return and put it aside. The danger of turning from creative messenger to addicted body is great, and many creators have succumbed, especially to the siren song of alcohol.

After taking drugs, Allen Ginsberg had a vision of William Blake. "I had the impression of the entire universe as poetry filled with light and intelligence and communication and signals. Kind of like the top of my head coming off, letting in the rest of the universe connected to my own brain." Ginsberg viewed the initial vision as the most important, most genuine experience he ever had, and he spent many years trying to recapture it through drugs and meditation.

Inspiration by Others' Creativity, Especially Works of Art and Music.   Many creators are inspired by others' creativity, especially by works of art and music produced by other artists. Art inspires. Music also inspires. Friendships between artists of different genres abound in biographical literature.

Artist Juan Miró described his neighborhood in Paris on Blomet Street from 1921 to 1927. He said that Blomet Street was a crucial place at a crucial time for him. The street represented friendship and a lofty exchange of ideas and discoveries among a superior group of creative people. Miró and his friends listened to music, talked, drank, and were poor struggling artists together. They also read Rimbaud and Lautreamont, Dostoevsky and Nietzsche. Other friends included writer Antonin Artaud, visual artists Jean Dubuffet and Juan Gris, and surrealists Andre Breton and Paul Eluard. His friend Ernest Hemingway bought his major breakthrough painting, "The Farm."

Thinkers and scholars routinely get inspiration from reading the works of others. French philosopher Michel Foucault found inspiration for his work *The Order of Things* in the works of Argentine playwright and novelist Jorge Luis Borges, who was making up an incongruous classification of animals from a fictional Chinese encyclopedia. Borges's audacious invention of this reference work inspired Foucault to consider the very nature of taxonomies, which to him were ceremonial categories that did not have life or place. His philosophical works have become must reading for postmodern thinkers.

In physics, the creation of the Manhattan Project put scientist Neils Bohr, Joseph Carter, Enrico Fermi, Richard Feynman, Hans Bethe, and Robert Oppenheimer, among others, together in a remote location in New Mexico, where they inspired each other to perfect the atomic bomb that was later dropped on Hiroshima and Nagasaki.

Inspiration from Dreams.   Many creators trust their dreams. The other side, the dark side, the night side, is very important to the creative process. Dreams have inspired many creative works. People who are highly creative often believe in their dreams. Dreams can have secret, esoteric symbols and meaning. Dreams can help them with their inventions and with creating art. Dreams can predict the future. They believe they can program their dreams. Creative people also try to remember their dreams, and they believe their dreams help them to solve problems.

The Surrealists encouraged creators to use their dreams as inspiration. Freudian psychology had a great influence on the Surrealists. Both Freud and Jung wrote extensively on the significance of dreams. Freud believed that dreams are wish fulfillment and Jung asserted that dreams capture the collective unconscious—the primitive archetypes lost to us in our waking state. Creators don't seem to care to use dreams' jolly, whimsical, dark, or brooding content for material.

The Inspiration of Novel Surroundings: Travel.   Travel seems to facilitate the creative process, perhaps because the novelty of sensory experience is inspirational, and a sense of naiveté is easy to maintain. Shifting our perspective by going to a new milieu, seeing how others do things differently, sleeping in strange rooms, eating exotic food can usher in great creative explosions.

Imagery

Imagery is also part of the creative process. The term *imagery* is psychological, the ability to mentally represent imagined or previously perceived objects accurately and vividly. Imagery is an attribute of imagination. Imagery is not only visual, but also auditory, tactile, olfactory, and gustatory. Three types of studies of creativity and imagery have been done: (1) biographical and anecdotal studies of creators telling about their personal imagery and how it inspired them; (2) studies which compared people's ability to create imagery and their scores on certain tests of creative potential; and (3) studies about creative imagery and creative productivity.

Guided imagery training goes on in schools and in business and industry. This training attempts to help people learn to manipulate images in their minds. Imagery is essentially spatial, and as such, concrete evidence of the mind's power to construct. Coaches teach athletes to image their performances before they do them; they visualize the ski run, the football play, or the course for the marathon. Studies have shown that athletes who use imagery perform better.

Imagination

Imagination in the creative process refers to a mental faculty whereby one can create concepts or representations of objects not immediately present or seen. The philosopher Aristotle, considered works of the imagination such as poetry, drama, and fiction, more true than history because the artist could fabricate truth from the elements of history rather than exhaustively tell all the facts. The artist is able to tell the truth on a deep level, being able to see the patterns, and the overarching themes, using the imagination. Working from the imagination is both stimulating and entertaining. Visual imagination is not the only kind that creators use. Composers imagine works in their "mind's ear," and mechanics imagine problems in their physical, spatial, array. Imaginative thought is also called daydreaming, and may be called night dreaming, as well as being called fantasy.

Of importance to educational psychology, children's play is the seed ground of adult imagination. Preschool children engage in make-believe. Story lines begin to develop in children's play as they grow toward kindergarten age. Games with rules follow, during the primary years. Then symbolic play continues, into adulthood, with video games, gambling, amateur theater, or the vicarious enjoyment of stories in books, movies, and on television.

Intuition

Intuition is part of the creative process. Intuition is having a hunch, "just knowing," having a gut feeling. Creative people trust and prefer to use their intuition. Everyone has intuition, but many don't trust intuition. Intuition is ambiguous, nebulous. Biographical information, testing, historical and archival research, and experimental studies have shown that creative people use intuition in doing their work.

Intuition is not verifiable by scientific or empirical means. Intuition seems to be a personality preference on the Myers Briggs Type Indicator (MBTI) for artists, scientists, writers, entrepreneurs, mathematicians, actors, and composers. The place of intuition in creating has long been honored. Plato thought that what we intuit was actually remembered from ancient imprints of the ideal, the true. Jung thought that intuition was a message from the collective unconscious of the archetypes of the deep human experience. The importance of intuitive perception of the world, of a nonconcrete but still tangible apprehension of underlying truth informs the creator's view of life.

Insight

Insight in the creative process is the ability to see and understand clearly the inner nature of things, especially by intuition. Several types of insight have been researched by cognitive psychologists The studies have shown that insight has the appearance of suddenness, requires preparatory hard work, relies on reconceptualization, involves old and new information; and applies to ill-structured problems.

Insight involves restructuring the problem so that it can be seen in a different way. Many notable creative works have originated from insights. When insight happens, we just have to say "Aha! So that's how it works. So that's the answer. So that's what it's all about. So that's what the pattern is." The most famous image of insight is that of Archimedes rising from the bathtub, saying "Aha!" and running down the street, after he discovered the principle of the displacement of water. The "Aha!" comes after knowing the field really well, and after incubation.

Incubation

Incubation as a part of the creative process occurs when the mind is at rest. The body is at rest. The creator has gone on to something else. The problem is percolating silently through the mind and body. But somewhere, inside, down there below the surface, the dormant problem is arising. A solution is sifting. Incubation was one of the steps in Wallas's four-part description of problem solving. Pyschologists speak of an "incubation effect," which may be caused by conscious work on the problem, and afterwards, overwhelming fatigue, where what doesn't work has been forgotten. While resting, the mind works on putting unlike things together. All the ideas may be assimilated through this time period. Then awareness comes and the answer is there. Experiments have shown that if people are given a problem and told to solve it right away, they solve it less successfully than if they are given the problem and told to go away and think about it. People often incubate while driving, sleeping, exercising, even showering.

Kary Mullis, a Nobel-prize winner, came up with PCR (Polymerase Chain Reaction) while driving.

Improvisation

The importance of improvisation in the creative process cannot be understated. To play your musical instrument without music in front of you is frightening to some who have learned to trust in their reading ability and not in their intuition and musical memory. The idea of "play" in improvisation is a necessity. Think of children making up the game as they go along, lost in imagination, forming teams and sides in a fluid all-day motion generated by the discourse of the moment.

Improvisation seems to be a key part of the creative process. Some writers say that writing is like playing jazz. The poet James Merrill used automatic writing as an improvisational technique; William Butler Yeats used automatic writing as inspiration for work. Improvisation underlies all creativity, but in music and theater, the performer cannot revise the work as writers or painters can. Improvisation in theater and music is almost always collaborative, and requires instant communication between people in the improvisation group. Improvisation reveals inner truth. Dance choreographers rely almost universally on improvisation in order to begin to make a dance. Martha Graham would begin to dance, outlining the pattern she wanted, and her dancers would imitate her. Then she would work on fixing the gestures so that the dancers would be moving together.

OTHER ASPECTS OF THE CREATIVE PROCESS

In the studies, biographies, and memoirs, several other aspects of the creative process seem apparent (Piirto, 2002, 2004): (1) the need for solitude, (2) creativity rituals, (3) meditation, and (4) creativity as the process of a life.

The Need for Solitude

The core of the creative process is solitude. Modern society believes that people are their best selves when they are in human relationships. People who don't have human relationships, who are not married, or in love, or in a family, are viewed as somehow sick. In creative people's lives, their work is often the most important thing. Creative people may be solitary, but that doesn't make them neurotic or unhappy. These experiences that take place when a person is alone need not occur with external stimuli, but there is something transcendental about such experiences. When the person is suddenly alone and able to concentrate, she is able to decipher what may have seemed too puzzling, and to unite ideas that may have seemed too different. Not being able to achieve solitude is a huge frustration for many creative people.

Solitude induces reverie. The state between sleeping and waking is relaxed, allowing images and ideas to come so that attention can be paid. What is important is a state of passivity and receptivity. Some people achieve this while cooking, cleaning, or sewing alone, walking in the woods, or during a long, boring drive. Virginia Woolf called solitude "real life" and went on to say, "I find it almost incredibly soothing—a fortnight alone." Visual artist Audrey Flack said that solitary working, helps the artist see her destiny. "When you are working, you are alone with yourself. You get in touch with your own destiny. Like entering a dream state, the tendency is to disbelieve that that state has validity. But that is the true reality."

Creativity Rituals

Ritual is repetitive practice. Ritual involves special places, special procedures, and special repetitive acts during or before creating. Rituals are sometimes personal. The artist Marlene

Ekola Gerberick described going to her studio, creating a circle, pacing around the current work she is making, lighting candles, picking up stones and feathers, all the while getting herself from the world of her outside life to her inner world of creating.

Ritual serves to remove the creator from the outer and propel her to the inner. Some people walk or exercise before creating, and they often get their best ideas while doing it. Some people go for a long drive. Some arrange their rooms or desks a certain way. Some like to work at a certain time of day. The approach to the work is ritualistic, and the work itself could be called, perhaps, the ceremony.

Meditation

Like creativity, meditation is in. A look at the books on the shelves at the local bookstore reveals an ongoing curiosity about eastern religions that continues from the 1960s. An astonishing number of writers, for example, have embraced Buddhism (Piirto, 2002). One suspects this is because of the attention paid to meditation, to solitude, to the going within oneself of that religious faith. Here is a partial list: Allen Ginsberg, Robert Bly, W. S. Merwin, Anselm Hollo, Anne Waldman, Gary Snyder, Jane Augustine, John Cage, William Heyen, Lucien Stryk, and Philip Whalen. Rock poet Leonard Cohen spent several years in a Buddhist monastery.

The vehicles for discovering one's self are breath control, meditational technique, visualization, imagery. Often the creative work follows the meditation, and the meditation is a preparatory ritual for the creative work. Creative people, mystics, and ascetics of all religions have known that meditation helps creativity.

Creativity as the Process of a Life

Others have viewed the creative process not merely as an altered consciousness, an immense concentration, an attainment of solitude, but as more. That is, we can look at the process of a creative person's life. The creative process is viewed these days as the province of every human being, and not just of the Einsteins, O'Keeffes, or Darwins of the world, or of those who make creative products such as music, or poems, or mathematical formulas. People's lives are their creative products.

In enhancing people's creativity, new age teachers sometimes use methods such as visualization, imagery, metaphorization, chanting, and the formulation of affirmations. People hold sacred objects such as quartz crystals and sit beneath pyramids. They go on vision quests and bang drums, chant in tones, and dance like dervishes, seeking inner peace and the guidance for living a creative life. Creativity is intertwined in the feeling of awe, of closeness to the essential, that results.

Other, less exotic methods such as writing in journals (Julia Cameron, Ira Progoff, and Natalie Goldberg), drawing (Betty Edwards and Peter Jones), crooning and engaging with the Mozart effect (Don Campbell), or dancing (Gabrielle Roth) are also employed in teaching people to be more creative, and thus to enhance the process of their lives. Again, the educational psychology of divergent production is notably absent.

An outgrowth of the humanistic psychology movement and of the work of such humanistic psychologists as Rogers, Maslow, and Perls, this quest for inner meaning has even made it to public television stations, where fund-raising is led by former high school guidance counselor, Wayne Dyer. The Open Center and the Omega Institute in New York, offer creativity-focused sessions such as intensive journal workshops, dream, singing, empowerment, improvisational theater, and dance workshops. Almost all the teachers of these workshops have written books that tell us how to enhance our creativity. All have in common the probing of the inner psyche, making one's life a work of art, and the attainment of inner peace through auto-therapy done by making creative products.

Thus, the postpositivist educational psychological idea that divergent production, the teaching and testing of Guilford's cognitive operations is creativity, has given way to the new educational psychology of creativity, a consideration and practice of what real creators in domains do when they are being creative.

TERMS FOR READERS

Creativity—The root of the words "create" and "creativity" comes from the Latin *creâtus* and *creâre*. This means, "to make or produce," or literally, "to grow." The word also comes from the Old French base *kere*, and the Latin crescere, and *creber*. Other words with these same roots are *cereal, crescent, creature, concrete, crescendo, decrease, increase,* and *recruit.* "Creativity" is a relatively new noun. The word does not appear in the 1971 *Oxford English Dictionary*. That creativity is an *ability* has been a false assumption made by educators since the early 1950s. The noun "creativity" seems to have origins in psychology. *The Dictionary of Developmental and Educational Psychology* in 1986 defined creativity as "man's capacity to produce new ideas, insights, inventions, or artistic objects, which are accepted as being of social, spiritual, aesthetic, scientific, or technological value."

Psychometrics—Testing and assessment of mental processes.

FURTHER READINGS

Gardner, H. (1993). *Creating Minds*. New York: Basic Books.

Guilford, J. P. (1967). *The Nature of Human Intelligence*. New York: McGraw-Hill.

Kaufman, J., and Baer, J. (Eds.). (2004). *Creativity in Domains: Faces of the Muse*. Parsippany, NJ: Lawrence Erlbaum.

Piirto, J. (2002). *"My Teeming Brain": Understanding Creative Writers*. Cresskill, NJ: Hampton Press.

———. (2004). *Understanding Creativity*. Scottsdale, AZ: Great Potential Press.

Simonton, D. (1995). *Greatness: Who Makes History and Why?* New York: Guilford.

CHAPTER 42

Reclaiming Critical Thinking as Ideology Critique

STEPHEN BROOKFIELD

Critical thinking is a contested idea, one with a variety of meanings claimed by different groups—including the subdisciplines of psychology—for very different purposes. Show up at a conference session on critical thinking and you will find yourself in the company of people who locate criticality within contradictory intellectual traditions. What count as examples of critical behaviors can be defined in terms that represent almost completely opposed political and economic interests. To a group of executives thinking critically could be the process by which they discover the unchecked assumptions underlying a faulty marketing decision that has reduced corporate profits. To union or community activists it may imply an unequivocal critique of capitalism and the fight for worker cooperatives or factory councils. Thinking critically in this latter view involves action, specifically that of galvanizing opposition to the relocation of U.S. factories to non-unionized countries with no inconvenient pollution controls. Clearly, then, how the term *critical* is used inevitably reflects the ideology and worldview of the user.

In American educational psychology it is the tradition of analytic philosophy that most strongly frames how critical thinking is currently conceived and taught. From this perspective to be critical is to be skilled at conceptual and argument analysis, to recognize false inferences and logical fallacies, to be able to distinguish bias from fact, opinion from evidence, and so on. This kind of relentless critique of unexamined and possible faulty assumptions is perhaps most famously articulated in the scientific method's principle of falsifiability where intellectual effort is devoted to investigating erroneous aspects of scientific procedures. The analytic philosophy tradition comprises a set of valuable, even essential, intellectual functions, but it focuses on critical thinking solely as a cognitive process requiring a facility with language or mathematical games. Criticality here neglects social and political critique. By way of contrast, critical psychologists evaluate the theories and practices of educational psychology in terms of how they maintain an unjust status quo.

This chapter takes as its starting point a provocative essay by Kincheloe (2000), "Making Critical Thinking Critical." Kincheloe argues that criticality is grounded in the critical theory tradition but that its political and ethical dimensions have been forgotten. In Kincheloe's view critical thinking is really "the ability of individuals to disengage themselves from the tacit assumptions of discursive practices and power relations in order to exert more conscious control over their everyday lives" (p. 24). This kind of critical distancing from, and then oppositional reengagement with, the dominant culture is the central learning task of life, according to the Frankfurt School, who used the term *ideology critique* to describe this activity. If we accept this conceptualization of critical thinking then educational psychologists concerned with its investigation would be compelled to research the degree to which learners were aware of power relations in the school (and wider community) and the ways in which learners attempted to challenge these relations when they were perceived as unfair or abusive. Obviously this makes educational psychology's assessment of critical thinking a much more complex task than simply administering a standardized test such as the CAAP Critical Thinking Test or Watson-Glaser Critical Thinking Appraisal. Assessing critical thinking that is conceived as ideology critique has a much closer connection to political economy and ethnography than it does to administering paper-and-pencil multichoice tests.

When I talk of critical thinking in this chapter, it is the ideology critique tradition I am chiefly invoking, particularly the work of theorists such as Gramsci, Althusser, and Marcuse. As a learning process ideology critique describes the ways in which people learn to recognize how unjust dominant ideologies are embedded in everyday situations and practices. As an educational activity ideology critique focuses on helping people come to an awareness of how capitalism shapes social relations and imposes—often without our knowledge—belief systems and assumptions that justify and maintain economic and political inequity. Conceptualizing critical thinking within this tradition unites cognition with political consciousness to define it as the ability to recognize and challenge oppressive practices. When informed by ideology critique one could argue that a prime indicator of critical thinking would be skepticism of the very standardized critical thinking tests generally used to assess it! Such tests would be investigated for the extent to which they were culturally skewed sorting devices that neglected sophisticated forms of everyday cognition and reproduced within the school those power relations taken for granted in the outside world.

Critical thinkers in the ideology critique tradition would also be engaged in action. A critical educational psychology does not separate the political from the cognitive. It views critical thinking as transformative in that it exists to bring about social and political change. Teachers who educate for critical thinking attempt to provide people with knowledge and understandings intended to free them from oppression. The point of critical thinking in this tradition is to generate knowledge that will change, not just interpret, the world. In this way, critical thinking qualifies for that most overused of adjectives, *transformative*. There is no presupposition of thought being distanced from social intervention or political action. On the contrary, the converse is true. Critical thought requires such intervention. Its explicit intent is to galvanize people into replacing capitalism with truly democratic social arrangements. One important measure of critical thinking, therefore, is its capacity to inspire action. In the evaluation literature this is referred to as consequential validity; that is, validity that asks for assessments of who benefits and who is harmed by an inquiry, measurement, or method. The knowledge it produces can be considered useful to the extent that it helps change the behavior of its unit of analysis (disenfranchised and alienated citizens acting in society).

Critical thinking as ideology critique therefore entails informed action in the world to fight ideological brainwashing and create democratic practices. In this tradition students who are critical thinkers can be recognized by their opposition to the lies their history texts tell them and by their alertness to those times when the media function as a mouthpiece for Conservative policy (as in Fox News's "fair and balanced" coverage of the American invasion of Iraq). Critically thoughtful students will most likely be challenging teachers to justify their actions, in particular the choice of certain curricula or evaluative procedures that are deemed to produce "official" knowledge. Ideology critique recognizes the expression of critical thought in students' calling school strikes, demonstrating in support of innovative teachers whose contracts are not renewed, and organizing to dismiss teachers who bully, either physically or symbolically. Critical thought is not the blind dismissal of the school status quo with no consideration as to what might replace it. It is thinking manifest in active claims by students of the right to be involved in shaping the classroom practices to which they are subject. On a broader level it is thinking through how schools might become sites that challenge dominant ideology and exclusionary practices. And on a macro-societal level it is thinking used to abolish the exchange economy of capitalism that commodifies human relations and turns subjects killed in foreign incursions into "collateral damage."

At the very heart of critical thinking is the skeptical analysis of dominant ideology. Ideology is viewed as an illusory system of false ideas that prevents people from correctly perceiving their true situation and real interests. If they are to free themselves from social repression, therefore, people must rid themselves of ideological illusion. In the critical theory tradition learning to resist ideological manipulation is the chief sign that someone can think critically. This tradition builds on Marx's views that the relations of production and material conditions of society determine people's consciousness. Blatantly unequal political and economic systems would endure unchallenged if the ruling class could get its ideas broadly accepted as the "objective" commonsense view of the world. In Marx and Engels's view the ruling class aims to represent its interest as the common interest of all members of society. It strives to universalize its ideas; that is, to convince the masses that ruling class conceptions of the world are the only rational, universally valid ones. When conceived as ideology critique, critical thinking educates people to recognize and oppose this kind of ideological manipulation. Critical thinkers view ideology as inherently duplicitous, a system of false beliefs that justify practices and structures that keep people unknowingly in servitude. If critical thinking is regarded as a form of ideology critique then the focus of its curriculum—the thing we are being critical about—is ideology. An early task of education for critical thinking, therefore, is to get learners to understand the concept of ideology.

Defined briefly, ideology is the broadly accepted set of values, beliefs, myths, explanations, and justifications that appears self-evidently true, empirically accurate, personally relevant, and morally desirable to a majority of the populace, but that actually works to maintain an unjust social and political order. Ideology does this by convincing people that existing social arrangements are naturally ordained and obviously work for the good of all. Its very normality and unremarkableness is a profound barrier to any critique. It is so hard to detect because it is embedded in language, social habits and cultural forms that combine to shape the way we think about the world. Ideology is equated with commonsense, a given, rather than being seen as a set of beliefs that are deliberately skewed to support the interests of a powerful minority. In recent years post-structuralists such as Foucault (1980) have clarified how knowledge and power entwine to create regimes of truth; that is, the collections of dominant ideas, frameworks of analysis, and forms of discourse that shape what we think are self-evidently obvious truths.

Strongly influenced by Marx and also by Gramsci's notion of hegemony, the French philosopher Louis Althusser deepened the understanding of ideology in his influential essay on ideology and ideological state apparatuses (1971). For Althusser ideology was a systematic form of thought control that ensured that people at all levels of the economic and social system accepted the system's basic reasonableness. Ideology intentionally obscured the fact that the system was based on certain values that furthered some interests over others. If ever the possibility of alternative values was seriously countenanced, then the system could be challenged. But if the system was accepted as a natural phenomenon needing no explanation or justification (because its essential rightness was so obvious) then the possibility of resistance evaporated.

Althusser believed that people lived naturally and spontaneously in ideology without realizing that fact. He argued that those who are ideological believe themselves by definition outside ideology. Consequently, one of the effects of ideology is the denial of any ideological influence by those laboring under such influence. Ideology never says, "I am ideological." In Althusser's view we can claim in all sincerity to be neutral, objective, and free of ideological distortion when this is really impossible. This conviction of their own nonideological nature extends even to those who manipulate the ruling ideology in the cause of exploitation and repression. To Althusser it was obvious that ideological managers such as educators would sincerely and strenuously deny the ideological character of their work. They would say "I'm just here to teach basic skills" or "I'm just here to teach the content/syllabus." Being immersed in ideology prevented them from stepping outside it and perceiving its social functioning.

How can people be so steeped in ideology without being aware of that fact? Althusser argued that this was made possible because an ideology always exists in an apparatus, and its practice, or practices; in other words, ideology is expressed in actions, not just in words. Ideology lives and breathes in our daily decisions, routine behaviors, and small-scale interactions. This takes into the world of Goffman's presentation of self in everyday life and also to Foucault's emphasis on the inscription of disciplinary power in the practices of daily life. Intimate gestures, routinized professional conduct, and conversational conventions all reflect a wider ordering of power relations that is unconsciously confirmed in these practices. The most subtle forms of ideology are buried in the modes in which concrete, day-to-day practices are organized. Ideology thus becomes less a clearly identifiable system of ideas and more a participation in actions, social games, and rituals that are themselves ideologically determined.

In the critical theory tradition coming to understand and challenge the workings of ideology is the core critical thinking process. If we think critically, so the argument goes, we stand a better chance of acting on the basis of instincts, impulses, and desires that are truly our own, rather than implanted in us. Since capitalism will do its utmost to convince us that we should live in ways that support its workings, we cannot be fully human unless we use critical thought to unearth and challenge the ideology that justifies this system. This is critical thinking's project. When we think critically we learn that the inclinations, biases, hunches, and apparently intuitive ways of experiencing reality that we had previously regarded as unique to us are, in fact, socially learned. We learn that what we thought were our idiosyncratic perspectives and dispositions are actually ideologically sedimented. Critical thinking as ideology critique helps us understand how we learn political ideals, morality, and social philosophy within the institutions of civil society such as schools, associations, clubs, families, and friendship networks. It shows us that the constructs and categories we use instinctively to understand our daily experiences are ideologically framed. What Williams (1977) calls our "structures of feeling" come to be seen as socially induced, learned from the cultural group and social class to which we belong. So critical thinking involves people learning how ideology lives within them as well as understanding how it buttresses the structures of the outside world that stand against them. What strikes us as the normal order of things is suddenly revealed through ideology critique as a constructed reality that protects the interests of the powerful.

CRITICAL THINKING AS COUNTER-HEGEMONY

One of the most important extensions to the understanding of how ideological control is created and maintained is Antonio Gramsci's analysis of hegemony. Hegemony describes the way that people learn to accept as natural and in their own best interest an unjust social order. In one of Gramsci's most invoked phrases, "every relationship of hegemony is necessarily an educational relationship" (1995, p. 157). People learn to embrace as commonsense wisdom certain beliefs and practices that work against their interests and serve those of the powerful. If hegemony works as it should then there is no need for the state to employ coercive forms of control—heavy policing, curfews, torture, assassination squads—to maintain social order. Instead of people opposing and fighting unjust structures and dominant beliefs they learn to regard them as preordained, part of the cultural air they breathe. In many ways hegemony is the conceptual bridge between the Marxist notion of dominant ideology and Habermas's idea of the colonization of the lifeworld by capitalism and technical rationality. It emphasizes how the logic of capitalism and the process of commodification seeps and soaks itself into all aspects of everyday life—culture, health care, recreation, and even intimate relationships.

Critical thinking to uncover hegemony requires a tenacity and commitment. As conceived by Marx and Engels ideology is taught by the ruling class who attempt to universalize their worldview. In hegemony, however, we teach ourselves dominant ideology, so that we become are our own enthusiastic controllers. The subtlety of hegemony lies in the fact that it is very difficult to peel away layers of oppression to uncover a small cabal clearly conspiring to keep the majority silent and disenfranchised. If there is any conspiracy at work here it is the conspiracy of the normal. The ideas and practices of hegemony—the stock opinions, conventional wisdom, and commonsense ways of behaving in particular situations that we take for granted—are part and parcel of everyday life. It is not as if these are being forced on us against our will. Hegemony's dark irony, its cruelty, is that people take pride in learning and then acting on the beliefs and assumptions that work to enslave them. In learning diligently to live by these assumptions people become their own jailers. By incorporating the concept of hegemony into the analysis of ideology Gramsci widens our understanding of how ideology contributes to the maintenance of social control. The emphasis shifts from understanding how the state or sovereign imposes a view of the world on a neutral, skeptical, or resentful populace, to understanding how people are willing partners with the ruling group actively colluding in their own oppression. Indeed, persuading people to accept their oppression as normal, even desirable, is the central educational task of hegemony.

Gramsci viewed critical thinking as the core process of education and something that all students could learn. For him the point of critical thinking is to help workers become aware of their oppression and organize for political transformation. The revolutionary party then becomes the educational agency charged with fostering this learning and transformation. Learning this kind of critical thinking is not easy since it involves adults deliberately distancing themselves from their childhood experiences and coming to see these as culturally constructed. But since in his view all humans are intellectuals—reasoning beings guided by dimly sensed philosophical beliefs—it is simply a case of making critical an already existing activity (i.e., thinking).

In his analysis of how we become critical across the lifespan Gramsci argues that it is in childhood that consciousness is socially, and relatively uncritically, formed. The child's consciousness is not an individually produced phenomenon; rather, it reflects the sector of civil society in which the child participates, and the social relations which are formed within family, neighborhood, and community. Thinking is always a social process in his view and the ruts and patterns of our cognitive pathways are etched by the pressure to conform to the ideas prevailing in our class, racial, ethnic, and gender groups. Gramsci writes that in acquiring a conception of the world we always belong to a particular grouping in which the majority shares the same mode of thinking and acting. For him childhood is a period of uncritical cultural immersion with true critical thinking more of an adult learning process.

Learning to recognize and challenge hegemony—the core critical thinking process for Gramsci—is linked to the development of political movements that fight class oppression, racism, sexism, and homophobia. Thinking critically is not an isolated internal decision or private mental act made by individuals somehow abstracted out from the world in which they move. It is a socially framed decision and, in Gramsci's view, linked to membership of a revolutionary party. The content of critical thinking (recognizing and contesting ruling class hegemony), the process of critical thinking (the methods and approaches people use to learn how hegemony works and how it can be countered), and the cognitive components of critical thinking (the concepts, categories, and interpretive forms that help people understand how hegemony works) all reflect the learner's situation—in contemporary terms, his or her location or positionality.

The major critical thinking project that consumed Gramsci's attention was the way in which workers developed a revolutionary class-consciousness and the way they then learned to act on this to change society and create a proletarian hegemony. This form of critical thinking involved two activities recognizable to educational psychologists today; learning to challenge common sense perceptions of the world (which he felt were often organized to reflect the dominant group's ideas) and learning to think independently (which happened as workers tried to distance themselves from prevailing habits of mind). If this learning occurred, Gramsci argued, people would be in a good position to blend revolutionary theory and practice. He studied these learning processes as they were lived out in the struggle for working-class revolution, and the learners he was most concerned with were political activists and organizers inside and outside the Italian Communist Party. But his analysis of learning has a contemporary resonance. Learning to think critically, for example, required the learner to work out consciously a particular conception of the world and then to engage in informed civic action based on that conception. For him critical thinkers were their own guides, refusing to accept passively and supinely from outside any molding of their personality.

How do people learn to do this? To Gramsci the elementary phase of developing critical thinking is found in the sense of being "different" and "apart." This feeling of separation provides an instinctive feeling of independence that progresses to the development of a single and coherent conception of the world. Here we can see the lexicon of self-directedness familiar within educational psychology, but of self-directedness as a deliberate break with, and a standing apart from, dominant ideology. A precursor to any form of authentic critical thinking, therefore, is the person's perception of herself as an outsider. The exercise of independent critical thought can have powerful political effects since an independent thinker often has more influence than a cadre of university academics. Gramsci is careful to point out, however, that independence of thought is not necessarily the same as the creation of original knowledge. One can experience critical thinking in a powerful way, even if what is being learned is already known to others. To discover a truth by oneself, without external suggestions or assistance, is to be authentically creative, even if the truth that is discovered is an old one. This independent critical coming to truth that others have already discovered (such as the realization that we collude in our own oppression) represents an important phase of intellectual maturity necessary to the discovery of new truth. Developing a critical awareness of how hegemony works, therefore, is the necessary precondition to learning how this state of affairs might be changed.

The elementary phase of critical thinking identified by Gramsci involves learning a basic sense of independence and separateness. This phase is then followed by a consciousness of one's own place in a hegemonic or counter-hegemonic group. Gramsci wrote that working people had two theoretical consciousnesses (or one contradictory consciousness). One of these was superficial and explicit, inherited from the past and uncritically absorbed from dominant authority. This superficially explicit conception of the world comprised the dominant ideas of the time. It worked to induce a condition of moral and political passivity that effectively nullified any serious political challenge to the established order. This first, superficial form of consciousness was hegemonic—a form of ideological control producing quietism and conformity. When circumstances conspired to have a group or class form itself into a movement to fight oppression, then the second consciousness—critical consciousness—began to emerge. It was to the furtherance of this second consciousness that critical thinking was directed. Thus, for Gramsci, critical thinking involved a struggle of radically different conceptualizations of the world and the creation of a radically different social system.

This is an unequivocal location of critical thinking in political struggle. Gramsci is saying that criticality is learned in the context of working-class activism and that a truer conception of reality is realized as working people understand their common situation and the need for collective action. Through critical thinking a worker comes to a consciousness of his solidarity with other workers. Critical thinking unites workers in a collective, practical transformation of the world. In Gramsci's analysis, the chief agent of facilitating critical thinking is the workers' revolutionary party. It is the party that organizes the workers' movement, triggers critical thinking and in so doing ensures political transformation. In this analysis educators are party members and activists, not classroom teachers who happen to have an interest in political change.

CRITICAL THINKING AS NECESSARY NEGATIVITY

A common theme in critical theory is that critical thinking begins with a rejection of what currently exists. This rejection is not seen as nihilistic or destructive, but rather as a necessary negativism. In an exploitative, falsely positive world, being negative is a hopeful act. One of the chief proponents of this view is Herbert Marcuse, who in *One-Dimensional Man* (1964) argued that we live in a society characterized by the cynical manipulation of needs by vested economic and technical interests. These needs are created by the dominant capitalist order and then internalized by us until they are indistinguishable from our most basic desires. We come to define ourselves, and the attainment of a fulfilled life, in terms of these needs. In such a society it is hard to identify revolutionary forces, since to be dissatisfied is taken as a sign of inadequacy or psychological disturbance. When the administered life becomes equated with the good life then the intellectual and emotional refusal to go along with dominant expectations appears neurotic and impotent. Thought that protests the given order of things is effectively anaesthetized by defining it as irrational or simply reframing it to fit the prevailing worldview.

Marcuse hypothesized that if we live in a society in which thought is circumscribed within certain limits that justify the correctness of the existing order, then critical thought must by definition exist outside of, and in opposition to, these limits. He argued that true critical thinking is necessarily distanced from the false concreteness of everyday reasoning. In his view an irreducible difference exists between the universe of everyday thinking and language on the one side, and philosophical thinking and language on the other. Critical thinking is conceptual in nature and deals with abstracts such as truth, beauty, fairness, or justice. Such abstraction is enhanced by a separation from the material practices of everyday life. Marcuse's equation of criticality with a learned capacity for abstract analysis and philosophical speculation challenges us to rethink our dismissal of conceptual analysis as an irrelevant game played only by ivory tower academics distanced from revolutionary struggle. For him critical philosophical thought is necessarily transcendent and abstract and subversive of the cynical opportunism that rules in everyday language and thought.

Not only does critical thinking operate at a necessary level of abstractness for Marcuse, it is also in an important sense negative. As articulated by Marcuse critical thinking is first and foremost critical negative. This is because critical thinking opposes the self-contentment of everyday common sense that is concerned to embrace the given, taken-for-granted aspects of life. Critical thinking starts with what's wrong with what currently exists, with illuminating omissions, distortions, and falsities in current thinking. In Newman's (1994) terms, critical thinking is about laying blame and defining enemies, both necessary precursors to informed social change. A negative appraisal of contemporary patterns of reasoning is the first step in developing a positive vision of the kind of thought that could replace what now exists. So what in the short term seems negative is in the long term positive. Marcuse argued that before we have the great liberation and the creation of what is to be, we need the great refusal, the rejection of what is. Those participating in the great refusal "reject the rules of the game that is rigged against them, the ancient strategy of patience and persuasion, the reliance on the Good Will in the Establishment, its false and immoral comforts, its cruel affluence" (Marcuse, 1969, p. 6). Saying no to a culture of domination is critical thinking as an act of hope.

What kind of education can prepare learners to think critically in the necessarily abstract and negative manner proposed by Marcuse? Based on his analysis it will be first and foremost a conceptual education. Marcuse was certainly very ready to give all kinds of strategic advice on direct political action, but he never left behind his fundamental conviction that learning to think conceptually was as much a part of the revolution as creating new political and economic structures. In the administered society of one-dimensional thought, any kind of conceptual abstract reasoning that challenges the emphasis on false concreteness is by definition critical. Hence, a fundamental task of education is to provide students with the conceptual instruments for a solid and thorough critique of contemporary culture, particularly the equation of happiness with consumer affluence.

Marcuse's insistence on people learning to think conceptually challenges practices lionized in progressive education. In particular, his position seems to stand against the celebratory aspects of experiential learning. In Marcuse's view living in a one dimensional society means that most people's experiences are falsely concrete; that is, focused chiefly on the acquisitive pursuit of material luxuries via short-term, instrumental action. Celebrating and dignifying these kinds of experiences—even integrating them directly into the curriculum—only serves to legitimize existing ideology. Following a Marcusean line of analysis, experiential learning has meaning only if it focuses on deconstructing experiences and showing their one-dimensional nature, and if it avoids the uncritical celebration of people's stories. Experiential learning conducted in a Marcusean vein is learning to recognize how the ways we perceive and construct experience have been colonized by the dominant language of consumerism. Marcuse implicitly questions the wisdom of "starting where the students are," long a prized tenet of the progressive education canon. If "where the students are" is living a falsely concrete existence, then we need to get as far away from where they are as is possible, chiefly by insisting on conceptual analysis. The struggle to think conceptually is, therefore, inherently critical. It is also always a political struggle to Marcuse, not just a matter of intellectual development. Political action and cognitive movement are partners here in the development of revolutionary consciousness.

CONCLUSION

If critical thinking is a form of ideology critique then teaching critical thinking is a form of political practice. A curriculum focused on helping people learn to think critically in this way would consider a series of questions. How can learners be helped to understand the omnipresence of dominant ideology? How can they learn forms of reasoning that challenge this ideology and that question the social, cultural, and political forms it justifies? How can they learn to unmask the flow of power in their lives and communities? How can they learn of the existence of hegemony— the process whereby people learn to embrace ideas, practices, and institutions that actually work against their own best interests—and of their own complicity in its continued existence? And, once aware of it, how do they learn to contest its all-pervasive effects?

The 2003 unilateral American invasion of Iraq provides a powerful example of what happens when critical thinking is discouraged and when a critical questioning of dominant wisdom is labeled as unpatriotic, un-American. Here was the case of a superpower proposing to invade another country and establish an occupying army on the argument that at some time in the future the country concerned might pose a threat to the superpower's interests. No matter that no unequivocally convincing evidence had been produced to demonstrate this possibility.

No matter either that most of the rest of the world, and the United Nations, vigorously opposed this action. Had the old Soviet Union engaged in such an act it is easy to imagine the calumny and condemnation we would have heaped on its leaders. Most frightening of all, perhaps, was the extent to which the majority of people had come to accept unquestioningly the subtle (but completely erroneous) suggestion that Iraq had somehow been responsible for the Al Queda terrorist attacks of September 11, 2001. Because a critical perspective on the invasion was curiously absent from dominant media a majority of the populace were polled as believing that the pilots of the planes that destroyed the World Trade Center were born or trained in Iraq.

It was not so much that TV companies and major newspapers granted outright approval of the war (the Fox network's enthusiastic propagandizing for "Shock and Awe" and "Iraqi Freedom" being a notable exception), but more that there was so little critical thinking regarding the Bush administration's justifications for it. No stream of public discourse emerged into the country's consciousness, or at least that part of it represented by mainstream media, to debate the wisdom, morality, effectiveness, or potentially fateful consequences of this invasion. To the extent that the decision to invade was made by a handful of people without a full public discussion of the facts or justifications involved—which would necessarily entail the presentation of a range of counterviews—it was undemocratic. A democracy is essentially a continuous conversation a group, community, or society conducts about how it will order its common affairs and about how it will use its members' limited energies and resources. The more people who get to air their preferences on these matters, the more likely it is that the decisions made will be morally acceptable to the majority. The minority who don't like some of these decisions will at least feel that they have had a fair hearing even if their arguments did not win the day. But if the minority feels they were never heard from in the first place, or that their voices when they spoke were not really listened to, then they will conclude, with complete justification, that these decisions are undemocratic.

Progressives have often lionized American public education as a movement to create and build democracy. It has a traditional concern to develop critical thinkers with the responsibility this necessarily entails of countering any process of brainwashing or ideological manipulation. But in 2003 it seemed as if the voices of dissent that one would expect were effectively marginalized. True, outlets such as *The Nation* magazine, or the *Pacifica Radio* network, continued to represent a view that was outraged by the Bush administration's acts. But such expressions of dissent could easily be seen as an example of Marcuse's repressive tolerance (Marcuse, 1965). Repressive tolerance is a tolerance for just enough challenge to the system to be allowed to convince people that they live in a truly open society. This kind of tolerance of a managed amount of diverse views functions as a kind of pressure cooker letting off enough steam to prevent the whole pot from boiling over. When repressive tolerance is in place the apparent acceptance of all viewpoints only serves to reinforce an unfair status quo.

In the context of an administration's determination to invade another country, the critical thinking required does involve some of the cognitive moves approved by educational psychology critical thinking tests such as distinguishing bias from fact, challenging the conflation of evidence and opinion, and recognizing when unwarranted assumptions are being made. But critical thinking as ideology critique frames these moves with a specific purpose. The biases we detect are that what exist must by definition be right and that those in power have the best interests of all at heart. The opinion we challenge is our own, deeply felt opinion that when we act enthusiastically and without apparent forethought we are therefore acting in a way that serves our best interests. And the unwarranted assumption we question is the assumption that being negative is somehow antihuman, pessimistic, and cynical. Education for critical thinking, on the contrary, teaches that negativity is positive and rejection the beginning of hope.

REFERENCES

Althusser, L. (1971). *Lenin and Philosophy*. New York: Monthly Review Press.

Gramsci, A. (1995). *Further Selections from the Prison Notebooks, Antonio Gramsci* (D. Boothman, Trans. and Ed.). Minneapolis, MN: University of Minnesota Press.

Kincheloe, J. L. (2000). Making critical thinking critical. In D. Weil and H. K. Anderson (Eds.), *Perspectives in Critical Thinking: Essays by Teachers in Theory and Practice*. New York: Peter Lang.

Marcuse, H. (1964). *One-Dimensional Man*. Boston, MA: Beacon.

———. (1965). Repressive tolerance. In R. P. Wolff, B. Moore, and H. Marcuse (Eds.), *A Critique of Pure Tolerance*. Boston, MA: Beacon Press.

———. (1969). *An Essay on Liberation*. Boston, MA: Beacon Press.

Newman, M. (1994). *Defining the Enemy: Adult Education in Social Action*. Sydney: Stewart Victor Publishing.

CHAPTER 43

Ideological Formation and Oppositional Possibilities of Self-Directed Learning

STEPHEN BROOKFIELD

Educational discourse surrounding the concept of self-directed learning demonstrates, depending on one's viewpoint, either its remarkable conceptual utility, or the co-optation and enslavement by corporate capitalism of a once subversive idea. From being regarded as a vaguely anarchistic, Illich-inspired threat to formal education, self-direction is now comfortably ensconced in the citadel, firmly part of the conceptual and practical mainstream. The marriage between self-direction and formal education seems to have settled into a comfortable and harmonious rut. Epistemologically contradictory approaches to researching self-direction (e.g., quantifying the hours spent in self-study and the number of resources consulted compared to understanding how authentic control is exercised and experienced) coexist like partners who know each others' faults but we have decided that something flawed is better than nothing at all. We can see a phenomenologically inclined naturalism sitting next to an experimental positivism without any visible rancor between them. What contentiousness exists is mostly confined to debates concerning the reliability and validity of measurement scales.

Self-directed learning is, however, one of the jewels in the crown of American ideology. Not surprisingly, then, it is often celebrated by educational psychologists as the culmination of intellectual development. Framed as the task of learning how to think for ourselves, or how to unleash the potential dormant within each of us, it conjures up frontier images of rugged individuals learning to actualize themselves into infinity. The folklore of the self-made man or woman elevates to near mythical status those who speak a narrative of succeeding against the odds through individual effort. This is the narrative often surrounding "adult learner of the year" awards bestowed on those who, purely by force of will and in the face of great hardship, claim their place at the table of higher learning. This is also the narrative that President Clinton's campaign team tapped expertly in its video *The Man from Hope* shown at his nominating convention. That anyone can be President was celebrated as a prized tenet of American culture. That this takes enormous amounts of money and years of courting, and co-optation by, big business interests remained unaddressed. Ultimately, self-directed learning is premised on the notion of individual choice, a crucial component of the ideologies of capitalism and liberty so revered in this culture. As such, an intellectual process viewed by educational psychology as existing solely within the cognitive domain has clear ideological underpinnings.

Self-directed learning also rests on a modernistic, and problematic, conceptualization of the self. A self-directed learner is seen as one who makes free and uncoerced choices from amongst a smorgasbord of enticing possibilities. The choices such a learner makes are held to reflect his or her desire to realize the strivings, dreams, and aspirations that lie at the core of his or her identity. So self-directed learning clearly depends on there being a 'self' to do the learning. This conception of the learner as a differentiated and self-contained individual entity has traditionally been at the core of educational psychology. In recent years, however, a growing body of critically inclined psychological work has questioned this conception. Educators such as Kincheloe (1999a,b) argue that we should talk of subjects rather than selves, and that subjects are produced and continually reproduced by culture and society. Such a conception of the socially produced nature of the self is central both to critical theory and postmodernism. Once self-directed learning becomes viewed as a social phenomenon, a process that is enacted within networks rather than located in the individual cortex, then it ceases to be a series of individualistic, dislocated decisions of interest only to educational psychologists. Instead it traverses the domains of critical social psychology and political economy and becomes of concern to political activists.

To critical educational psychologists the predominance of the concept of self-directed learning illustrates the tendency of humanistic educators to collapse all political questions into a narrowly reductionist technical rationality. From the perspective of a critical educational psychology, the early free spirit of self-direction has been turned (through the technology of learning contracts) into a masked form of repressive surveillance—one more example of the infinite flexibility of hegemony, of the workings of a coldly efficient form of repressive tolerance. What began as a cultural challenge, a counter hegemonic effort, has taken a technocratic, accommodative turn. It is certainly highly plausible to see the technology of self-directed learning—particularly the widespread acceptance and advocacy of learning contracts—as a highly developed form of surveillance. By interiorizing what Foucault (1980) calls the "normalizing gaze" (teacher developed norms concerning what's acceptable) through their negotiations with faculty, learning contracts transfer the responsibility for overseeing learning from the teacher to the learner. This is usually spoken of as an emancipatory process of empowerment in which educators are displaying an admirable responsiveness to student needs and circumstances. But, using Foucault's principle of reversal (seeing something as the exact opposite of what it really is) learning contracts can be reframed and understood as a sophisticated means by which the content and methodology of learning can be monitored without the teacher needing to be physically present.

This chapter questions the view that self-directed learning can be studied, and facilitated, as if it were the product of a monological consciousness. It argues instead that such learning is always ideologically framed and never the innocent, unfettered expression of individual preference. Drawing on a critical theory perspective the chapter calls into question the foundational belief of some educational psychologists that people make free choices regarding their learning that reflect authentic desires felt deeply at the very core of their identity. Ideology critique—the core critical thinking process of critical theory—rejects self-directed learning's ideal of learners making autonomous choices among multiple possibilities. Instead it alerts us to the way that a concept like self-direction that is seemingly replete with ideals of liberty and freedom can end up serving repressive interests. The chapter concludes with a discussion of how self-directed learning can be reclaimed as an inherently critical process. If in 2002 and 2003 there had been widespread self-directed learning projects focused on researching the accuracy of the arguments, justifications, and assumptions regarding the proposed unilateral invasion of Iraq it is unlikely that that there would have been so little public questioning of the Bush administration's justifications for it. In this atmosphere of jingoistic self-justification it seemed as if self-directed learning's best role was to act as some kind of force for political detoxification. If adults could be encouraged to discuss a range of different perspectives on the invasion it would be much harder for the administration's supporters and ideological managers to equate criticism of its actions with a lack of patriotism. To this degree, self-directed learning can be the fulcrum of a vigorous democratic discourse.

In educational psychology the image of how self-directed learning works is premised on a particular concept of the self. This views each individual learner as self-contained and internally driven, working to achieve her learning goals in splendid isolation. The self is seen as a free floating, autonomous, volitional agent able to make rational, authentic, and internally coherent choices about learning while remaining detached from social, cultural, and political formations. Viewing the individual learner's self this way allows educational psychologists to administer intelligence tests purporting to measure the IQ possessed by each discrete self. Intelligence itself becomes treated as a static, integrated phenomenon replicable across contexts. A self-contained concept of the self also allows educational psychologists and teachers to set up learning contracts to achieve the ends of self-directed learners. Such contracts are regarded as if they were legally binding arrangements between consenting, self-contained entities. The same conceptualization of the self allows adult educational psychologists to create scales to measure people's self-directed learning readiness as if this were an objectively verifiable phenomenon like one's heart rate or blood pressure. Ehrenreich (1990) writes that in this conception of individualism "each self is seen as pursuing its own trajectory, accompanied by its own little planetary system of values, seeking to negotiate the best possible deal from the various 'relationships' that come along. Since all values appear to be idiosyncratic satellites of the self, and since we have no way to understand the "self" as a product of all the other selves—present and in historical memory—we have no way of engaging each other in moral discourse, much less in a routine political argument" (p. 102).

A critical theory perspective points out three problems with this notion of the self within educational psychology. First, it emphasizes that the self cannot stand outside the social, cultural, and political streams within which it swims. In Kincheloe's (1999a) words self-directed learning should be informed by "a sociopolitical cognitive theory that understands the way our consciousness, our subjectivity, is shaped by the world around us" (p. 5). From this perspective what seem like purely personal, private choices about learning inevitably reflect the contradictory ideological impulses within us. Second, a critical perspective warns that conceiving self-direction as a form of learning emphasizing separateness leads us to equate it with selfishness, with the narcissistic pursuit of private ends regardless of the consequences of this pursuit for others. This is, of course, in perfect tune with capitalist ideology of the free market, which holds that those who deserve to survive and flourish naturally end up doing so.

Thirdly, a critical perspective points out that a view of learning that regards people as self-contained, volitional beings scurrying around in individual projects is also one that works against collective and cooperative impulses. Citing an engagement in self-directed learning, people can deny the existence of common interests and human interdependence in favor of an obsessive focus on the individual. Translated into classroom practices, this conception of self-directed learning supports individual projects, individual testing, and rewards individual merit. It works against collective and collaborative forms of learning in which projects, test results, and merit are cocreated by people engaging with their environment.

A self-directed learning stance focused on the individual as a fully integrated being disconnected from broader social currents also allows wider beliefs, norms, and structures to remain unchallenged and thereby reinforces the status quo. This conceptualization of self-direction emphasizes a self that is sustained by its own internal momentum needing no external connections or supports. It erects as the ideal culmination of psychological development the independent, fully functioning person. Fortunately, this view of a human development trajectory that leads inevitably to the establishment of separate, autonomous selves has been challenged in recent years by work on gender and critical developmental psychology. This work questions the patriarchal notion that atomistc self-determination is both an educational ideal to be pursued as well as the natural end point of psychological development. In its place it advances a feminist valuing of interdependence and a socially constructed interpretation of identity.

The critical theory tradition unequivocally condemns the separatist emphasis of self-directed learning within educational psychology and demonstrates how this emphasis makes an engagement in common cause—within and outside classrooms—difficult for people to contemplate. A separatist conception of self-direction severs the connection between private troubles and wider social and political trends and obscures the fact that apparently private learning projects are ideologically framed. In the rest of this chapter I wish to explore two contributions to critical theory that inform this critique of self-directed learning. The first is Erich Fromm's (1941) notion of automaton conformity, briefly defined as the self-conscious desire of people in contemporary culture to strive to be as close to an imagined ideal of normality as possible. Although Foucault does not build centrally on Fromm's idea of automaton conformity, I believe Fromm raises issues that are very close to Foucault's own articulations of disciplinary power, self-surveillance, and the technology of the self (Foucault, 1980). The second idea is that of one-dimensional thought as articulated by Herbert Marcuse (1964). Marcuse argued that under contemporary capitalism our thought processes are predetermined by the overwhelming need we feel to avoid challenging the system. One-dimensional thought is wholly instrumental, focused chiefly on making the current system work better. There is little impulse to generate learning projects that challenge the system. If we do feel such impulses we dismiss them as irrational Utopianism or signs of approaching neuroticism. The logic of Marcuse's position is that in a culture of one-dimensional thought self-directed learning projects will be framed to underscore the legitimacy of the existing order. I end the chapter by trying to reposition self-directed learning as an inherently radical process.

SELF-DIRECTED LEARNING AS AUTOMATON CONFORMITY

In *The Sane Society* (1956a) the critical theorist and social psychologist Erich Fromm laid out a character analysis of the personality type required for capitalism to function effectively. At the center of his analysis was capitalism's need for ideological standardization. In Fromm's view modern mass production methods required the standardization of workers' personalities to conform to a particular characterlogical mold. Capitalism needed people who were willing to be commanded, to be told what is expected of them, to fit into the social machine without friction. Such individuals are educated to crave conformity, to feel part of a mass that feels the same impulses and thinks the same thoughts in synchronization. They devote a great deal of psychic energy to ensuring that they conform to an imagined ideal of what it means to be "normal." This is the basic thesis of *Escape from Freedom* (1941) where Fromm attempts to explain the rise of fascist and totalitarian regimes.

In *Escape from Freedom* (titled *The Fear of Freedom* outside the USA) Fromm argued that the decline of traditional mores and the growth of secularism had made people more and more aware of the fact that they had considerably increased freedom to choose how to live and what to think. However, rather than bringing a sense of pleasurable control this recognition was a source of existential terror to most people. The central thesis of *Escape from Freedom* is that the isolation, insecurity, and alienation of modern life has resulted in many people experiencing a sense of powerlessness and insignificance. Faced with the void of freedom people turned to two avenues of escape —submission to a totalitarian leader, as happened in fascist countries or a compulsive conforming to be just like everybody else.

Of these two avenues it is automaton conformity that is the most subtle and intriguing, and ultimately the most alienating. Individuals attempt to escape the burden of freedom by transforming themselves into cogs in a well-oiled machine of society. People might be well fed and well clothed but they are not free. Instead they have succumbed to automaton conformity and become cogs in a bureaucratic machine, with their thoughts, feelings, and tastes manipulated by the government industry and the mass communications that they subtly control. Through automaton conformity people escape the anxiety produced by the awareness of their freedom. By imagining themselves to be like everybody else, they are saved from the frightening experience of aloneness. The subtlety of automaton conformity is that the pressure to conform is applied internally, not externally, an example of disciplinary power in action. The authority people submit to by conforming is anonymous—the authority of imagined common sense, public opinion, and conventional wisdom. In pursuing automaton conformity people become their own controllers making sure they don't step out of line by daring to think deviant thoughts or engage in deviant behaviors.

The power of anonymous authority comes from its all-pervasive, yet invisible, nature. Like fish unaware of the water in which they live, citizens swim unsuspectingly in the ocean of anonymous authority. They are surrounded by an atmosphere of subtle suggestion which pervades their social life without them ever suspecting that there is any order which they are expected to follow. Under the enveloping influence of anonymous authority individuals cease to be themselves, adopting entirely the kind of personality offered to them by cultural patterns. Their concern is to become exactly the same as everybody else. Any anxiety people might feel about this kind of existence concerns whether or not they are sufficiently assiduous in pursuing and realizing the pattern of conformity. The automaton conformist's credo can be summarized thus; "I must conform, not be different, not 'stick out'; I must be ready and willing to change according to the changes in the pattern; I must not ask whether I am right or wrong, but whether I am adjusted, whether I am not 'peculiar', not different" (1956a, p. 153).

If Fromm's analysis is correct, then self-directed learning as the expression of individual yearnings through which people realize their core identities is clearly nonsensical. To attempt to measure such yearnings as if they were the authentic product of individual consciousness is also misconceived. These yearnings have been ideologically implanted in us as part of capitalism's desire to produce a personality type that will support its continued functioning. Any desires we experience to learn new skills or explore new bodies of knowledge will, by definition, be framed by our desire to think and learn what we imagine others are thinking and learning. And one of the chief sources for finding out what others are thinking and learning will be the mass media, which themselves are capitalist corporations. In their desire to attract the largest viewing audience—and thereby charge the highest possible rates for advertising—media are careful to offend the fewest possible consumers possible. The images they project, the interpretations of current events they present as self-evident, and the desires they embody, constitute the conformist norm toward which people gear their behavior.

Although Fromm was a social critic he was also a practicing psychologist producing best sellers such as *The Sane Society* (1956a) and *The Art of Loving* (1956b). When he turned his psychologist's eyes on educational practices he professed himself alarmed at the way these underscored the force of automaton conformity. Education had become completely commodified, in his view, with colleges concerned to give each student a certain amount of cultural property, a sort of luxury-knowledge package with "the size of each package being in accord with the person's probable social prestige. Knowledge becomes equated with content, with fixed clusters of thought that students store." In this system teachers are reduced to bureaucratic dispensers of knowledge. This commodified content, transmitted bureaucratically, is alienated from learners' lives and experiences. In contemporary classrooms the students and the content of the lectures remain strangers to each other, except that each student has become the owner of a collection of statements made by somebody else. Educational psychology contributed to this transmission of canned sensibilities to students by its refusal to consider adequately the undeniable intersection of students' biographies with the ideology of automaton conformity. Indeed, Fromm so despaired of schooling's potential to counter automaton conformity's power that he believed this challenge could only be mounted in adulthood. In his opinion to understand properly how one's identity, potential, and IQ is socially constructed a person must have had a great deal more experience in living than he or she has had at college age. For many people the age of 30 or 40 was deemed to be much more appropriate for learning.

SELF-DIRECTED LEARNING AS ONE-DIMENSIONAL THOUGHT

The second idea from critical theory that informs this chapter's analysis of self-directed learning is Herbert Marcuse's idea of one-dimensional thought. Marcuse argued that in advanced industrial society the most pernicious oppression of all is that caused by affluence. Like Fromm, Marcuse believed that people had been lulled into stupefaction by the possession of consumer goods and believed themselves to be living in democratic freedom. In reality, Marcuse argued, our needs have been manipulated to convince us we are happy. Consequently a condition of disaffection lurks beneath the carapace of everyday life. If we could just see our alienated state clearly we would want to liberate ourselves from it. But we have learned to regard half-buried feelings of dissatisfaction as irrational symptoms of neurosis.

This vision of a society controlled by technological advances and smoothly functioning administration is most fully laid out in *One Dimensional Man* (1964), Marcuse's most celebrated book. One dimensional thought—instrumental thought focused on how to make the current system work better and perform more effectively—is the most pervasive mechanism of control that Marcuse elaborates. When people think this way they start to conceive of the range of possibilities open to them in life within a framework predefined by the existing order. This order then determines the focus of self-directed learning projects. People assume that all is for the best in society, that things are arranged the way they are for a good reason, and that the current system works for the benefit of all. In this system philosophical thought, even of an apparently critical kind, serves only to keep the system going. Paranthetically, self-directed learning projects—even if they appear to be the expression of a robust individualism—are, by definition, subservient to the system's needs. In a one-dimensional culture problems of meaning and morality, such as how we should treat other people, what it means to act ethically, or how we can make sense of death, are defused of metaphysical dimensions and turned into operational difficulties to be addressed by techniques and programs. Thus, operational and behavioral ways of thinking become the chief features of the larger universe of discourse and action.

One-dimensional thought ensures its own continuance by using the educational system to train people to feel a deep need to stay within their existing frameworks of analysis. Any self-directed learning conducted thus becomes geared to reinforcing these frameworks. Although avoiding divergent thinking seems like an individual decision, it is in reality the result of a massive indoctrination effort intended to stop people questioning what they see around them. The purpose of this system-preserving effort is to ensure that the needs and the satisfactions that serve the preservation of the Establishment are shared by the underlying population. The apogee of the administered society is reached when everyone shares the same deep-seated need to preserve the existing social order, but each believes this to be an idiosyncratic feature of his or her own personality. Social control is assured if the conflation of social into individual needs is so effective that they are deemed to be identical. In such a situation self-directed learning has no potential to disturb the system since its projects will have been framed to keep the system intact.

The picture Marcuse paints in *One-Dimensional Man* of the administered society dominated by technology, consumerism, restricted language, and falsely concrete thought processes that only confirm the correctness of the existing order, is dismal indeed. Scientific management and rational production methods might have improved people's standards of living but at a price—the destruction of nature and diminution of the soul—that people are not so much willing to pay, as completely oblivious to. The administered society has extended its tentacles into the deepest recesses of the psyche to produce a seemingly instinctual concern to toe the line. If there is any truth to this dismal vision then self-directed learning is always co-opted, an expression of our need to make sure things stay as they are. We may genuinely believe ourselves to be generating learning projects that reflect only our particular needs and circumstances, but such projects are, by definition, compromised. The all-pervasive effects of one-dimensional thought have subtly predisposed us to learn things that keep the system intact.

SELF-DIRECTED LEARNING AS AN OPPOSITIONAL PRACTICE

In this section I want to challenge the arguments I have been making up to now by contending that self-directed learning *could* become an oppositional practice if its political dimensions could be made explicit. Despite its accommodative tendencies there is still something intrinsically critical, freeing, and empowering to many people about the idea of self-direction. People understand that embedded in the idea is some strain of resistance that sets learners in opposition to powerful interests and against institutional attempts to mandate how and what people should learn. So I believe that self-directed learning can be reinterpreted with a political edge to fit squarely into the tradition of emancipatory education. The case for reframing self-direction as an inherently political practice rests on two arguments neither of which is adequately acknowledged in educational psychology. The first argument is that at the heart of self-direction is the issue of control, particularly control over what are conceived as acceptable and appropriate learning activities and processes, and that control is always a political issue involving questions of power. The second argument is that exercising self-direction requires that certain conditions be in place regarding access to resources and that these conditions that are essentially political in nature. Let me take each of these themes in turn.

The one consistent element in the majority of definitions of self-direction is the importance of the learner exercising control over all educational decisions. What should be the goals of a learning effort, what resources should be used, what methods will work best for the learner, and by what criteria the success of any learning effort should be judged are all decisions that are said to rest in the learner's hands. This emphasis on control—on who decides what is right and good and how these things should be pursued—is also central to notions of emancipatory education. For example, when talking about his work at Highlander the radical educator Myles Horton (1990) stressed that "if you want to have the students control the whole process, as far as you can get them to control it, then you can never, at any point, take it out of their hands" (p. 152). Who controls the decisions concerning the ways and directions in which people learn is a political issue highlighting the distribution of educational and political power. Who has the final say in framing the range and type of decisions that are to be taken, and in establishing the pace and mechanisms for decision-making, indicates where control really resides.

Self-direction as an organizing concept for education therefore calls to mind some powerful political associations. It implies a democratic commitment to shifting to learners as much control as possible for conceptualizing, designing, conducting, and evaluating their learning and for deciding how resources are to be used to further these processes. Thought of politically, self-direction can be seen as part of a populist democratic tradition which holds that people's definitions of what is important to them should frame and instruct governments' actions, and not the other way round. This is why the idea of self-direction is such anathema to advocates of a core or national curriculum, and why it is opposed so vehemently by those who see education as a process of induction into cultural literacy. Self-directed learning is institutionally and politically inconvenient to those who promote educational blueprints, devise intelligence measures, and administer psychological tests and profiles that attempt to control the learning of others. Emphasizing peoples' right to self-direction also invests a certain trust in their wisdom, in their capacity to make wise choices and take wise actions. Advocating that people should be in control of their own learning is based on the belief that if people had a chance to give voice to what most moves and hurts them, they would soon show that they were only too well aware of the real nature of their problems and of ways to deal with these.

If we place the self-conscious, self-aware exertion of control over learning at the heart of what it means to be self-directed, we raise a host of questions about how control can be exercised authentically in a culture that is itself highly controlling. Marcuse and Fromm reveal an inauthentic form of control where people feel that they are framing and taking key decisions about their learning, all the while being unaware that this is happening within a framework that excludes certain ideas or activities as subversive, unpatriotic, or immoral. Controlled self-direction is, from a political perspective, a contradiction in terms, a self-negating concept as oxymoronic as the concept of limited empowerment. On the surface we may be said to be controlling our learning when we make decisions about pacing, resources, and evaluative criteria. But if the range of acceptable content has been preordained so that we deliberately or unwittingly steer clear of things that we sense are deviant or controversial, then we are controlled rather than in control. We are victims, in effect, of self-censorship, willing partners in hegemony.

Hegemony describes the process whereby ideas, structures, and actions come to be seen by people as both natural and axiomatic—as so obvious as to be beyond question or challenge—when in fact they are constructed and transmitted by powerful minority interests to protect the status quo that serves these interests so well. A fully developed self-directed learning project would have at its center an alertness to the possibility of hegemony. Those engaged in this fully realized form of self-directed learning would understand how easily external control can unwittingly be internalized in the form of an automatic self-censorship in the instinctive reaction that "I can't learn this because it's out of bounds" (that is, unpatriotic, deviant, or subversive). A fully authentic form of self-direction exists only when we examine our definitions of what we think it is important for us to learn for the extent to which these end up serving repressive interests.

I have argued that being in control of our learning means that we make informed choices. Making informed choices means, in turn, that we act reflectively in ways that further our interests. But informed choices can only be made on the basis of as full a knowledge as possible about the different options open to us and the consequences of each of these. This leads me to the second political condition for self-directed learning, that concerning the unconstrained access to resources necessary for the completion of learning projects.

How much control can really be said to exist when the dreams we dream have no hope of being realized because we are struggling simply to survive? Any number of supposedly self-directed initiatives have foundered because those attempting to assume control over their learning found themselves in the invidious position of being denied the resources to exercise that control properly. Being self-directed is a meaningless idea if you are too weary at the end of the day to think clearly about what form of learning would be of most use to you, or if you are closed off from access to the resources necessary for you to be able to realize your self-designed projects. Being the arbiter of our own decisions about learning requires that we have enough energy to make reflectively informed choices. Decisions about learning made under the pressure of external circumstances when we are tired, hungry, and distracted, cannot be said to be fully self-directed.

For learners to exercise control in any meaningful sense they must not be so buried under the demands of their daily work that they have neither time, energy, nor inclination left over to engage in shaping and making decisions about their own development. Action springing from an immediate and uninformed desire to do something, anything, to improve one's day-to-day circumstances can be much less effective than action springing from a careful analysis of the wider structural changes that must be in place for individual lives to improve over the long term. If the decisions we make for ourselves are borne out of a desperate immediate need that causes us to focus only on what is right in front of us rather than on the periphery or in the future, if we choose from among options that are irrelevant to the real nature of the problem at hand, or if our range of choices has been framed by someone else, then our control is illusory. In this regard, decision framing is as important as decision making in a self-directed learning project. Understood thus, we can see that central to a self-directed learning effort is a measure of unconstrained time and space necessary for us to make decisions that are carefully and critically examined and that are in our own best long-term interests.

It may also be the case in a self-directed project that I decide I want to learn something that I consider essential for my own development, only to be told that the knowledge or skills involved are undesirable, inappropriate, or subversive. A desire to explore an alternative political ideology is meaningless if books exploring that ideology have been removed from the public library because of their 'unsuitability', or, perhaps more likely, if they have never been ordered in the first place. In a blaze of admirable masochism I may choose to undertake a self-directed learning project geared toward widening my understanding of how my practice as an educator is unwittingly repressive and culturally distorted. In doing this I may have to rely primarily on books because my colleagues are convinced of the self-evident correctness of their own unexamined practice. Yet I may well find that the materials I need for this project are so expensive that neither I, nor my local libraries, can afford to purchase them. In an ironic illustration of Marcuse's (1965) concept of repressive tolerance, critical analyses of professional practice are often priced well beyond the pockets of many who could benefit from reading them. Again, I may need physical equipment for a self-directed effort I have planned and be told by those controlling such equipment that it is unavailable to me for reasons of cost or others' prior claims. If I decide to initiate a self-directed learning project that involves challenging the informational hegemony of a professional group, I may find that medical and legal experts place insurmountable barriers in my path in an effort to retain their position of authority. So being self-directed can be inherently politicizing as learners come to a critical awareness of the differential distribution of resources necessary to conduct their self-directed learning efforts.

Self-directed learning is a good example of the process whereby subjugated, radical knowledge, is co-opted or reframed to underscore conformity with the system. Yet I do not believe we should give up on the oppositional potential of this practice. If we can demonstrate convincingly the political dimensions to an idea that is now unproblematized within educational psychology, and if we can prize the concept out of the slough of narcissistic, self-actualization in which it is currently mired, then we have a real chance to use this idea as one important element in rebuilding a critical practice of education. Self-directed learning could become a highly effective, politically charged Trojan Horse.

FURTHER READING

Belenky, M. F., Clinchy, B. M., Goldberger, N. R., and Tarule, J. M. (1986). *Women's Ways of Knowing: The Development of Self, Voice, and Mind*. New York: Basic Books.

Ehrenreich, B. (1990). *Fear of falling: The inner life of the middle class*. New York: Perennial.

Foucault, M. (1980). *Power/Knowledge: Selected Interviews and Other Writings, 1972–1977*. New York: Pantheon Books.

Fromm, E. (1941). *Escape from Freedom*. New York: Holt, Rinehart and Winston.

———. (1956a). *The Art of Loving: An Enquiry into the Nature of Love*. New York: Harper and Row.

———. (1956b). *The Sane Society*. London: Routledge, Kegan and Paul.

Goldberger, N., Tarule, J., Clinchy, B., and Belenky (1996). *Knowledge, Difference and Power: Essays Inspired by Women's Ways of Knowing*. New York: Basic Books.

Horton, M. (1990). *The Long Haul*. New York: Doubleday.

Kincheloe, J. L. (1999a). The foundations of a democratic educational psychology. In, J. L. Kincheloe, S. R. Steinberg, and L. E. Villaverde (Eds.), *Rethinking Intelligence: Confronting Psychological Assumptions about Teaching and Learning*. New York: Routledge.

———. (1999b). Trouble ahead, trouble behind: The post-formal critique of educational psychology. In J. L. Kincheloe, S. R. Steinberg, and P. H. Hinchey (Eds.), *The Post-Formal Reader: Cognition and Education*. New York: Falmer.

Marcuse, H. (1964). *One-Dimensional Man*. Boston, MA: Beacon.

———. (1965). Repressive Tolerance. In R. P. Wolff, B. Moore, and H. Marcuse (Eds.), *A Critique of Pure Tolerance*. Boston, MA: Beacon Press.

Morss, J. R. (Ed.). (1996). *Growing Critical: Alternatives to Developmental Psychology*. New York: Routledge.

CHAPTER 44

Literacy for Wellness, Oppression, and Liberation

SCOT D. EVANS AND ISAAC PRILLELTENSKY

If there were tests about what constitutes the public good, most of us would fail miserably, including those of us with university degrees. Lack of numerical and verbal literacy is bad enough, but there is another type of ignorance with similar or even greater negative consequences: Moral and political illiteracy. This is the type of ignorance that results from not knowing how to challenge dominant ideas about what our society should be like. If we are to begin questioning the status quo, we need to understand what wellness is, how oppression obstructs it, and how liberation can enhance the former and resist the latter.

We learn more and more about how to control nature but fall short of resolving basic human predicaments. This is not because social problems are insolvable, but because there are powerful groups interested in keeping things the way they are. Unless we educate ourselves about the role of power in wellness, oppression, and liberation, we will never be able to challenge current structures of inequality, a major impediment in human, organizational, and community development.

Psychologists and educators have studied well-being in the narrowest sense of the word. Usually, they have limited their approach to subjective reports of happiness. They have conceptualised wellness in individualistic terms devoid of social context. But if they were remiss in studying wellness from multiple levels of analysis, they have completely ignored questions of oppression and liberation. Power differentials are absolutely crucial in the genesis and transformation of wellness, oppression, and liberation. Without a specific literacy on these topics, the most we can expect from psychologists and educators is slight amelioration of inimical conditions. To encourage the transformation of conditions that lead to suffering and injustice, we discuss wellness, oppression, and liberation at five levels of analysis: personal, interpersonal, organizational, community, and social. Following this conceptual orientation we suggest literacy for wellness and liberation and roles for agents of change, including educators, psychologists, parents, policy makers, community organizations, and youth.

WELLNESS

Wellness is a positive state of affairs, brought about by the combined and balanced satisfaction of personal, interpersonal, organizational, community, and social needs. Notice that our definition extends beyond the individual. Although the person is the ultimate beneficiary of wellness, he or she cannot attain high levels of satisfaction and fulfilment unless other domains achieve adequate levels of satisfaction as well. Human beings are interdependent on each other and on organizational, communal, and societal structures. Each one of the five domains of wellness must meet certain needs for it to thrive and for wellness as a whole to flourish.

Wellness as a whole takes place when its five components meet certain needs and when they act in concert. This creates a synergy that is hard to achieve without the satisfaction of needs of any one element. Omissions or neglect in any one domain have negative repercussions for that particular domain and for other spheres as well. In this sense, the five nodes of wellness operate as a web in which the weakness of one diminishes the strength of all, and the strength of each enhances the resilience of the whole. Once this view of wellness is adopted, we can no longer define wellness in merely personal or interpersonal terms. It is an interdisciplinary conceptualisation that defies reductionism. From an ecological perspective, wellness can exist but in incipient forms at each of its subcomponents. It is only when they interact and strengthen each other that the synergy of wellness can emerge. The satisfaction of personal needs such as growth and love cannot be fulfilled in the absence of meaningful relationships, which, in turn, are affected by norms of interpersonal violence regnant in the culture—a culture which is reproduced in organizations and communities through social norms and economic determinants such as consumerism, mass media, and the like. The links among the various components of wellness are not hard to discern. It is only when we resort to myopic disciplinary lenses that we miss the big picture of wellness.

In each and every case, components of wellness are units and parts at the same time. Each of the five elements is a unit, in and of itself, and part of holistic wellness at the same time. Arthur Koestler introduced in science the notion of holons. A holon is an entity that is whole and part at the same time. Personal wellness may be viewed as a unit—consisting of physical, psychological, and spiritual domains—but at the same time it is only a part of holistic wellness, which is achieved when personal, interpersonal, organizational, community, and social wellness come together. The wellness of each domain is codependent on the wellness of others. In the following sections we discuss the needs and determinants of the various components of wellness and conclude with illustrations of their synergic properties.

Personal Wellness

Physical, psychological, and spiritual components cocreate personal wellness. Physical needs include health, growth, adequate stimulation for brain development, nutrition, exercise, and an active lifestyle overall. Psychological needs entail a sense of control, self-determination, self-esteem, hope, and optimism. Meaning, development, and transcendence are some of the spiritual needs of personal wellness. A cursory inspection of these needs reveals their dependence on other domains of wellness. For we cannot achieve control over our lives if others deprive us of it, much as we can have little hope in inhospitable communities and war-torn societies.

Interpersonal Wellness

This component of wellness reflects qualities of relationships. Interpersonal wellness occurs when a relationship is based on caring, compassion, respect for diversity, and collaboration and democratic participation. People can experience interpersonal wellness in some relationships but not in others. As with personal wellness, this domain is dependent on others. An organizational climate that promotes participation is more conducive to wellness among workers than one that is dictatorial or repressive.

Organizational Wellness

Organizations achieve different levels of wellness depending on how well they meet certain needs—both for the people who work within the organization and the people who are affected by it in the community. Clear roles, positive climate, balance of economic with social and environmental mission, accountability, effectiveness, and participatory decision-making processes are basic needs organizations must meet for all stakeholders to prosper. An imbalance among the various needs is an ever-present risk. Many corporations put economic interests over and above social and environmental aims, resulting in damage to communities: poor wages, unacceptable working conditions, violation of environmental rules, and others. Organizations are appropriately located at the middle of the various wellness components, as they mediate among persons and society.

Community Wellness

Communities experience varying levels of wellness, depending on the satisfaction of certain needs, such as sense of cohesion, social capital, safety, transportation, adequate housing, access to recreational facilities, well-resourced schools, opportunities for participation in decisions affecting the community, and level of control over what happens in the neighborhood. In the absence of these needs, children suffer from poor educational systems, people are afraid to walk the streets, and isolation ensues.

Social Wellness

We distinguish between community and social wellness in terms of physical proximity and level of policies affecting the population. With respect to the former, the community is proximal to where people live. Society is a larger physical construct than the immediate neighborhood. With respect to the latter, social wellness is largely determined by policies that affect nations as a whole, such as access to universal health care or lack thereof, the presence of safety nets and unemployment benefits of lack thereof, progressive taxation systems or lack thereof. Societies that support the unemployed and single mothers, that offer day care for young children, and that regard health care as a universal right attain higher levels of wellness than societies that discriminate on the basis of economic opportunity. Consequently, social wellness cannot be achieved when the need for universal health care, adequate safety nets, housing, and decent public schools are not met. In summary, these are needs for justice and equality. In their absence, only those with privilege can access services and resources that support personal development.

The Synergy of Wellness

Throughout the various components of wellness we have tried to illustrate how closely connected they all are. Wellness is maximized when individuals enjoy meaningful relationships in formal and informal organizations, when communities are safe and prosperous, and when societies are just and equitable. It is interesting to note that in wealthy societies where the gap between the rich and the power is smaller, people live longer and are healthier than in less equitable ones. This is but one example of how social policies affect health and well-being. Another example concerns the positive effects of social cohesion on levels of education, welfare, tolerance, and crime. Clear positive effects have been found in states and communities where people volunteer more and are more engaged in civic life.

OPPRESSION

Oppression entails a state of asymmetric power relations characterized by domination, subordination, and resistance, where the dominating persons or groups exercise their power by the process of restricting access to material resources and imparting in the subordinated persons or groups self-deprecating views about themselves. It is only when the latter can attain a certain degree of political literacy that resistance can begin. Oppression, then, is a series of asymmetric power relations between individuals, genders, classes, communities, and nations. Such asymmetric power relations lead to conditions of misery, inequality, exploitation, marginalization, and social injustices.

Oppression is a condition of domination where the oppressed suffer the consequences of deprivation, exclusion, discrimination, and exploitation imposed on them by individuals or groups seeking to secure economic, political, social, cultural, or psychological advantage. Oppression consists of *political* and *psychological* dimensions. We cannot speak of one without the other. Psychological and political oppression coexist and are mutually determined.

Personal Oppression

The dynamics of oppression are internal as well as external. External forces deprive individuals or groups of the benefit of personal (e.g., self-determination), social (e.g., distributive justice), and interpersonal (e.g., collaboration and democratic participation) wellness. Often, these restrictions are internalized and operate at a psychological level as well, where the person acts as his or her personal censor. Some untoward psychological conditions such as low self-esteem and excessive anxiety derive from internalized oppression. Personal oppression, then, is the internalized view of self as negative, and undeserving of resources or increased participation in societal affairs. This derives from the use of affective, behavioural, cognitive, material, linguistic, and cultural mechanisms by agents of domination to affirm their own superiority. Psychological dynamics of oppression entail surplus powerlessness, belief in a just world, learned helplessness, conformity, obedience to authority, fear, verbal, and emotional abuse.

Interpersonal Oppression

This type of oppression derives from relationships where a powerful person dominates another individual or group by restricting their self-determination, opportunities, and growth. This type of oppression is characterized by power differentials and is often called emotional abuse or neglect, although at times it can also be physical or sexual abuse. This type of oppression can take place in families, schools, workplace, or other community venues.

Organizational Oppression

This expression of oppression takes place where repressive norms and regulations deprive workers or people affected by the organization of their rights and dignity. Boarding schools where children have been physically, sexually, and emotionally abused are prototypical examples of oppressive organizations where the powerless (e.g., children) are taken advantage of and dominated by the powerful (e.g., priests, school masters). Work environments can also be oppressive. Employers often take advantage of fearful illegal farm workers and deprive them of basic working conditions.

Community Oppression

Entire communities may be oppressed by discrimination, lack of opportunities, and exclusion. Racism, ableism, and classism exemplify the oppression and unjust treatment of certain groups in society. As with previous instances of oppression, power differentials and abuse of power characterize this type as well.

Social Oppression

At the broadest level, oppression is the creation of material, legal, military, economic, or other social barriers to the fulfilment of self-determination, distributive justice, and democratic participation. This condition results from the use of multiple forms of power by dominating agents to advance their own interests at the expense of persons or groups in positions of relative powerlessness. Some political mechanisms of oppression and repression include actual or potential use of force, restricted life opportunities, degradation of indigenous culture, economic sanctions, and inability to challenge authority.

The Synergy of Oppression

It is often the case that oppressed individuals become abusive themselves—at home, at work, in the community—thereby perpetuating oppressive cycles. Oppressive cultural norms, work environments, and relationships are often internalized, resulting in personal harm and diminished opportunities in life. In many ways, oppression resembles a chain reaction that starts with oppressive and repressive social policies and ends up with repressed individuals in abusive relationships. History is replete with examples of abominable policies readily embraced by otherwise law-abiding citizens. The Nazi treatment of Jews, the treatment of slaves in the United States and the treatment of Blacks under Apartheid are but few examples.

LIBERATION

Liberation refers to the process of resisting oppressive forces and the state in which these forces no longer exert their dominion over a person or a group. Liberation may be from psychological and/or political influences. There is rarely political or social oppression without a concomitant psychological or personal expression. Repressive cultural codes become internalized and operate as self-regulatory, inhibiting defiance of oppressive rules. Liberation is about overcoming the barriers to defiance. Liberation is the process of overcoming internal and external sources of oppression (freedom from), and pursuing wellness (freedom to).

Personal Liberation

Freedom from internal and psychological sources includes overcoming fears, obsessions, or other psychological phenomena that interfere with a person's subjective experience of well-being. Liberation to pursue wellness, in turn, refers to the process of meeting personal, relational, and collective needs. As we shall note below, the process of personal liberation cannot really start until a certain degree of literacy and awareness has been reached. In the absence of systemic explanations of suffering, individuals blame themselves for their oppression. Emancipation requires a new language, the language of agency, possibility, and opportunity.

Interpersonal Liberation

To liberate oneself from oppressive relationships requires courage and support from others. It is very rare that people leave abusive relationships without social and emotional support. Much suffering occurs because of abusive relationships where the powerful instill hopelessness in victims. Interpersonal liberation means asserting one's power and exercising more control over one's life. Abused women who liberate themselves from abusive partners have much to teach us about the difficulties of leaving and the joys of having left.

Organizational Liberation

Groups affected by oppressive policies of institutions strive to organize to challenge the status quo. Many stakeholders internal and external to organizations are affected by repressive policies. Unfortunately, we don't know enough about how workers organize to overcome organizational oppression. Much of the literature in this field has been characterized by inadequate accounts of organizational oppression. Wittingly or unwittingly many authors mask real issues of oppression and frame them in terms of incompetent leaders or disgruntled workers.

Community Liberation

Personal suffering and struggles are often explained in terms of private ineptitudes divorced from systems of domination and exclusion. This dynamic often applies to gay, lesbians, ethnic minorities, and other communities subjected to discrimination. In a positive outcome, people discern the political sources of their psychological experience of oppression and rebel against them. However, research on the process of empowerment indicates that individuals and communities do not engage in emancipatory actions until they have gained considerable awareness of their own oppression. Hence, the task of overcoming oppression should start with a process of literacy. It is through this kind of education that those subjected to conditions of injustice realize the sources of their oppression.

Social Liberation

Liberation from social oppression entails, for example, emancipation from class exploitation, gender domination, and ethnic discrimination. Social movements demonstrate the power of large masses united in the pursuit of justice. Such was the case with the women's movement and the civil rights movements in the United States. Through processes of political literacy and political organizing, marginalized groups gained rights and protections that had been hitherto the exclusive province of white males. Unfortunately, social movements today are fragmented by lack of solidarity.

The Synergy of Liberation

The process of liberation starts with political literacy, according to which marginalized populations begin to gain awareness of oppressive forces in their lives and of their own ability to overcome domination. This awareness is likely to develop in stages. People may begin to realize that they are subjected to oppressive norms. The first realization may happen as a result of therapy, participation in a social movement or readings. Next, they may connect with others experiencing similar circumstances and gain an appreciation for the external forces pressing them down. Some individuals will go on to liberate themselves from oppressive relationships or psychological dynamics such as fears and phobias, whereas others will join social movements to fight for political justice.

The evolution of critical consciousness and literacy can be charted in terms of the relationship between the psychological and political dynamics of oppression. The level of critical awareness of a person or group will vary according to the extent that psychological mechanisms obscure or mask the external political sources of oppression. In other words, the more people internalize oppression through various psychological mechanisms, the less they will see their suffering as resulting from unjust political conditions. Internalized psychological oppression can completely obscure the political roots of oppression.

LITERACY FOR WELLNESS AND LIBERATION

In the introduction to the thirtieth anniversary edition of Brazilian educator Paulo Freire's *Pedagogy of the Oppressed* (1970), Richard Shaull suggests that there is no such thing as a neutral education process. Education functions either to facilitate the younger generation's conformity or to foster their critical reading of reality and their ability to transform it. This is the essence of what we mean by literacy for wellness and liberation. Literacy for wellness and liberation is a worthy goal, not only for oppressed populations, but for the entire population as well. Critical consciousness has the potential to enhance wellness and liberation. Paulo Freire describes critical consciousness, or conscientization, as learning to perceive social, political, and economic contradictions, and taking action against an oppressive reality. Literacy, in this sense, is the understanding of how power dynamics operate to enhance opportunities or to perpetuate oppression in personal and collective life. Education is not about knowledge per se, but about ideas; it is about engaging in dialogue to generate thought, explanation, and understanding. It is a way of knowing.

It is important to discuss the developmental implications of this kind of critical knowing. This level of understanding suggests a cognitive structure that allows individuals to free themselves from the constraints of the present moment. This mature level of understanding involves the capacity for systemic reasoning, or the ability to see interconnections and to critically reflect on them. Various theorists have described this critical stage of development in different ways. Constructivist knowing, postformal thinking, postinstitutional ego system, reflective judgement, informed commitment, cultural literacy, and transformative learning are just some illustrative concepts. Regardless of the precise terminology, the central factors in this type of literacy are the ability to challenge internalized images of established ways of life, and the understanding of synergy of various components of wellness. Although reaching this stage of development is no easy task, it should be, nevertheless, as Lawrence Kholberg famously wrote, the aim of education.

The history of social movements and positive social change reveals that consciousness-expanding strategies had been amply used to promote critical literacy. Gains around workplace struggles, achievements in peace and justice, and the liberation of minorities, women, and other groups all involved efforts to promote critical consciousness. The context for consciousness raising and human development is everyday activities. Everyday life encounters, purposeful action, and social situations can be valuable contexts for people and groups to challenge assumptions, values, and practices that tend to be taken for granted. The many forms of media that youth and adults are exposed to can also be important tools and opportunities for critical reflection. Literacy can be promoted in these everyday activities through the use of challenging questions, alternative perspectives, and reflective dialogue about the consequences of prevailing social realities.

Critical literacy can also be promoted in the professional practices of teachers, social workers, educational psychologists, and policy makers. Redefining these practices to bring the values of justice, wellness, and liberation to the foreground can have a profound impact on human development and the transformation of oppressive systems. Implementing strategies to redesign these practices is difficult and involves inherent risks. It will require collective commitment and study, experimentation, organizational openness, and systems of support. In the next section, we offer ideas for ways that citizens and professionals can become agents of change.

ROLES FOR AGENTS OF CHANGE

Different people in different roles can promote literacy for wellness. These agents of change can promote wellness and liberation and resist oppression through literacy, not any literacy, but participatory literacy. For each of these groups of people, action presupposes the development of one's own literacy for wellness and liberation.

Roles for Teachers

Classroom teachers can facilitate the development of literacy for wellness and liberation by attending to their own personal and professional development, by the use of critical pedagogy, and by acting as agents of change in their own schools and communities.

In Personal and Professional Development.   It is important for teachers to attend to their own development, most importantly, their own critical consciousness. Unfortunately, this is not the central aim of many training programs. Teachers must seek out ways to expand their own awareness of critical events in the world. They should also seek to impart that knowledge to their students. More difficult than learning about external events is reflection about how we, in our personal and professional roles, contribute to injustice and oppression.

In the Classroom.   Central to literacy for wellness and liberation, and, for that matter, all effective learning is the "teacher-student" relationship. Teachers need to be skilled at student-centered, constructivist approaches to learning. Additionally, a joyful and participatory environment in the classroom helps students feel respected, valued, and capable. Teaching in this type of setting should inspire personal reflection and consciousness-raising and promote the values of personal as well as collective well-being. Teachers should take care to utilize diverse cultural references, theories, authors, and perspectives as well as intentionally tap into the experiences and wisdom of students.

This requires that teachers cast off any ties to the banking method of education (teacher deposits knowledge into students) and, instead, embrace the problem-posing method of teaching Through skillful posing of people's problems in their relation with the world, teachers can enter into meaningful dialogue with students who then become joint owners of the process. To quote Freire,

Students, as they are increasingly posed with problems relating themselves in the world and with the world, will feel increasingly challenged and obliged to respond to that challenge . . . Their response to that challenge evokes new challenges, followed by new understandings; and gradually, the students come to regard themselves as committed (p. 81).

There are numerous examples of this in our schools today. In our local community, we often hear stories of problem-posing methods being used to help students learn and apply critical thinking. In one example, a fifth-grade science teacher charged with having to deliver a lesson on endangered species joined with students to research the problem and to explore the issue in depth. This led to the conclusion that humans have played, and continue to play, a major role in the elimination of species. They then explored the possibilities for doing things differently in the world.

In the School.   Teachers can also play an important role in creating organizational wellness in their own schools. Schools, unfortunately, are often not settings that promote human development and well-being. Teachers can help to create a school community that is just, participatory, supportive, and caring. They can help reduce power dynamics, especially between the adults and the students in the setting, and can do this by advocating for ways that students can play meaningful roles in the ongoing functioning of the school organization.

In the Community.   Teachers can work to break down the barrier between students and community by working to immerse students in the community and by bringing the community into the classroom. Service-learning, field research, and experiential learning are tested ways of increasing student learning in relation to the world. Teachers can also bring the world into the classroom, inviting guests to share their special gifts and expertise with students.

Teachers can also become active agents of change in the school reform process. This might entail bringing their expertise to local planning sessions, school board meetings, parent-teacher-student organizations, and local government. This involvement also requires that teachers become active in their local and national teachers unions. On a larger scale, teachers may choose to join organizations and movements for reform such as Rethinking Schools, Educators for Social Responsibility, Teaching for Change, and the Teacher Union Reform Network, among others.

Roles for Parents.   Parents can be agents of change by fostering political and moral literacy at home, and by taking an active role in their child's school. Implicit in these suggested roles is the understanding that parents can best foster the well-being of their children by attending to their own development of political and moral literacy.

In the Home.   Parents can have a tremendous impact on the young person's critical consciousness; primordially by helping them to become critical consumers of media. There are many opportunities to dialogue with youth about programs and news we watch on television, and articles we read in newspapers, magazines, and on the Internet. Parents can join with young people in "trying on" alternative perspectives, dialoguing about the content, and exploring what is behind the many messages we receive from the media on a daily basis. Parents and their children can also act by writing letters to the editor and advocating responsible news reporting. Additionally, parents can encourage and support their child's participation in local community organizations, neighborhood groups, and social movements.

In the Community.   As difficult as it is, parents need to be active in the schooling of their children. This means participating in parent-teacher-student organizations, attending school board meetings and forums, and getting involved in organizations working toward education reform. Parents can be agents of change by becoming aware of how power impacts the well-being of schools and by working for a more just and equitable allocation of resources in the public schools. As their children get older, parents can ask them to accompany them to various events to help them develop literacy and civic awareness.

Roles for Counselors

Counselors can be agents of change with their counselees, in organizational settings, and in the community.

In Counseling.   Counselors should avoid psychologizing problems and victim-blaming approaches. Professional helpers such as psychologists and counselors often prescribe personal solutions to collective problems. Counselors can instead join with their counselees to learn about ways that "societal violence" gets replayed through individuals. A shift in discourse from the medical model to a critical language of oppression and empowerment is needed. We can help students and families trace links between their issues and individual, social, economic, political, and cultural dynamics. Therapeutic methods such as narrative therapy help individuals to externalize the problem and work to reauthor their story based on the new awareness. Counselors can catalyze processes of personal empowerment and liberation, and can enhance literacy by facilitating critical consciousness. The goal is personal and collective empowerment and social change. There is an additional role for counselors in linking students and colleagues to external services, support groups, and organizing groups.

In the Organization.   Often overlooked is the role that counselors can play in the development of organizational wellness. Counselors can be facilitators of a caring organizational community. Along with teachers and administrators, they can encourage democratic participation in the settings and include youth in leadership roles. They can mediate differences, help to reduce power differentials, and propose visions of empowerment and justice. They can also help build an organizational culture that promotes people's dignity, safety, hope, and growth and relationships based on caring, compassion, and respect.

In the Community.   It is important for professional helpers to disseminate the need for caring and compassion in both the "proximal" and "distal" forms. Distal forms of caring involve work at the system level to help create conditions that promote wellness and liberation. Counselors can speak out in the community to help raise awareness of how power differentials and community conditions impact wellness, oppression, and liberation. Counselors can accomplish this in a variety of ways, including letter writing, contributions to newsletters and trade magazines, "teach-ins" and training, participation in community groups as well as local and national social movements. Proximal forms of caring, in turn, refer to the acts of compassion we engage in with individuals with whom we work or for whom we care in our immediate environments.

Roles for Educational Psychologists

Scan any Educational Psychology textbook, journal, or encyclopedia and you'll generally discover a focus on such concepts as motivation, assessment, comprehension, achievement, cognitive development, learning processes, learning styles, behavioral objectives, and instructional models. Largely missing in the field of Educational Psychology are theories, research, and interventions that address sociopolitical development, moral and political literacy, wellness, justice, oppression, and liberation. What is needed is a *critical* educational psychology that acknowledges the limits of traditional psychology, that challenges power differentials, and that encourages the transformation of conditions that lead to suffering and injustice.

Educational Psychologists can take the lead in researching the ways in which social conditions and oppressive school settings impinge on the learning and well-being of young people. They can be steadfast in their refusal to partial out the context in learning, teaching, and growing. They can develop theories and interventions that enhance the critical consciousness of students and teachers and advocate for settings that foster empowerment and community. In teacher training programs, they can prepare teachers to be agents in fostering literacy for wellness and liberation. Educational psychologists can take the lead in questioning basic assumptions about whether schools as they are currently arranged are the best places for learning to occur. Armed with research, sound theories, and ideas for action, they can then work to impact educational policy.

Roles for Educational Policy Makers

The literacy objectives we have described in this chapter cannot be accomplished under the public schools status quo. Critical pedagogy or teaching for moral and political literacy requires a different commitment and it requires resources. Teachers cannot be expected to do the things we suggest when their classes are overstocked with students, when there are limited opportunities for professional development, when they have to provide money for their own supplies, and when they are unable to take students out into the community. These objectives are not possible in an educational culture that places priority on assessment, universal academic standards, and authoritarian accountability. Literacy for wellness and liberation requires a whole new approach to educating young citizens.

As long as we consider the status quo as unchangeable, the policies we design will be limited in their effectiveness to create schools that serve a broader purpose in society. Conventional policy formulation is often hindered by prevailing social, economic, and cultural realities. Policies are often formulated with full awareness that they will not deal effectively with the overarching problems. In this case, the problem is a lack of attention to the sociopolitical development needs of young people and the educational system's lack of vision in promoting wellness and liberation. What we advocate for is what Gil (1998) calls radical policy practice. This is a holistic approach that eschews incremental policy adjustments and, instead, suggests transformations of entire policy systems.

Roles for Community Organizations

Community organizations can be partners with schools, parents, and young people in promoting wellness and liberation. Organizations can offer an array of opportunities for people to be engaged in learning about and addressing community problems. They are natural holding environments for the development of critical consciousness, providing opportunities for people to develop a critical awareness of the disempowering social conditions facing them. Additionally, they can help youth and their families channel their frustration and anger, caused by societal ills, into constructive involvement in activities and movements pursuing wellness, social justice and liberation.

Community organizations, along with their members and clients, can make their voice heard in school systems and community decisions. Proactive organizations can look for ways to bring their wisdom, and the wisdom and voice of their constituents, to the table. Community organizations can also play an educative role by holding "teach-ins," speaking and presenting to groups, and partnering with groups to research community issues. They can help raise awareness by providing political and civic education and opportunities for engagement. Organizations can be more proactive by taking a stand on social issues, advocating for meaningful change, and lobbying (within allowed limits) their representatives for policies that enhance well-being and liberation.

Organizations should also pay attention to their own organizational wellness. The work of community-based organizations is difficult and taxing. Special care is needed to create and maintain a workplace that is nurturing, supportive, and participatory. Additionally, individuals in community organizations need opportunities to develop their own literacy for wellness and liberation. Personal and professional development opportunities should abound and leaders can play an important role in developing an open organizational culture that values questioning, diverse perspectives, and creativity.

Roles for Young People

Many social movements were driven by the energy and creativity of young people. Youth can be agents of change. With proper supports and gentle coaching, young people can act as researchers, teachers, consultants, project leaders, committee members, presenters, writers, and experts. Courageous adults can help young people serve as full members on school boards and committees, as well as on community and organizational boards and commissions. Young people can not only act, they can appeal to others to act as well. They can work in solidarity with other youth and adults to raise awareness, write letters, start media campaigns, and generally organize for social change. Young people can fight for and demand roles in the settings that affect their lives. And through their actions, they can remind the community and the world about the need to live up to the principles outlined in International Convention of the Rights of the Child[1]—especially Article 12, which speaks to young people's right to participation.

The principle affirms that children are full-fledged persons who have the right to express their views in all matters affecting them and requires that those views be heard and given due weight in accordance with the child's age and maturity. It recognizes the potential of children to enrich decision-making processes, to share perspectives and to participate as citizens and actors of change.

CONCLUSION

To encourage the transformation of conditions that lead to suffering and injustice, we need to develop our own moral and political literacy and work to develop it in others. The critical capacity to challenge dominant ideas about society, reject oppression, and promote liberation is a major pathway to wellness. In this chapter, we have suggested roles for agents of change. Youth, parents, organizations, and educational professionals alike can enhance their personal and collective critical consciousness, a critical precursor in the creation of healthy and just societies.

Educational psychologists can facilitate well-being in schools and communities by paying more attention to the role of power and structures of inequality in their own research and practice. This requires a widening of the disciplinary lens to capture the big picture of wellness. It requires attention to the political as well as psychological dimensions of wellness, and it requires a focus on external as well as internal factors. By making these issues part of the disciplinary dialogue, educational psychologists can move beyond amelioration and begin to transform conditions that lead to suffering. A critical educational psychology may be the first step toward the promotion of this dialogue.

TERMS FOR READERS

Conscientization—Learning to perceive social, political, and economic contradictions, and to take action against oppressive elements of reality.

Critical Consciousness—A mental faculty, a way of knowing the world that involves the ability and inclination to pose questions (critical thinking), to disembed from the present and grasp historical themes, and to critically analyze causality in our relationships with specific aspects of reality. It is also characterized by the power to perceive, respond to critical needs, and reconstruct reality through engagement with others and through conscious, responsible, creative relationships with reality.

Liberation—The process of resisting oppressive forces and the state in which oppressive forces no longer exert their dominion over a person or a group. Liberation is about overcoming the barriers to defiance. Liberation is the process of overcoming internal and external sources of oppression (freedom from), and pursuing wellness (freedom to)

Oppression—A series of asymmetric power relations between individuals, genders, classes, communities, and nations. Such asymmetric power relations lead to conditions of misery, inequality, exploitation, marginalization, and social injustices. Oppression is a condition of domination where the oppressed suffer the consequences of deprivation, exclusion, discrimination, and exploitation imposed on them by individuals or groups seeking to secure economic, political, social, cultural, or psychological advantage

Wellness—A positive state of affairs brought about by the combined and balanced satisfaction of personal, interpersonal, organizational, community, and social needs.

NOTE

1. Only two countries, Somalia and the United States, have not ratified this celebrated agreement. Somalia is currently unable to proceed to ratification, as it has no recognized government. By signing the Convention, the United States has signaled its intention to ratify—but has yet to do so.

FURTHER READING

Freire, P. (1970). *Pedagogy of the Oppressed*. New York: Continuum.

Gil, D. G. (1998). *Confronting Injustice and Oppression: Concepts and Strategies for Social Workers*. New York: Columbia University Press.

Mustakova-Possardt, E. (2003). *Critical Consciousness: A Study of Morality in Global, Historical Context*. Westport, CT: Praeger.

Prilleltensky, I., and Nelson, G. (2002). *Doing Psychology Critically: Making a Difference in Diverse Settings*. New York: Palgrave/Macmillan.

CHAPTER 45

Transformative Learning: Developing a Critical Worldview

EDWARD TAYLOR

There is an innate drive among all humans to understand and make meaning of their experiences. It is through established belief systems that adults construct meaning of what happens in their lives. Since there are no fixed truths and change is continuous, adults cannot always be confident of what they know or believe. Therefore, it becomes imperative in adulthood that we seek ways to better understand the world around us, developing a more critical worldview. As adults, we need to understand how to negotiate and act upon our own meanings rather than those that we have uncritically assimilated from others, gaining greater control over our lives (Mezirow, 2000). Developing more reliable beliefs about the world, exploring and validating their dependability, and making decisions based on an informed basis is central to the adult learning process. It is transformative learning theory that explains this psycho-cultural process of constructing and appropriating new or revised interpretations (beliefs) of the meaning of one's experience.

[It] is a process by which we attempt to justify our beliefs, either by rationally examining assumptions, often in response to intuitively becoming aware that something is wrong with the result of our thought, or challenging its validity through discourse with others of differing viewpoints and arriving at the best informed judgment. (Mezirow 1995, p. 46)

Transformative learning is uniquely an adult learning theory, abstract, idealized, and grounded in the nature of human communication. Despite the keen interest in the field of adult education with transformative learning theory over the last twenty-five years, as a theory and an area of learning it has been overlooked by the literature in educational psychology. Much of this oversight seems to be the result of the field's primary interest in learning of children and the lack of awareness of adult learning. This chapter is an effort to address this concern.

There are multiple interpretations of the nature and process of transformative learning and how it is fostered in the classroom. They range from a view of transformation as a lifelong process of individuation grounded in analytical (depth) psychology rooted in the work of Carl Jung to a cosmosological view of transformation involving a deep structural shift of consciousness that alters the way one views and acts in the world within a broad cultural context (O'Sullivan, 2002).

To be consistent with the theme of this handbook, this discussion will focus on defining the varying conceptions of transformative learning and transformative education from a more social psychological lens. These include Mezirow's rational transformative learning model, Freire's (1970) emancipatory view of transformation, and O' Sullivan's cosmoslogical view of transformation. As the reader engages in these different perspectives of transformative learning he or she will see that the centrality of the individual as the object of study becomes less central as the discussion moves from one perspective to another, to the final perspective, where individual change has becomes more peripheral and change in society becomes more central. In addition, at the end of the section on the various conceptions on transformative learning a discussion will be provided about its relationship to constructivism, illustrating its close connection to the field of educational psychology.

MEZIROW: A RATIONAL TRANSFORMATION

Transformative learning from Mezirow's perspective is a constructivist theory that is partly developmental, but more a rational learning process of construing a new or revised meaning of one's experience in order to guide future action. Transformative learning offers an explanation for change in meaning structures that evolve from two domains of learning based on the epistemology of Habermas' communicative theory. First is *instrumental* learning, which focuses on learning through task-oriented problem solving and determination of cause and effect relationships— learning to do, based on empirical-analytic discovery. Second is *communicative* learning, which involves in understanding the meaning of what others communicate (e.g., ideas, feelings, values). When these learning domains involve critical assessment of significant premises and questioning of core personal assumptions, transformative learning is taking place. Transformative learning attempts to explain how our expectations, framed within cultural assumptions and presuppositions, directly influence the meaning we derive from our experiences. It is the revision of meaning structures from experience that is addressed by the process of a perspective transformation within transformative learning.

Perspective transformation explains the process of how adults revise their meaning structures. Meaning structures act as culturally defined frames of reference that are inclusive of meaning schemes and meaning perspectives. *Meaning schemes*, the smaller components, indicative of specific beliefs, values, and feelings that reflect interpretation of experience. They are the tangible signs of our habits and expectations that influence and shape a particular behavior or view, such as how an adult may act when they are around a homeless person or think of a Republican or Democrat. Changes in meanings schemes are a regular and frequent occurrence.

A *meaning perspective*, on the other hand, is a general frame of reference, worldview, or personal paradigm involving a collection of meaning schemes forming a large meaning structure containing personal theories, higher-order schemata, and propositions. The frame reference provides criteria for judging or evaluating the world adults interact with. The frame of reference is composed of two dimensions, habits of mind and a point of view. Habits of mind are, habitual means of thinking, feeling, and acting influenced by underlying cultural, political, social, educational, and economic assumptions about the world. The habits of mind get expressed in a particular point of view. For example, my point of view as a liberal Democrat are expressed by my emphasis on ensuring rights for those that are often marginalized, the need for family wage, and a more transparent government. This point of view reflects a collection of beliefs and feelings that shape how the learner makes meaning of experiences (Mezirow, 2000).

Mezirow argues that meaning perspectives are often acquired uncritically in the course of childhood through socialization and acculturation, most frequently during significant experiences with parents, teachers, and other mentors. They reflect the dominant culture that we have been socialized into. Over time, in conjunction with numerous congruent experiences, these perspectives become more ingrained into our psyche and changing them is less frequent. In essence, they provide a rationalization for an often, irrational world and we become dependent upon them. These meaning perspectives support us by providing an explanation of the happenings in our daily lives but at the same time they are a reflection of our cultural and psychological assumptions. These assumptions constrain us, making our view of the world subjective, often distorting our thoughts and perceptions. They are like a "double-edged sword" whereby they give meaning (validation) to our experiences, but at the same time skew our reality.

Meaning perspectives operate as perceptual filters that organize the meaning of our experiences. When we come upon a new experience, our meaning perspectives act as a sieve through which each new experience is interpreted and given meaning. As the new experience is assimilated into these structures, it either reinforces the perspective or gradually stretches its boundaries, depending on the degree of congruency. However, when a radically different and incongruent experience cannot be assimilated into the meaning perspective, it is either rejected or the meaning perspective is transformed to accommodate the new experience. A transformed meaning perspective is the development of a new meaning structure. This development is usually the result of a disorienting dilemma due to a disparate experience in conjunction with a critical reappraisal of previous assumptions and presuppositions. It is this change in our meaning perspectives that is at the heart of Mezirow's theory of perspective transformation—a worldview shift. A perspective transformation is seen as the development of a more inclusive, discriminating, differentiating, permeable, integrative, critical worldview. Although less common, it can occur either through a series of cumulative transformed meaning schemes or as a result of an acute personal or social crisis, for example, a death of a significant other, divorce, a natural disaster, a debilitating accident, war, job loss, or retirement. Often these experiences are stressful and painful and can threaten the very core of one's existence. A perspective transformation can be better understood by referring to an example given by an individual who experienced a perspective transformation as a result of living in a different culture. Harold, an American, describes his change in perspective (worldview) in response to living in Honduras for two years as a Peace Corps volunteer:

I definitely see the world in a whole different light than how I looked at the world before I left. Before I left the states there was another world out there. I knew it existed, but didn't see what my connection to it was at all. You hear news reports going on in other countries, but I didn't understand how and what we did here in the States impacted on these people in Honduras, in South America, Africa, and Asia. Since I did not have a feeling for how our lives impacted their lives. It was as if the U.S. were almost a self-contained little world. After going to Honduras I realized how much things we did in the States affected Hondurans, Costa Ricans. How we affected everyone else in the world. I no longer had this feeling the U.S. was here and everybody else was outside. I felt that the world definitely got much smaller. It got smaller in the sense of throwing a rock in water it creates ripples. I am that rock and the things I do here in the States affect people everywhere. I feel much more a part of the world than I do of the U.S. I criticize the U.S. much more now than I would have in the past.

Mezirow has identified phases of perspective transformation based on a national study of women returning to college who participate in an academic reentry program after a long hiatus from school. The study involved in-depth interviews of eighty-three women from twelve programs in Washington, California, New York, and New Jersey. From the data, he inductively identified a learning process that began with a disorienting dilemma, such as returning to school, to include a series of experiences, such as a self-examination with feelings of guilt or shame, critical assessment of assumptions, the sharing of this discontent with others, exploration and experimentation with new roles and ideas, developing a course of action, acquiring new skills and knowledges, taking on roles, building competence, and ultimately the development of a more inclusive and critical worldview.

Transformative learning is also seen as way of thinking about the education of adults. Fostering transformative learning in the classroom includes the most significant learning in adulthood, that of communicative learning. Communicative learning involves critically examining the underlying assumptions of problematic social, political, cultural ideas, values, beliefs, and feelings—questioning their justification through rational dialogue. Mezirow does not see fostering transformative learning as an "add-on" educational practice or technique. He views it as the very essence of adult education, such that the goal of transformative learning is to help learners become more autonomous thinkers so they are able to negotiate the meaning-making process rather than uncritically acting on the meaning of others. Ideal conditions to strive for when fostering transformative learning in the classroom include: (a) a process that ensures learners have information that is thorough and valid; (b) a classroom environment that is safe, free from oppression and coercion; (c) learners who are encouraged to be open to varied and contested perspectives and are willing to assess and validate these perspectives as objectively as possible; (d) methods that promote and encourage critical reflection about the inherent underlying assumptions and related consequences; (e) an equitable opportunity to question, dialogue, and reflect on the various issues; and (f) and an overall goal of striving for objectivity and rational consensus.

This approach to education rests on the belief that there is inherent purpose, logic, and ideal associated with transformative learning. Significant learning in the classroom involves the transformation of meaning structures through an ongoing process of critical reflection, discourse, and acting on one's beliefs in relationship to the larger sociocultural context. It is this approach that provides a rationale for educators in choosing the best practices for fostering transformative learning.

PAULO FREIRE: AN EMANCIPATORY TRANSFORMATION

Paulo Freire (1970) was a radical educational reformist from Brazil (Latin America), who portrayed a practical and theoretical approach to emancipation through transformative education. His work is based on experiences with teaching adults who had limited literacy skills in the Third World, where he used an educational method that was such a threat to those in power he was exiled from Brazil in 1959. Freire wanted people to develop a theory of existence, which views people as subjects, not objects, who are constantly reflecting and acting on the transformation of their world so it can become a more equitable place for all to live. This transformation, or unveiling of reality, is an ongoing, never ending, and a dynamic process. Unlike Mezirow's emphasis on personal transformation and the choice to act politically, Freire is much more concerned about a social transformation via the unveiling or demythologizing of reality by the oppressed through the awakening of their critical consciousness, where they learn to become aware of political, social, and economic contradictions and to take action against the conditions that are oppressive. This awakening or kindling of one's critical consciousness is the consequence of his educational process. In Freire's (1970) words: "[The] more radical he [sic] is, the more fully he enters into reality so that, knowing it better, he can better transform it. He is not afraid to confront, to listen to see the world unveiled. He is not afraid to meet the people or enter into dialogue with them. He does not consider himself the proprietor of history or of men [sic], or the liberator of the oppressed; but he does commit himself, within history, to fight at their side" (pp. 23–25).

The latter quote reflects most accurately the intent of his work, that of fostering an emancipatory transformative process. The process is *conscientizaçao* or conscientization (Freire 1970), where the oppressed learn to realize the sociopolitical and economic contradictions in their world and take action against its oppressive elements. For Freire education is never neutral. It either inculcates through assimilation of unquestioned values of the dominant group reinforcing the status quo or it liberates by encouraging critical reflection (ideological critique) of the dominant values and taking action to improve society toward a more just and equitable vision.

Like Mezirow, Freire sees critical reflection central to transformation in context to problem posing and dialogue with other learners. However, in contrast, Freire sees its purpose based on a rediscovery of power, while more critically aware learners become, the more they are able to transform society and subsequently their own reality. Essentially Mezirow's view of transformation does not go far enough, such that personal transformation is seen as in and by itself, sufficient. He links himself conceptually to Freire (conscientization is critical reflection), but draws back at the concept of acting for social change and justice. For Mezirow, a transformation is first a personal experience (confronting epistemic and psychological distorted assumptions) that empowers persons to reintegrate (not questioning the dominant assumptions) or act on the world (confronting sociolinguistic distorted assumptions), if they choose. However, for Freire transformation is more of a social experience: by the very act of transformation, society is transformed. There are only two ways for humans to relate to the world, that of integration and adaptation. Integration involves the critical capacity to act on the world as a Subject and adaptation is an Object, acted upon by the world. Transformative learning from Freire's perspective is seen as emancipatory and liberating, both at a personal and social level. An outcome of transformative learning is that of voice where the learner acquires the ability to construct his or her own meaning of the world.

Three broad concepts/methods, some of which are the most often alluded to by other educators and scholars, reflect Freire's basic beliefs and practices about fostering an emancipatory transformation. First is his illumination of the domesticating effect of traditional education by teachers in their narrative "bank deposit" approach to teaching. Freire (1970) states that most teaching reflects the teacher as the expert where he or she provides a gift of knowledge, depositing into the minds of the students, who in an unquestioning manner, receive, repeat, and memorize the information as if they have nothing to contribute in return. Since the "banking" approach to adult education will not induce students (the oppressed) to reflect critically on their reality, he proposes a liberating education couched in acts of critical reflection, not in the transferal of information, that of a problem-posing and dialogical approach to teaching.

A second concept that is at the core of this problem-posing approach of education is that of praxis. Praxis is the moving back and forth in a critical way between reflecting and acting on the world. The idea of reflection is the continual search for new levels of interpretations with a new set of questions with the intent to critique former questions. Action happens in concert with reflection; it is a process of continually looking over our shoulders at how our actions are affecting the world. Furthermore, praxis is always framed within the context of dialogue as social process with the objective of tearing down oppressive structures prevalent both in education and society. Third is the horizontal student-teacher relationship. This concept of the teacher working on an equal footing with the student seems couched in the Rogerian ideology, whereby the student-teacher dialogue is built upon a foundation of respect and mutual trust. This approach provides an educational atmosphere that is safe, where anything can be shared and talked about and is an obvious setting for raising one's consciousness and facilitating an emancipatory transformation. Freire's philosophy of education reflects an emancipatory perspective inherent of both a personal and social transformation of which neither can be separated. It is the combination of both the biography of the personal and that of the social that sets the stage for emancipation. Transformative learning from this perspective occurs when the learner becomes aware of their history and biography and how it is embedded in social structures that foster privilege and oppression of persons based with power. Furthermore, it is through the practice of critical reflection, problem posing, and dialogue that transformative learning is fostered—accomplishing its primary objective of democratizing our social world.

O'SULLIVAN: A PLANETARY TRANSFORMATION

O'Sullivan's (2002) perspective of transformative learning is cosmological in nature. This is a visionary view of transformation, planetary in scope that includes a comprehensive understanding about the universe as a whole. More specifically, transformative learning from O's Sullivan's view:

Involves experiencing a deep, structural shift in the basic premises of thought, feeling, and actions. It is a shift of consciousness that dramatically and permanently alters our way of being in the world. Such a shift involves our understanding of ourselves and our self-locations, our relationships with other humans and with the natural world; our understanding of relations of power interlocking structures of class, race, and gender, our body awareness's; our visions of alternative approaches to living; and our sense of the possibilities for social justice and peace and personal joy. (p. 11)

A transformation from this perspective is about radical change or restructuring of the main-stream culture, involving a significant rupture from the past. It is a transformation that dramatically alters the way people relate to the world around them. The focus of this view of transformation is much more about the nature of the new perspective and the kinds of education that needs to be fostered, and less about the learning process experienced by an individual. Essentially, the goal of transformative education from a cosmological perspective is about the development of a planetary consciousness within a broad cultural context. This is where individuals come to recognize and appreciate the importance of fostering a sustained world habitat of interdependency working against the constant environmental degradation caused by the global competitive market. It is a conscious recognition that the present system is no longer viable or appropriate for fostering sustainable living. Transformation requires a reorganization of the entire system, developing a world habitat that effectively challenges structural forces of the market place to where people in their everyday lives, create an environmentally viable world.

Transformative education involves three distinctive modes of learning, a tripartite of education for survival, for critique, and for creativity. Survival education involves coming to terms with a world system that is contributing to the current ecological crisis. On an individual level it focuses on issues not often associated with learning, that of dealing with the dynamics of denial, despair, and grief about the present state of the world around us. These mechanisms must be dealt with at length before a transformation of the consciousness and behavior can begin. O'Sullivan identifies the task at hand, as a form of cultural therapy, involving critique (critical resistance education) and fostering critical reflection. There are several dimensions to a critical resistant education. One dimension involves recognizing the mechanistic and overly dependent and destructive nature of the western worldview concerning the natural environment. It also means fostering a cosmological view of the world that is holistic, interdependent, and interconnected, where individuals recognize and appreciate their place in the world as a whole. A second dimension is confronting the saturation of the consciousness, that of where our present knowledge/information makes us unconscious of what is happening to the world around us. O'Sullivan argues that a diversity of information is needed about the world and its present environmental condition. The third dimension of critical resistance is that of fostering a critical examination of power structures that foster a dominant worldview, particularly those structures that support the foundations of patriarchy and imperialism.

The third mode of transformative learning is that of fostering of a visionary education—a planetary consciousness. Specifically, it involves articulating a holistic context that challenges the present hegemonic structures that foster the global market vision. One approach is the development of narratives, or stories that are of significant power that bring to light the complexity associated with environmental issues, to offer new and more viable possibilities for living, and identify roles that people can take that foster change in the present system. A second dimension of this visionary education is that of a vision of development that overcomes the limitations of the mainstream conceptions of development, that of a dynamic of wholeness that encompasses the entire world. The third dimension of a visionary education that contributes to transformative learning, is bringing attention to the impact the first world (Western) has on others the lives of others in the world. More specifically, it means fostering a sense of community, a sense of place, and encouraging diversity within and between communities. Essential to this sense of place is a civic culture, where individuals play an active role of caretaking the environment and keeping a watchful and critical eye on the government. The last theme of this vision means recognizing the significance of the sacred. Transformative learning must address the topic of spirituality, a spiritual destiny, where there is a greater emphasis on nurturing the soul and spirit, and less emphasis on materialism.

These three views of transformative learning offer varied perspectives on the nature of significant paradigmatic transformation and its relationship to the larger sociocultural context. Mezirow's work is much more centered on the individual and the nature of change. However, as discussed in greater detail, essential to significant personal change is the larger personal and historical context. Freire moves away from the individual somewhat, with more attention given to the goal of the transformation, that of fostering political awareness and social justice. Similarly, is the work by O'Sullivan, who spends even less time on the individual nature of change, and more on articulating a transformative vision and educational practices that foster change. Despite the differences between these varied and contested perspectives of transformation, there are several core premises that they share to a greater or less extent that reflect a situated, socially constructed view of adult learning. Furthermore, these core premises have implications for the practice of adult education and educational psychology.

Four common themes are the centrality of experience, critical reflection, rational discourse, and the significance of context in the process of transformation. The first theme, experience is much more central to the work of Mezirow and Freire. It is the learner's experience that is the starting point and the subject matter for transformative learning. Experience is seen as socially constructed, so that it can be deconstructed and acted upon. It is personal experience that provides the grist for critical reflection and critique. In particular, it is shared learning experiences that are most significant to fostering transformative learning. Shared experiences provide a mutual base from which each learner makes meaning through group discussion and personal reflection. The group often subjects the meanings that learners attach to their experiences to critical analysis. Group discussion often disrupts the learner's worldview and stimulates questioning and doubt in learners about their previously taken-for-granted interpretations of experience.

The second theme, critical reflection, imbued with rationality and analysis, is considered a distinguishing characteristic of transformative learning. It is in adulthood where individuals begin to become aware of half-truths, unquestioned conventional wisdom, and power relationships and how he or she is being shaped by their own history. Critical reflection involves questioning the integrity of personal, social, cultural, and political assumptions and beliefs based on prior experience. It often occurs in response to an awareness of a contradiction among our thoughts, feelings, and actions. These contradictions are generally the result of distorted epistemic (nature and use of knowledge), psychological (acting inconsistently from our self-concept), and sociolinguistic (mechanisms by which society and language limit our perceptions) assumptions. In essence, we realize something is not consistent with what we hold to be true and act in relation to our world. It is the process of giving attention to the justification for what we know, feel, believe, and act upon in the world.

The third theme of transformative learning is rational discourse. Rational discourse is the essential medium through which transformation is promoted and developed. However, in contrast to everyday discussions, it is used when there is a need to question the appropriateness, integrity, and authenticity of what is being asserted. Rational discourse in transformative learning from Mezirow's perspective rest on the following assumptions: (a) it is rational only as long as it meets the conditions necessary to create understanding with another; (b) it is to be driven by objectivity; (c) all actions and statements are open to question and discussion; (d) understanding is arrived through the weighing of evidence and measuring the insight and strength of supporting arguments; and (e) the primary goal is to promote mutual understanding among others. It is within this social constructivist arena of rational discourse that experience and critical reflection is played out. Discourse becomes the medium for critical reflection to be put into action, where experience is reflected upon and assumptions and beliefs are questioned, and where meaning schemes and meaning structures are ultimately transformed. This is similar to the notion of double-loop learning discussed by Argyris and Schön, where an individual reexamines current ways of knowing and acting in the world.

A fourth theme is context and its relationship to the process of transformative learning. Broadly speaking this refers to contextual factors that include the surroundings of the immediate learning event, made up of the personal, professional, and historical situation of the individual at that time and the more distant background context involving the familial and social history that has influenced the individual growing up. Research on transformative learning, in the response to Mezirow's somewhat decontextualized view of learning, has identified personal contextual factors as: a readiness for change, the role of experience, and a predisposition for transformation. Recent research on sociocultural contextual factors, inclusive of related historical and geographical influences, has identified life histories, prior educational experiences, and historical events as having influence on transformative learning. An example, in a study involving Jewish women reentering the workforce after a long hiatus revealed that their personal transformation could only be fully understood by considering their earlier married years, and that their return to employment outside the home was not a random event, but a response to historical circumstances, where women in general were finding voice and identity outside the family. This research on others on transformative learning reveals a conception of learning that is situated, not bound by the narrow confines of the psychological, but instead constructed personally and historically across the confines of the body, activity, and cultural setting.

Transformative learning theory offers a way to make meaning of how adults develop a more critical, inclusive, and discriminating worldview. A worldview that is politically conscious, socially and culturally aware, and tolerant of the ambiguity often associated with our postmodern world. In addition, transformative learning provides a framework for educators to help them guide their practice in an effort to foster transformative learning in the classroom. In addition, further understanding can emerge when discussed in relationship to constructivism and to educational psychology.

A CONSTRUCTIVIST PERSPECTIVE OF TRANSFORMATIVE LEARNING

Many of the processes of transformative learning are consistent with what is understood in educational psychology as constructivism. It is a view that knowledge does not exist exclusively outside the learner and/or that knowledge can be transferred from the teacher or expert to the learner (e.g., Bruner, Ausubel, Piaget, Vygotsky). Instead it is a view of learning that is seen as more meaningful, where the learner is an active participant in the learning process creating and interpreting knowledge, not transferring, but rooted and shaped by personal experience. This is particularly important when trying to make sense of the adult learner and how they engage learning in the classroom. Adults have significant life experiences and it this rich personal experience that is essential to the meaning-making process both for constructivism and transformative learning. As previously mentioned it is the centrality of experience in conjunction with critical reflection and dialogue that helps make sense of how adults develop and transform their knowledge structures—their personal views of the world.

Kegan (2000) helps further illustrate transformative learning relationship with constructivism by discussing the transformation as an epistemological transformation, rather than behavioral or simply the process of acquiring greater knowledge. This epistemological transformation is reflected in two processes. One is a constructivist process of meaning forming or making, where perceiving is both an act of interpreting and conceiving. The second, and most significant to transformative learning, is the reformation of meaning-making. "We do not only form meaning, and we do not only change our meanings; we change the very form by which we are making meaning. We change our epistemologies" (pp. 52–53). Greater understanding of the dynamics of this change can be found in constructive developmental psychology (e.g., Kegan; Piaget; Kohlberg). During the transformative process the learner developmentally moves from a place where his or her values and beliefs are informed and defined by others, uncritically assimilated, toward a place or he or she develops an internal authority, making personal choices, critically, developing a self-authoring view of the world. This developmental view of transformative learning encourages a lifelong view of learning, where learners are capable of having several transformations of knowing during their lifetime.

Another way to add further understanding of the different perspectives of transformative learning to look at them through three forms of constructivism, psychological, social and sociological, as discussed by Woolfolk (2001). Psychological constructivism is concerned with "individual knowledge, beliefs, self-concept, or identity . . ." (p. 330), similar to Mezirow's view of transformative learning, where the primary focus is on significant change in the inner psychological life of adults. New understanding for the adult learner is derived from reflection on thoughts and actions. Although in contrast to Piaget, Mezirow would see social interaction, particularly dialogue with others as a key mechanism in fostering change in thinking. This emphasis on the social moves the analysis into the next form of constructivism, that of social constructivism. Rooted predominantly in the work of Vygotsky, this form of constructivism held "that social interaction, cultural tools, and activity shape individual development and learning" (p. 330). Vygotsky sees cognition not solely determined by innate factors, but is the product of the activities rooted in place, context, and culture. Consequently, the situation, the context, in which an adult learns, is a crucial determinant how adults will make sense of the learning experience. It is the emphasis on situated knowing connected to the essentiality of language that consistent with the previous factors identified significant to transformative learning, that of the role of context and dialogue. Research has shown that other concepts introduced by Vygotsky help broaden the constructivist emphasis of transformative learning. They include the nature of change in relationship to the zone of proximal development (interdependent process of development), using a holistic approach of analysis, the emphasis on language mediation within collaborative group settings (dialogue with others), and the importance of studying phenomena in process as opposed to performance outcomes.

The third form of constructivism, sociological, sometimes called constructionists, "does not focus on individual learning" (Woolfolk, 2001, p. 331) instead it is concerned with how public knowledge is created. Freire and O'Sullivan, similarly, emphasize the importance of discussing not only how knowledge is socially constructed, but more importantly, foster an awareness, a consciousness, of the dominant culture and its relationship to power and positionality in defining what is and is not knowledge in society. Further, all perspectives of transformative learning, like constructivist, encourage collaborative dialogue across diverse perspectives, fostering critique and questioning of dominant discourses.

By engaging transformative learning theory through a lens of constructivism, it not only sheds light on its inherent relationship to much in the field of educational psychology, but further illustrates the importance of recognizing the unique nature of learning across the lifespan, that of learning as an adult.

TERMS FOR READERS

Cosomology—Stephen Toulin, a philosopher, in his book *The Return of Cosmology* (1985) refers to it as an ambition by humans to speak and reflect upon the natural world as a whole.

Transformative Learning—Explains how adults' expectations, framed within cultural assumptions and presuppositions, directly influence the meaning individuals derive from their experience. It is a learning process where adults transform their worldview (paradigmatic shifts) as a result of developing more reliable beliefs about the world, exploring and validating their dependability, and making decisions based on an informed basis.

FURTHER READING

Freire, P. (1970). *Pedagogy of the Oppressed*. New York: Seabury Press.

Kegan, R. (2000). What "form" transforms? A constructive developmental approach to transformative learning. In J. Mezirow and Associates (Eds.), *Learning as Transformation*, pp. 35–70. San Francisco, CA: Jossey-Bass.

Mezirow, J. (1995). Transformation theory of adult learning. In M. R. Welton (Ed.), *In Defense of the Lifeworld* (pp. 39–70). New York: SUNY Press.

Mezirow, J., and Associates (Ed.). (2000). *Learning as Transformation*. San Francisco: Jossey-Bass.

O'Sullivan, E. (2002). The project and vision of transformative education. In E. O'Sullivan, A. Morrel, and M. A. O'Connor (Eds.), *Expanding the Boundaries of Transformative Learning*, pp. 1–13. New York: Palgrave.

Woolfolk, A. E. (2001). *Educational Psychology* (8th ed.). Boston, MA: Allyn & Bacon.

CHAPTER 46

The Impact of Apartheid on Educational Psychology in South Africa: Present Challenges and Future Possibilities

J. E. AKHURST

Ten years after the first democratic elections in South Africa, the schooling system in the country is facing numerous challenges. The legacies of the apartheid system and its impact on many aspects of schooling form a major part of these challenges. Many schools were sites of the struggle where learners rebelled against the oppressive regime. The apartheid system targeted education as the place where discriminatory policies could best be reproduced, and it is therefore the school system that has needed urgent attention. Thus, one of the major tasks in the development of a democratic and equitable society has been the reconstruction of education.

In 1990, Nicholas wrote, "Psychologists in South Africa have the daunting task of responding ethically to the many psychological problems that may result from apartheid" (p. 50). We might then ask, "What has been the role of educational psychology, and how might this division of professional psychology make a contribution to educational reform?" The purpose of this article is to explore this question.

In South Africa, educational psychology is not a unitary field: it covers both what are termed School Psychology and Educational Psychology in the United States of America. Thus, the application of psychological theory to the broader field of education, as by teachers and administrators, as well as the "work" of qualified and registered psychologists who work with learners, are both covered in SA educational psychology. The focus of practitioners may thus be both on the broader political, social, and economic issues and their impact on the lives of learners and educators, as well as on the specifics of tackling everyday management and learning issues of learners whose performance is compromised in various different ways. All of this needs to be responsive to the context of ongoing change in the educational arena.

Since 1994 (when the first democratic government was elected), policy makers and developers have been working on reforming the education system from its base—beginning with the underpinning principles and rationales. The system has been gradually refocused toward an outcomes-based education (OBE) system, with implications at every level of delivery. A fully retooled curriculum has been the result, and though there were hopes of it being fully in place by the millennium, it has now been more realistically adapted and termed *Curriculum 2005*, to be fully implemented for learners aged seven to sixteen by 2005. In no small part, the difficulties encountered during the implementation of the new curriculum relate to the legacies of apartheid still evident in the system. One of these legacies relates to the marginalizing of educational psychology in the past, and the relatively minor role it still plays in influencing policies and practice.

In order to understand the position of South African educational psychology, it is necessary first to explore the impact of apartheid on education. Then, the current status of educational psychology is briefly presented, in the context of contemporary social issues. To follow on, we look at ways in which both academic and professional educational psychology may have to work, in order to begin to address the complex problems that exist in the psychosocial systems of schools and communities. Finally, suggestions for interventions are offered to demonstrate potential future directions for the field, and suggest opportunities for collaboration between professionals in the developed world and their counterparts in South Africa.

BACKGROUND TO APARTHEID

Apartheid emerged in South Africa as the over-arching policy of the Nationalist government after their 1948 election to power (by a whites-only electorate). These developments were the result of a number of influences on Afrikaans-speaking South Africans. Two of the most powerful were the impact of the wars with Britain at the turn of the twentieth century (leading to great bitterness and resentment) and people's experiences of the great depression of the 1930s, when many were reduced to "poor white status". The development of Afrikaner identity became important as people strove to become emancipated from their experiences of unemployment and poverty. Furthermore, after the 1939–1945 war, there was a heightened awareness of the impending shortage of white employees in the labor market as the economy improved, especially in the professional, technical, administration, and management fields. In South Africa, these developments led to a vision of prosperity and dignity for the Afrikaner, and since the group was a minority, Black South Africans were seen as a potentially great threat to these aspirations.

Over the following decades, apartheid policies developed into a system of White power based on beliefs of racial superiority (echoing Nazi sentiments). This led to differential policies related to land ownership and rights of access to certain areas (eventually expressed in the notorious pass laws), job reservation for people of different groups, and separate development. In schools, Christian National Education was introduced for White learners and Bantu Education for Black learners, with all of these policies guarded by a vigilant and often brutal police force. Thus citizens of South Africa had vastly differing experiences of living conditions and standards, all based upon racial differences. A major expression of this was in the education system.

THE IMPACT OF APARTHEID ON EDUCATION

All spheres of social life were radically affected by the inequalities resulting from apartheid. Apartheid was not only expressed in unequal treatment of people, but philosophically influenced the very levels of what knowledge was considered to be legitimate for different groups, as expressed through the education system. In this section, the philosophies and practices in education will be outlined, including the limited role of psychology in the system, and illustrating how the legacy of apartheid is still very visible in education today.

Separate Schools

Although the school system was in broad terms a dual one, influenced by the policies of Bantu Education or Christian National Education for Black and White learners respectively, the situation became much more complex toward the end of the apartheid era. This was influenced by the unfolding policies of distinct homelands and separate development for many different groupings.

The concept of differing education for Blacks and Whites was evident in SA pre-1948 (when the Nationalist government came into power), but was built into a monolithic system from the 1950s by Dr. H. Verwoerd (who went on to become the prime minister before being assassinated in 1965). As early as 1936, there existed policies favoring the White child, in preparation for a dominant position in society, and limiting the education of the Black child, who was to be directed toward a subordinate position. From 1948, more blatantly racist sentiments were expressed in the policy-making.

The policies of Bantu Education led to a highly controlled type of education, preparing people mainly to take on menial tasks in the workplace. Learners were equipped with limited skills and attitudes, such as obedience and compliance, and critical thinking was not encouraged. The authority of the teaching staff was to be unquestioned, and the words of the textbooks reified. Teachers were poorly trained, with limited qualifications, and often had only basic second-language skills (the language in which they were expected to teach). Many became indoctrinated by the system, accepting policies with little question. For Black learners, instruction was in their home language until the end of the fourth year of education, but from the fifth year they were expected to learn through the medium of the Afrikaans language or English (depending on the controlling provincial education department). Many Black learners therefore dropped out of school at grade 5 because the change in medium of instruction led to great difficulties, particularly for those who had little contact with people speaking the language in which they had to learn. The continued imposition of education in Afrikaans, seen by black learners as the language of the oppressor, was one of the factors that sparked the famous Soweto riots of 1976.

When a more complex "Differentiated Education System" was introduced in the 1970s, along with the development of the self-governing "homelands" (an attempt to provide some autonomy for Black people in certain areas), further divides in the levels of education of different groups opened. This spawned more controlling departments of education, depending on the locality of the schools (rural or urban) and specific ethnic group. By the 1980s there were seventeen education departments in the four South African provinces, and schools were resourced according to the race group they served. Whites were provided with well-resourced schools in terms of buildings, facilities, and teaching staff (with low educator to learner ratios), and Blacks had poorly resourced schools. So-called coloreds and people of Asian origin were "in-between" in terms of provision and resources.

Within the education system for White learners, designed to "fast-track" especially Afrikaans-speaking learners into work in which they would take responsible positions, the hidden agendas of the Nationalist government were evident. English-speaking South Africans were gradually drawn into the fold by propaganda such as the talk of *swart gevaar* (danger from black people) and the threats of communism, and in 1967 the philosophies of Christian National Education (CNE) were announced. At its core, CNE entrenched White supremacy as based in the authority of God and pronounced that children should be molded as future citizens. Various systems in white schools were put in place to ensure conformity and "molding" of learners. There were Nazi-like overtones in the system, where White learners were to learn to "guard their identity" and to render "service" which was in response to their gratitude and loyalty to their people and country. Thus, the shaping of learners into desirable persons with correct attitudes (as determined by the government) underpinned various activities in schools: examples are discussions of civic responsibility, quasi-military marching, singing of the anthem, and prayers around the flag. Teachers had to be vigilant for any deviance from these activities, which needed to be corrected.

From a psychological perspective, the focus of education was on conformity to the group rather than a focus on the individual, with responsibility and obedience to authority (those placed in such positions being seen as God's representatives), rather than individual rights, being paramount. School Guidance was introduced into all White schools as a part of this system of indoctrination, with learners being assigned tutors who would keep a careful watch over their development. Psychology as a subject was viewed by the policy-makers as subversive, and was replaced by the philosophy of *Fundamental Pedagogics* (to be discussed below). Psychometric testing was developed to assist with "correct" job placement, and favored White learners, since they were tested in their home language. Whilst there was some psychometric testing in Black schools, this was mainly a bureaucratic window-dressing exercise and the results were never discussed with the learners, if the tests were returned to the schools at all.

The School Guidance syllabi for Black and White learners are an example of the different ways in which the Nationalist government strove to maintain social control. For Whites, there were emphases on conformity to ruling party attitudes and beliefs, and adherence to group norms, whilst for Blacks the emphasis was on preparation to be workers who were obedient to those in authority.

There are thus gross disparities between schools that have emerged from the different education departments, with the most poorly serviced schools being in the rural areas. The influence of the Nationalist ideologies was pervasive in education, and still endures in many schools even though there have been great efforts to change this. In the following section, I describe the underpinning philosophy.

Fundamental Pedagogics

Fundamental Pedagogics (FP) was derived from a Dutch theorist in phenomenology (Langeveld), and became the most influential philosophy in SA education. The resulting principles became the foundations of training in education in the Afrikaans-speaking universities and subsequently in most teacher-training colleges. In FP special terms were developed to drive attitudes to practice, such as "ortho-didactics" (right teaching methods), "pedo-diagnosis," and "pedo-therapy" (using the prefix "pedo" to emphasize the difference between children and adults). Many university departments of educational psychology developed separately from departments of psychology, often situated in different faculties, due to education taking the more conservative stance of FP, and developing rigid outlooks on the aims, purposes, and methodology of teaching.

FP provided a theoretical basis, which was congruent with CNE because it supported an hierarchically structured education system, in which educators were regarded as purveyors of knowledge, superior to their learners due to their training and their conformity to Nationalist policies of education. The thrust of pedagogy was to emphasize the knowledge and wisdom of those placed in positions of authority, and the relative powerlessness of the learner who was expected to conform to the dominant group norms.

FP developed a theory of deviance where the "different" or "conspicuous" learner was seen as a person challenging the social realities and the normative principles of the society. Educators were therefore encouraged to identify such a learner in order to "re-orientate" (i.e., "indoctrinate") the young person to be able to resist what were seen as "onslaughts of foreign ideologies" both from the more liberal first world, and from communism. Educators were bound by strict syllabi, encapsulated in textbooks carefully vetted by the education departments, and little deviance from the laid-down content of the syllabus was tolerated. This was further entrenched by a well-structured examination system from grade 5, leading to teaching being focused on examinations for learners from about age ten onward.

In the authoritarian system that emerged, learners were not encouraged to think independently or question, rote learning became the chief means of success, and decisions were generally made for the learner. Eventually, it was hoped that learners would be inculcated with a philosophy of life in which the person would make conforming decisions without critical thought. Thus, learners were not encouraged to be individuals exercising free choice (as encouraged by humanistic philosophies of psychology), but rather were to be persuaded by those who knew better.

Teacher competencies were therefore judged by their adherence to the philosophies and system described above, and teachers were themselves expected to obey those higher up the ladder in the system. The systems of inspection in schools, and of promotions being given only to those who did not challenge the system, further perpetuated and entrenched the system. Many teachers therefore developed relatively passive styles, having little influence and becoming cogs in the system rather than feeling that they could in any way change the *status quo*. The full routines and demands of both the classroom and extra-mural activities stifled teacher motivation, and teachers undertook their tasks with little question or critique, often willing to accept less than adequate conditions of service.

Guidance and Counseling in Schools

In the 1930s, psychologists were appointed to three of the White provincial education departments (Cape, Transvaal, and Orange Free State); and the fourth province, Natal, followed in 1944. The main focus of these psychologists was career guidance. A commission in 1948 recommended the appointment of guidance teachers to schools, and the first Vocational Guidance Officers were appointed in the 1950s. The provision of guidance in schools became a statutory requirement for whites-only schools in the National Education Policy Act of 1967. During the 1970s, guidance teachers were appointed, with such titles as "teacher counselors," "teacher psychologists" or "vocational guidance teacher," depending on the education authority. School Guidance was seen as having some benefit to the individual, but more importantly it was mandated to benefit the career development needs of the country. There is no term in Afrikaans to permit a direct translation of the word "counseling," with *voorligting* (guidance) being the term preferred, since the work was directive in nature.

In more conservative regions, a "tutorship program" was established, whereby educators were given the responsibility to monitor the progress and development of learners. Tutors were to keep a file of notes on each pupil, gathering information from other members of staff on conduct, home background, achievement, personality, appearance, health, leisure pursuits and religious participation. The purpose of this was to develop a form of surveillance and control over the learner, and to "guide" the young person if any activities were contrary to what were seen to be acceptable norms. In order to accomplish this, the tutor was instructed to build relationships of trust with children, to enable the "guiding" to take place. Learners' rights to privacy were therefore infringed, so that they could be subtly influenced.

The syllabi for School Guidance were vague with little available resource material. Also, since Guidance was viewed as different from examinable subjects, it was not accorded as much status, and was allocated to mostly untrained teachers, in order to fill up timetables. It was therefore widely viewed as a waste of time by educators and learners alike in the examination-driven system. Although a few schools developed sophisticated systems of guidance, much depended on the views of the school principal, and his or her attitudes to the careers and educational guidance.

Posts for School Guidance teachers were created in Black schools from 1981 (a response to the 1976 Soweto uprisings). However in Black schools, School Guidance was viewed with distrust, firstly because it was a government-imposed solution, and secondly due to resistance to the role of "moral guidance" described above. Differences in the provision of School Guidance thus became another tool for the promotion of discrimination.

Because of these politically formalized differences, entrenched over the decades of apartheid rule, the majority of the Black population had little access to or understanding of formal Western psychological counseling. The majority of Black schools had no counselors of any sort, due to staff allocations, even though posts may have existed. The attitude that Guidance was a waste of time as a non-examinable subject was pervasive, and teachers given Guidance responsibilities lacked training and resources. The result is that generations of learners had little if any careers guidance, and left school with minimal knowledge of the options or opportunities available to them.

Individuals with Special Needs

Provision for special needs was determined, as for general education, by the race group of the learner, with White learners having far greater provision made for remedial and specialized education than Black learners. Although Whites made up about 17 percent of the population, there were sixty-four specialized schools across the four provinces; whereas for learners of all other race groups, there were only thirty-four comparative schools provided. The ratio of the number of learners in a special school compared to those in mainstream was 1:62 for White learners compared to 1:830 for Black learners.

In KwaZulu Natal (the province in which the author worked), learners in white schools prior to 1992 who were potential candidates for specialized education had to be tested by a psychologist in order to ascertain the appropriate placement. In the for-Whites Natal Education Department, there was a ratio of 3,000 learners to one school psychologist. In certain primary schools, remedial teachers worked alongside mainstream teachers, and a number of remedial schools where learners were placed for more intensive assistance for up to two years were also created. For learners with limited intellectual ability, certain primary schools had special classes, and a handful of special secondary schools were also created to accommodate those making inadequate progress in mainstream. There were also schools for the visually-, aurally- and physically-disabled. The situation for Black learners was not comparable, with a learner to psychologist ratio of 1:30,000 in the former KwaZulu government schools. Psychological assistance was therefore inaccessible to those in need of assistance, with most learners in special need remaining in mainstream by default or dropping out of school.

There were thus great disparities in the provision for individuals with special needs, and the needs of the majority of Black children in this category were not met. The situation is further compounded by the existence of greater number of children with disabilities in developing countries compared to developed nations. Conditions of poverty and social disadvantage, and the interaction of intrinsic factors with contextual disadvantages contribute to this. Inadequate resources in mainstream schools and very limited specialized provision have led to a totally inadequate and divided system having been inherited from the past.

Conflict in Schools

Whilst it is not possible here to give extensive detail regarding schools as a site of the struggle against the apartheid government, it is necessary to note the impact of the conflict on the schools for Black learners. The Soweto riots of 1976 marked the beginnings of youth organizing themselves against the regime, and the mid-1980s were characterized by boycotts of schools as a way of indicating resistance. Learners became more organized through joining student movements, and whereas at first the struggle focused on educational issues, it broadened out to include the wider struggle of the people living in the urban "townships" of the time.

The impact on children, of either being involved in or witnessing the horror of violent police and youth clashes, or the nightmare of being caught in the crossfire of political factions engaged in battles in the townships, must not be underestimated. Families were extensively affected by

the violence with many fleeing the violence or moving their children into safe areas, sometimes hundreds of kilometers away. Many families experienced the death and/or injury to their
members. Politicized youth derided their elders for previously being passive, and parents and
caregivers found it difficult to have any influence over young people. Young people left school
prematurely and the slogan "liberation now, education later" was often chanted. The cohort of
young people at this time have often been termed the "lost generation," since their education was
severely compromised and many drifted into adulthood with limited prospects of employment.
The psychological impact of the destruction of community life, schools being gutted, young people roaming around with nowhere to go, and the trauma of recovering from horrific experiences
and grief was extensive, yet very little psychological intervention was possible (or available).

One of the effects of the violence was that it seriously impaired relationships between learners
and teachers. Teachers were fearful of the armed and angry youth, and were often threatened.
They would thus be absent from school for extended periods of time, and learners became a
law unto themselves. The writer knows of teachers who had to face learners armed with guns
or knives in the classroom, and there were schools where security guards were employed in an
attempt to provide for occupants' safety. Teachers thus retreated into passivity and a technicist
approach to teaching, becoming even more syllabus and textbook bound, and communicating at
a minimal level with learners.

THE LEGACIES OF APARTHEID AND THEIR IMPACT ON
FUTURE DIRECTIONS

Since 1994, there has been little redress of past imbalances in Black schools, other than some
teachers being "re-deployed" in order to even out the teacher to learner ratio differences between
schools from the different departments. Whereas the racial composition of the formerly privileged
White schools has changed, often considerably, to be more inclusive, former Black schools have
mostly remained single race schools. The urban–rural divide remains very problematic, in that
many teachers who have become accustomed to urban life are resistant to being placed in rural
schools where there might not be electricity, a telephone, or in remote areas even running water!
Whilst every effort has been made by policy makers to provide a new curriculum, and to strive to
equalize the provision of education, the problems remain extensive as a result of the influences
described earlier.

The legacy of apartheid is therefore still evident in South African society, particularly in
school education. Remnants of the education system described above are still extensive, with
previously White schools well-resourced, and previously Black schools still lacking in many
basic amenities and being overcrowded. However, the legacies of apartheid go much deeper than
physical provision of amenities—they are to be seen in the attitudes and approaches of many
teachers, and thus influence many learners.

From the second phase of education onward, large numbers of young people display characteristics of passivity, apathy, lack of interest, and motivation related to schooling. There is little
communication between home and school, and schools are regarded by many as a necessary evil
rather than being places of excitement and learning. Parents are mostly not involved in schools,
many having been intimidated as learners, and thus being afraid of educators. This is further
exacerbated by teachers often living outside of the area in which they teach, and doing little to
initiate contact with parents and other community members.

Many teachers were attracted to the work in earlier decades because their tertiary education
would be government-sponsored and they were thus sure of employment. Such teachers often
lack interest in teaching or the motivation to give of themselves. Some of them also became
militant as trade unionists, demanding their rights, but there has as yet been limited recognition of

the need for individual teachers to take responsibility for their roles in the lives of young people. The culture of teachers being late for class and absenteeism is still evident in many schools, and this has a great impact on the attitude of learners because of what they see modeled by their educators.

Whilst it might seem that the preceding two paragraphs are very critical of teachers, this must be seen in the context of their own previous education and training, as well as their emergence from the struggle. There is no doubt that there are many dedicated educators who give unstintingly of themselves, and herein lies the hope for education in South Africa. Many teachers engage in tertiary studies in order to improve their qualifications and competencies, and there is great potential for such further education to have an impact on practice in schools. It is in this realm that educational psychology has a central role to play, and such courses are proving to be popular choices.

The malaise affecting teaching extends to Higher Education to some extent. Many university lecturers pay lip service to policies of empowering students to become critical thinkers and leaders, and a limited number challenge academic practices that do not foster such approaches. Some of this relates to the tensions of research-led demands but greater teaching loads for academics. Many lecturers, in order to cope, continue to function in a more traditional "transmission" mode, where lectures are content-driven, and many students still use the rote-learning practices they developed in school.

Although there is a greater awareness of the fact that educators at all levels need training in democratic and liberal theory and practice, particularly in reflective practice which evaluates attitudes to and understandings of learning, the process of change has been slow. A dominant mode still in existence is that "experts" have access to knowledge and "the answers", and there is little explicit development of thinking skills or widespread debate about knowledge as a socially constructed and dynamic entity. Since authoritarian practice was so entrenched by the apartheid regime, it is harder to shift in SA than in many other countries.

In the apartheid years, the few posts available for psychologists in education were largely in the White education departments. Much of the work of psychologists was limited to psychometric testing with little time for therapeutic intervention (perhaps to limit any influence psychologists might have had). Given the post-apartheid economic constraints and reorganization in education, along with views of some administrators that psychology is auxiliary rather than central to the educational endeavor, the number of provincial departmental posts for psychologists has diminished, and educational psychology has all but disappeared as an influence in educational policy making. Yet, it is evident that various forms of psychological intervention at a group, community, and organizational level have the potential to offer a great deal to assist in rebuilding postapartheid education.

Emerging research data indicates the need for psychological interventions in schools. There is the need for creative interventions to be implemented and researched, since the traditional School Psychology model of working with individual learners cannot be utilized in such a resource-limited context. Innovative interventions include Teacher Support Teams, Career Focus Groups, and Peer Help Programs. Whole-school community-based interventions are important and the potential for building on these developments needs to be explored. Furthermore, the HIV/AIDS pandemic as well as poverty-related diseases pose a great challenge for both the health system and the education system, because of the effects on children and youth. Many children are already orphaned, and their performance in schools is adversely affected by the emotional impact of their grieving, as well as often having to cope with added responsibilities at home. Then, there are a growing number of infected children and teenagers, compounding the difficulties in schools. School-based programs to respond to these challenges are therefore a high priority, and educational psychologists have the skills to be able to implement these.

In the new curriculum, there is support for skills-based educational programs, with the learning outcomes of such programs being the focus of attention. OBE has been developed as a concept which it is hoped will influence all levels of education. The underpinning philosophy of the approach is far more learner-centered than previously, and such methods as cooperative and collaborative learning are favored, with continuous assessment being preferred to the previous examination system. Whilst the government has extensive work to do in implementing educational reform, it must be applauded for identifying the destructiveness of the central tenets of the previous system, and for providing an alternate philosophy as a basis for education. The challenges in moving toward implementation, given the dysfunctions in the system and the extent of the remedial work that is needed, are daunting, and there is no doubt that it will take many years for educational reform to take hold more broadly.

From the above, it is clear that educational psychology has a potentially important role to play in reconstructing education, and providing programmatic responses to the challenges in schools. There are encouraging signs. For example, the book *Educational Psychology in a Social Context*, by Donald et al., (2002) is the first South African text specifically designed to discuss the theoretical application of Educational Psychology to the challenges described. Then, in professional psychology, the current chair of the Psychological Society of South Africa (PsySSA, the equivalent of the American Psychological Association), is an educational psychologist— illustrating the way in which educational psychology has the potential to become a far more central role-player professionally. There are also many creative projects known to the writer where educational psychologists are working in difficult settings without a fanfare or without writing up these interventions. Such workers need the support of their colleagues.

Educational psychologists will face difficulties in delivering appropriate services related to the policy of inclusive education. Consensus is lacking among educational psychologists about their preferred role, and among educators in schools, regarding their expectations of educational psychology services. Learners with special need are particularly in need of attention, and the equipping of mainstream teachers to deal with these learners should be a priority. There is also the need, more broadly, for a reappraisal of psychological interventions in schools. Certain alternative interventions have been noted above, and the lessons from these interventions must form the basis of wider programs. Theory and practice need to be considered together, in order for practice in schools to be improved. Theory from educational psychology and community psychology enables new ways of thinking about problems, and also provides tools for creating solutions. There is a shortage of person-power in South Africa, and major efforts will need to be made to support and enable educational psychologists to make a difference.

CONCLUSION

In this article I have endeavored to uncover some of the influences of apartheid on education in South Africa from the perspective of an educational psychologist. No doubt there are other influences that I have neglected to mention, and the impact of apartheid is far-reaching. The apartheid system violated the human rights of generations of people, and its legacies live on as the new government struggles to make the fundamental shifts necessary to unpick the intricacies of its influence and evil intent. A number of writers have written of the massive scale of the conceptualizing, legislating, planning, and implementing of such a comprehensive transformation agenda.

One decade of democracy has passed. The challenge in the next decade will be to find innovative strategies to implement the educational change that the new curriculum facilitates. This involves turning the democratic and learner-centered principles of OBE into practice. Educational psychologists need to become more active in utilizing psychological theories for the purpose of developing the potentials of educators and learners in schools. This will require the role of the educational psychologist to be expanded beyond that of working with individual children to include advocacy, mediation, and facilitation, with practitioners engaging in systemic work in schools and communities. Political negotiation and influence are necessary in these tasks, since many educational decision-makers will need to be convinced to channel limited resources in such directions. A part of the work will thus need to be in the researching, evaluating, and writing-up of initiatives that are making a difference (e.g., the article by de Jong, 1995, listed below). Educational psychologists must determinedly take up their role as scientist practitioners. In these activities, educational psychologists would benefit from the collaboration and support of their colleagues from around the world. Educational psychology has, I believe, a central role to play, and the way is now clearer than before for transformational work to take place in schools.

FURTHER READING

Basson, C. (1987). School psychological services in white schools in the Republic of South Africa. In C. Catterall (Ed.), *Psychology in the Schools in International Perspective* (pp. 155–167). Columbus, OH: International School Psychology Steering Committee.

Cross, M. (1999). *Imagery and Identity in South African Education: 1880–1990.* Durham, NC: Carolina Academic Press.

de Jong, T. (1995). The educational psychologist and school organization development in the reconstruction of education. *South African Journal of Psychology*, 26, 114–119.

Donald, D., Lazarus, S., and Lolwana, P. (2002). *Educational Psychology in Social Context.* Cape Town, South Africa: Oxford University Press.

Dovey, K., and Mason, M. (1984). Guidance for submission: Social control and Guidance in schools for black pupils in South Africa. *British Journal of Guidance and Counselling*, 12(1), 15–24.

Leach, M. M., Akhurst, J., and Basson, C. (2003). Counseling psychology in South Africa: Current political and professional challenges and future promise. *The Counseling Psychologist*, 31(5), 619–640.

Nicholas, L. J. (1990). The response of South African professional psychology associations to apartheid. In L. J. Nicholas and S. Cooper (Eds.), *Psychology and Apartheid.* Johannesburg, South Africa: Vision/Madiba.

Watts, A. G. (1980). Career guidance under apartheid. *International Journal for the Advancement of Counselling*, 3, 3–27.

CHAPTER 47

Implications of Cultural Psychology for Guiding Educational Practice: Teaching and Learning as Cultural Practices

PATRICK M. JENLINK AND KAREN E. JENLINK

INTRODUCTION

Psychology, in particular educational psychology, has struggled with a crisis of identity in recent years, beset by questions of allegiances, values, and sense of place within education and society (O'Donnel and Levin, 2001). Historically, educational psychology has focused on prioritizing precision and theoretical parsimony over understanding the phenomena of learning as situated in educational contexts such as schools; contexts that do not lend to precision and parsimony (Turner and Meyer, 2000). Emergent in the ongoing debate and direction in educational psychology as an evolving field is the place of cultural psychology—cultural historical activity theory—as an important consideration in reconstructing the identity of educational psychology in relation to educational practice, and more importantly, in reconstructing our understanding of cognition and learning within the situated nature of human activity in educational settings.

Cultural-historical, sociocultural, sociohistorical, and cognitive theorists have advanced differing perspectives of learning in the past two decades, which have been instructive in helping to develop new understandings of how both students and teachers learn (Brown et al., 1989; Engeström et al., 1999; Fosnot, 1996; Lave, 1988; Rogoff and Lave, 1984; Vygotsky, 1978). Premised on the situatedness of learning, historically, socially, and culturally, a cultural psychology—cultural-historical activity theory—perspective (Cole, 1996) understands that learning occurs while individuals (students and teachers alike) participate in the sociocultural activities within and across the various communities of practice in which membership is held and practiced. The situated nature of learning is transformative, reflexively shaping and being shaped by the learner's cognitive and cultural processes and practices, and view of reality as the learners participate within and across communities of diversity and difference (Cole, 1998).

In this chapter, the authors will examine the use of cultural psychology for guiding educational practice, in particular educational practice in relation to learning and teaching in cultural–historical contexts where children come from many different home cultures, ethnicities, languages, and social classes. The authors undertake to: (1) examine the relationship between culture and activity; (2) explicate, using activity theory as a guiding framework, patterned ways of conduct of educational practice as activities or cultural practices, examining the import of mediational tools and artifacts in relation to educational practice (as situated in diversity-rich contexts); and (3) extend the author's positions concerning the implications of cultural psychology for guiding educational practice—the choice of activities or cultural practices.

CULTURAL PSYCHOLOGY—A RELATIONSHIP OF CULTURE AND ACTIVITY

Cultural psychology is an interdisciplinary field that has emerged at the interface of anthropology, psychology, and linguistics. Its aim, in part, is that of examining ethnic and cultural sources of psychological diversity in relation to emotional functioning, moral reasoning, social cognition, and human development. A central thesis of cultural psychology, originating in the Russian cultural–historical school of thought, according to Michael Cole, is "that structure and development of human psychological processes emerge through culturally mediated, historically developing, practical activity" (Cole, 1996, p. 108). In his conceptualizing a second cultural psychology, Cole elected to bring cultural artifacts, both ideal and material, to the foreground of understanding learning. In this perspective, artifacts are viewed as products of human history, situated socially and culturally: culture is moved to the center in relation to artifact-mediated action within human activity systems. Culture, for Cole (1996), is an artifact-saturated medium of human life, further explicated as an "immense, distributed, self-regulating system consisting of partial solutions to previously encountered problems" (p. 294). Explicating his theoretical perspective of cultural psychology, Cole is concerned with a conception of culture adequate to the theories and practices related to an artifact mediated perspective of learning as activity, adopting an activity theory framework to further elaborate his cultural–historical notion of learning.

Cultural–Historical Activity Theory

A distinctive notion of cultural–historical activity theory is that learning is mediated within/by culture and its products. Learning is also understood as being historical and having social origins. Suggested as a main discipline to the cultural–historical psychology approach is human activity that is constructive. As summarized by Davydov (1995), "the genuine, deep determinants of human activity, consciousness and personality lie in the historically developing culture, embodied in various sign and symbol systems." Cultural–historical theory, then, suggests that individuals engage in goal-directed activities within cultural contexts while relying on "others" who are more experienced, and using artifacts to mediate learning. Mediation occurs within "zones of proximal development" (Vygotsky, 1978), wherein less experienced individuals are assisted by more experienced "others" through mediated assistance: mediated assistance through cultural artifacts, both ideal and material in nature.

Situating Cognition

Situating cognition refers to learning within the context of practice, to the relationship between learners and the properties of specific contexts. Situating cognition reflects an understanding of knowledge as knowing about, which is a perceptual activity that always occurs within a context (Prawat and Floden, 1994). As Brown et al. (1989) explain, learning is always situated and progressively developed through situated activity. Learning involves more than acquiring a set of self-contained entities; it involves building a contextualized appreciation of these entities as artifacts, as well as for the situations through which these artifacts have value.

Mediating situated cognitive activities may be understood as a relationship between more experienced and less experienced individuals. In this relationship, more experienced others use conceptual as well as physical artifacts as tools for mediating cognitive reasoning and problem solving. Vygotsky's concept of zone of proximal development (ZPD) is instructive in understanding this relationship. He defined the ZPD as the distance between the actual development level of the learner and the level of potential development "determined through problem solving under ... guidance or in collaboration with more capable peers" (Vygotsky, 1978). The zone is where mediated assistance, such as teaching or facilitating, (through the resources of a more experienced other as cultural agent) and the individual (student or teacher as learner) development potential interface.

Extending the concept of ZPD into human activity systems, Engeström explained mediation as "the distance between the present everyday actions of the individuals and the historically new form of the societal activity that can be generated as a solution" (Engeström, 1987). Mediation, then, represents the use of cultural artifacts (ideal and material) to assist less experienced individuals, less cognitively and consciously aware individuals, to learn in situ—as situated cognitive development within communities of practice.

Artifact Mediation—Three Levels of Artifacts

A central principle of cultural–historical theory, as Cole (1996) explains, is the use of artifact mediation: semiotic mediation through the use of different levels of artifacts. All human actions are mediated by the use of cultural artifacts: culture is defined as a system of shared meanings and as the social inheritance embodied in artifacts. Thus, culture mediates human interactions, shaping and in turn being shaped by the use of artifacts. Artifacts are, as Cole explains,

an aspect of the material world that have been modified over the history of its incorporation into goal-directed action. By virtue of the changes wrought in the process of their creation and use, artifacts are simultaneously *ideal* (conceptual) and *material*. They are ideal in that their material form has been shaped by their participation in the interactions of which they were previously a part and which they mediate in the present. (p. 117)

Defined in this way, the distinction between the ideal and material properties of artifacts both affirms the inseparability of the material from the symbolic and affirms the equal force of mediating human actions through use of artifacts whether one is considering language or a more concrete artifact such as a pencil.

Importantly, in cultural–historical theory, Cole (1996) identifies three levels of artifacts, including primary artifacts (words, writing instruments, words, telecommunication networks, a mythical cultural personages, etc.); secondary artifacts (traditional beliefs, norms, constitutions, etc.); and tertiary artifacts (imagined worlds, creative representations, play, schemas, scripts, notions of context, etc.). These three levels of artifacts enable semiotic mediation of human action; most importantly they animate learning with the cultural-historical nature of human interaction in educational settings.

Internalization/Externalization

Cultural–historical activity theory explains that internalization/externalization processes regulate human actions/interactions within cultural activities. Internalization is a transformational process with changes in the structure of activity; internalization is the transfer onto an internal psychological plane of external performances. The process of internalization is, in part, an appropriation of cultural knowledge, as ideal/conceptual artifacts, and therein contributes to the reproduction of culture. In contrast, externalization creates new artifacts that enable the transformation of culture.

Internalization of external experiences is derived from social interactions that are mediated through use of artifacts, and as such, internalization is simultaneously an individual and a social process. Relatedly, externalization is also an individual and a social process through which the application of schemas and cognitive processes work to create/transform existing semiotic, ideal/conceptual, and material artifacts, and animate learning. Conceived as a representational activity, internalization is a process that occurs simultaneously in social practice and in the mind. The appropriation of semiotic artifacts—symbol systems—as an internalization process translates into the transformation of communicative language into inner speech. Internalization processes are those through which individuals construct minds in interaction with the external social world(s) of other individuals.

Legitimate Peripheral Participation

The notion of legitimate peripheral participation (Lave and Wenger, 1991) is the process through which individuals who enter a community of practice, recognized as peripheral participants (less experienced members of the community), appropriate a community identity (personal epistemology) through emergence in the practices of the community. Wenger explains that, "Because learning transforms who we are and what we can do, it is an experience of identity. It is not just the accumulation of skills and information, but it is a process of becoming – to become a certain person, or conversely, to avoid becoming a certain person" (Wenger, 1998). As an individual engages in a community of practice, or a community of learners, he or she would assimilate an identity (like-mindedness) similar to the members of that community. This is accomplished by providing for opportunities to engage in the patterned ways of conducting practice, first observing and then practicing. Situating the peripheral participant within activity contexts of the community, mediating the participant's learning through cultural artifacts of the community, and assisting the peripheral participant to appropriate the shared beliefs and meanings of the community through its culture, cognitively develops the peripheral participant over time to move from the periphery to a more central participation. Mediation of an individual's actions and practices, through cultural artifacts in social interaction, is the essential precondition for cognitive and social development.

Mediated Agency—The Authority of Cultural Artifacts

In activity theory, Wertsch and Rupert (1993) explain that agency refers to who it is that carries out the action, and by extension in cultural–historical activity theory, mediated agency refers to "individual(s)-operating-with-mediational-means." If the focus on mediated agency is on the actions of participants within communities of practice, and more specifically its focus is on social dimensions of consciousness—mediational means employed in mental functioning, either intermental or intramental functioning (Wertsch, 1985). Mediated agency is concerned with how forms of social interaction maybe internalized to form individual mental processes; cognitive reasoning processes.

Mediated agency understands that human action is fundamentally shaped by the mediational means it employs, within situated activities of learning and practice. Relatedly, it is understood that appropriate mediational means (artifacts) are necessary to create solutions to problems, to engage in reasoning and to have certain thoughts. Mediated agency also acknowledges that shaping human action through the use of cultural artifacts does not imply simply a static body of knowledge or practices. Rather, it recognizes that tensions arise through the interaction between mediational means and the individuals using them, which results in a continuous process of transformation and creativity (Wertsch and Rupert, 1993).

An inherent property of mediational artifacts (means) is that they are culturally, historically, and institutionally situated within and across culture(s). Therefore, because of the sociocultural situatedness of mediational means, mediated agency focuses on the cultural–historical "situatedness" of cognitive reasoning. Mediated agency, then, fosters the creation of new ideas and practices through focusing on existing cultural artifacts as mediational means (Wertsch and Rupert, 1993). Importantly, individuals engaged in mediated agency draw on the authority of cultural artifacts to mediated situated cognitive reasoning and development. Equally important, recognizing the inherited cultural authority of artifacts means recognizing the shared values, beliefs, and meanings within the artifacts, and how this inheritance may contribute to cultural reproduction and/or transformation.

Social Inheritance of Cultural–Historical Activity

Within cultural–historical activity theory, as Cole explains, culture is conceived of "as human being's 'social inheritance.' This social inheritance is embodied in artifacts, aspects of the environment that have been transformed by their participation in the successful goal-oriented activities of prior generations" (Cole, 1998, p. 291). As a learner engages in external social activity, mediated by different levels of artifacts, his or her internal cognitive reasoning processes, cognitive schemas, and knowledge structures are transformed; conversely, through his or her schemas (Cole, 1996), cognitive activities construct and orchestrate social processes. The social inheritance of culture is acquired through mediated activity, and may simultaneously be transformed to reflect new artifacts constructed through interactions within various social activities.

Social inheritance of cultural artifacts includes the three levels of artifacts identified by Cole (1996), and therein the importance of analyzing the artifacts to determine their cognitive as well as political implications is important. All human actions are mediated, and the selection of mediating artifacts by more experienced others reflects the use of culture to either reproduce existing cultural patterns; patterned ways of conducting educational practice, and ways of learning. Within a diversity-rich context, multicultural and multiracial considerations are necessary to ensure that mediation of learning reflects artifacts responsive to the diversity of the individuals within and across situated activities designed for cognitive development of mind. Equally important, is that the artifact selection acknowledges how social inheritance—the shared beliefs and meanings embodied in artifacts—instructs the process of internalization, and may serve to reproduce cultural patterns that are ideologically bound in dominant politics as opposed to transform cultural patterns into possible alternative futures.

Cultural–historical activity theory recognizes that the conduct of educational practice as situated learning, mediated by cultural artifacts, creates patterned ways of learning and practice within social contexts defined by their historicity and spatial qualities. Patterned ways of learning reflect an inseparable relationship between the material and symbolic in human reasoning (Blanton et al., 1998). Internalization of cultural artifacts, symbolic (ideal) and material, appropriates, in part, cultural knowledge and ways of knowing and being; a patterned way of conducting practice. Outwardly, material artifacts are used to impact on objects; to externalize artifacts is to work to change patterned ways of conducting practice. In contrast, artifacts that are psychological in orientation work inwardly and outwardly to enable self-regulation and the regulation of others, patterning group dynamics, regulating shared thinking and negotiated meaning (Brown and Duguid, 2000).

PATTERNED WAYS OF CONDUCTING EDUCATIONAL PRACTICE—AN ACTIVITY THEORY FRAMEWORK

Educational practice—teaching, learning—is social and cultural in nature, taking place within and across human interactions mediated by artifacts and guided by sociocultural rules. Educational practice is a process of learning *to be* and learning *about* that are deeply intertwined within communities of practice. Situated within communities of practice (Chung and Chen, 2002), we "learn 'how' through practice; and through practice, we *learn to be*" (Barab and Plucker, 2002). Educational practice also has both temporal and spatial qualities, that is, practice is patterned over time and defines, while simultaneously being defined by, the space in which the practice is lived. In this sense, the individual as learner is shaped (through internalization) by the culture as a process of mediation using various artifacts. Relatedly, the individual's practice shapes (through externalization) the culture and transforms it, constructing new artifacts that replace existing ones, creating alternative realities animated by social imaginaries (tertiary artifacts as mediating influences).

Understanding how practice is patterned—how learning is mediated through cultural artifacts as the learner *learns to be*—is instructed by the use of cultural–historical activity theory in the form of an activity system framework. Cultural–historical theorists, in referring to activity, are not simply concerned with *doing* as disembodied action, but more importantly they are concerned with action that is *doing to transform* some object (that which is acted upon through action/practice), with the focus on the culturally, historically contextualized activity of the entire system, rather than a singular activity (Cole, 1996; Cole and Engeström, 1993).

Cultural–Historical Activity Systems

Cultural–historical activity is predicated on the understanding that an individual's schemas—cognitive frameworks—for thinking are developed through problem-solving actions conducted in specific contexts whose social structures are based on historical, culturally grounded actions. In this sense, activity theory is concerned with the historical origins of a phenomenon or activity and the cultural patterns of practice. Importantly, cultural–historical theory focuses on the interconnections, with and across cultures, which instruct human activity and work to form systems of activities such as teaching and learning situated within a classroom.

An activity system, then, consists of subjects (individuals or groups that act) and an object (that which serves as the focus of the activity), as well as the mediating tools and artifacts (ideal and material: first, second, tertiary levels) that mediate the relations of subject and object. An activity system also consists of sociocultural rules (informal, formal, technical) that guide practice and activity. Relatedly, an activity system involves a community (comprised of individual members who share in purpose) and a division of labor that reflects both the horizontal division of tasks and the vertical division of power and status. Figure 47.1 illustrates the relationship of these elements of the activity system as related to diversity-rich learning contexts (adapted from the work of Cole and Engeström (1993) and Cole (1996). The activity system for a diversity-rich context focuses on the processes of how individuals develop in relation to the involvement with others while using and transforming cultural artifacts within cultural–historical situated contexts. This activity system recognizes the multilayered and multivoiced nature of activities within diversity-rich contexts. Tensions within the system (see a, b in Figure 47.1) arise as individuals and groups interact and contradictions are introduced as part of the transaction between the activity system and other systems, between mediated agency and individual needs, or between the peripheral participant and the patterned practices of the community.

Cultural–historical activity theory understands that the human activity system learns, expands, and transforms itself. In this sense the system is organic and self-organizing, experiencing crises and contradictions that create tensions. Such tensions require the activity system to self-critically examine and reorganize; to change in response to externally introduced contradictions (i.e., such as mandated curriculum, high-stakes testing) or innovations from another system. Importantly, the activity system is seen as a heterogeneous entity—there are diverse voices, perspectives, and

Figure 47.1
Human Activity System for Diversity-rich Contexts

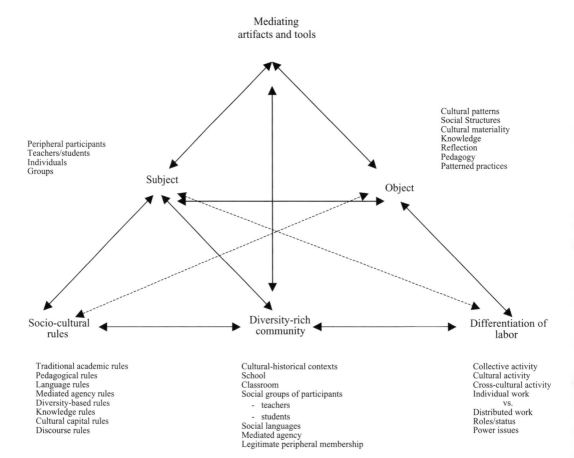

Discourse
Critical reflection
Inquiry activity
Knowledge—cultural, formal, etc.
Technical tools—computer, software
Symbol-based tools—Language
Process-based tools
Diversity-based—multicultural

Mediating
artifacts and tools

Cultural patterns
Social Structures
Cultural materiality
Knowledge
Reflection
Pedagogy
Patterned practices

Peripheral participants
Teachers/students
Individuals
Groups

Subject

Object

Socio-cultural
rules

Diversity-rich
community

Differentiation of
labor

Traditional academic rules
Pedagogical rules
Language rules
Mediated agency rules
Diversity-based rules
Knowledge rules
Cultural capital rules
Discourse rules

Cultural-historical contexts
School
Classroom
Social groups of participants
- teachers
- students
Social languages
Mediated agency
Legitimate peripheral membership

Collective activity
Cultural activity
Cross-cultural activity
Individual work
vs.
Distributed work
Roles/status
Power issues

cultures represented in the system. The heterogeneity of an activity system is defined, in large part, by its multicultural and multiracial makeup. The system is also defined by its historicity. Through its heterogeneity and historicity the system is bound in a complex contexts shaped by historical discourse and practices of disciplining and difference that have shaped its development. Relatedly, an activity system constitutes the minimal meaningful context in and through which to understand human praxis. That is, to understand how activity is distributed as tasks (division of labor) across subjects (those more experienced and those less experienced) and within the tasks, the artifacts individuals and groups use to accomplish the distributed tasks, all of which occur in relation to as well as within and across communities of practice.

An Activity System Framework: Implications for Practice

Cultural–historical activity theory is useful in understanding how individuals and groups learn, particularly in illuminating how teacher educators or teachers or students choose particular artifacts such as pedagogical tools to guide and conduct their practice. An activity systems framework, predicated on cultural–historical theory, focuses attention on the predominant value systems and social practices that characterize the contexts in which learning occurs.

Relatedly, an activity theory framework works to illuminate the cultural goals of reproduction, development, or transformation and the ways in which learning environments are structured, socially, to promote attainment of these goals (Cole, 1996). Where cultures are infused with alternative possibilities of individual and societal realities, alternative futures are promoted through ways in which cultural activity is structured. A central concern of cultural–historical activity theory is to examine the kinds of culturally defined artifacts that shape existing realities through mediated activity, and to understand the kinds of culturally defined artifacts necessary to create alternative futures that motivate individual's activity in order to facilitate mediation of one another's learning that transform, learning that creates alternative futures.

An activity theory framework for understanding patterned practices within activity systems situated in diversity-rich contexts includes certain key elements. These include the activity setting, identity, artifacts (tools), appropriation, and multivoicedness.

Activity Settings

Activity settings are those contexts that mediate the development of consciousness and the acquisition of cultural knowledge and skills. Examining the relationships within and across activity settings in a diversity-rich context illuminates motives that encourage patterned practices that serve to bring the peripheral participant into the community of practice. Activity settings are instructed by sociocultural rules that provide constraints and guidance to support learners' efforts to *learn to be* a member of the community. Activity settings in diversity-rich contexts have cultural histories that require certain relationships, mediated by artifacts and tools, in which participants adopt a general agreement of purpose and meaning. Recognizing that multiple and competing desired outcomes often coexist within an activity setting is important, as is the understanding that tensions arise from competing outcomes. Activity settings are often individual constructions, that is, they are constructed through the interactions of individuals, influenced by the mediated agency of a more experienced other. Thus, there may be multiple activity settings within a situated context, constructed by the various participants engaged in different activities. Activity settings are defined, in part, by the boundaries constructed through mediated interactions. Such boundaries are not insular, but coexist as sets of relationships, overlapping one with another. The cultural history and cultural spatiality of activity settings create complex systems of social interactions that must be understood in relation to mediated agency and human development.

Identity

Identity is shaped and at the same time shapes the social interactions and relationships of individuals within the activity setting. Activities, mediated through cultural artifacts, pass on a social inheritance to participants. In effect, activities are part of a larger system of relations in which they have meaning—an activity system—and from which individual and group identity is shaped. Understanding this aspect of cultural–historical activity, as identity shaping within situated contexts of practice, is to understanding the broader implications of *learning to be* in diversity-rich contexts. Communities of difference bring to the foreground the need for mediated agency that recognizes the ethnic, cultural, linguistic, social, and economic diversity that define social interactions, and importantly situate learning within complex systems of cultural knowledge and shared meaning. Agency and identity share an important relation in that the more experience member (such as a teacher) of a community of practice (activity setting) serves as the mediating agency for less experienced individuals, and importantly mediates not only the cognitive development in terms of reasoning ability, but also mediates the development or formation of identity of the less experienced participant as he or she is brought into the community. Recognition of cultural, ethnic, racial, linguistic differences as well as cognitive maturity contributes to the shaping of identity. Mediating social interaction and shaping of identity enables the individual to appropriate necessary artifacts and acquire the social inheritance within these artifacts, and to construct an identity commensurate with the community of practice.

Diversity-Based Artifacts

Mediated agency within diversity-rich contexts implicates the use of cultural tools and artifacts—ideal, material, psychological—in the mediation of cognitive development; acknowledging the need for selecting artifacts that are responsive to the needs of diverse individuals as well as the need to select artifacts that engender an appropriate social inheritance that works to transform the patterned ways of conducting practice in educational settings. Importantly, understanding the cultural–historical origins of the individuals is necessary for identifying the conceptual, material, and practical tools used in mediating learning and social interaction toward moving from legitimate peripheral participation to a more central role in the community of practice. Herein, mediated agency must focus on Cole's (Cole, 1998, p. 292) three levels of artifacts, recognizing that first and second level artifacts (conceptual and material [physical]) are necessary, but not sufficient in mediating the diversity of individuals, if mediation is to transform practice. The third level of artifacts, which reflect the use of social imaginaries and creativity to foster alternative possible futures, is essential to the externalization of culture. Mediated agency must understand the historical origins of individuals, as well as the culturally patterned nature of practice, recognizing that social practice is both temporal and spatial, defined by social interactions over time and by the nature of the place in which human activity is conducted. Diversity-based artifacts are carefully selected to transform the individual and at the same time, to transform the patterned conduct of educational practices.

Appropriation

Appropriation refers to the process through which individuals adopt artifacts/tools available for use in particular social spaces/places such as classrooms and schools. In part, appropriation is the internalizing ways of cognitive reasoning inherent in cultural artifacts. Through appropriation, shared meanings, values, and beliefs embedded in cultural artifacts are acquired by individuals engaged in mediated actions situated within activity settings. Here the question of types of social structures, patterned ways of conducting practice prevalent in different activity settings is important. Equally important is the question of how such structures and patterned practices mediate appropriation of particular cultural knowledge and skills as well as mediate the development of consciousness of individuals. For the legitimate peripheral participant, appropriate occurs over time, situated within activity settings. Within diversity-rich contexts, legitimate participation on the periphery requires legitimation of multivoicedness and a recognition that participants have different cultural, ethnic, linguistic, and economic needs. Mediated agency works to create a safe and just activity setting in which individual actions are mediated with diversity-appropriate artifacts/tools. Appropriation can occur at different levels of artifacts/tools, including ideal or conceptual, material or practical, and social imaginary or creative schema. Factors affecting appropriation include social context of learning and the individual characteristics of the learner. Mediating the appropriation of cultural artifacts through activities situated in diversity-rich contexts is a process of cultural transformation and cognitive-cultural human development.

Multivoicedness

Multivoicedness reflects a diversity of beliefs, values, culture, ethnicity, race, and sexual preference. It is based on the principle that "every form of human interaction contains within it many different selves, arranged in multiple, overlapping, and often-contradictory ways" (Brown, Collins, and Duguid, 1989, p. 41). Diversity-rich contexts represent multicultural/multiracial/multiperspectival differences that define communities of difference that exist within and across—cross-cultural—activity settings or communities of practice. Multivoicedness also reflects a level of consciousness of complexity of historical origins of individuals and their respective cultures, noting the need for appropriating artifacts from within and across different cultures. Situating learning in diversity-rich contexts recognizes that such contexts are social constructions, through mediated human interaction, and that the recognition of differences is fundamental to the development of individual and group identity within and across activity settings within the larger activity system (such as a school). Multivoicedness also recognizes that the voices of the less experienced (legitimate peripheral participant) and of the more experienced participant must be recognized and heard, therein mediating asymmetry of power relations within communities of practice and distributing social tasks and work equitably and justly.

FINAL REFLECTIONS

Cultural–historical theory, and by extension cultural–historical activity theory, in diversity-rich contexts, is fundamentally concerned with mediated human development in relation to recognizing difference in human growth and potential. Its concern for the cultural–historical nature of human development makes it an important consideration in understanding learning in educational contexts. Cultural–historical activity theory illuminates the importance of context, in particular the historical and cultural origins, as related to learning. An importance of this perspective is that it situates learning within social contexts, and therein moves the focus from the individual to the setting of human activity. A second importance of this perspective is that it provides a theoretical basis for analysis and understanding of the patterned conduct of educational practices within diversity-rich contexts. Importantly, cultural–historical activity theory provides a framework for understanding the interactions of individuals and the different contexts in which they learn, and for understanding how individuals appropriate cultural artifacts, through mediated agency in diversity-rich contents.

REFERENCES

Barab, S. A., and Plucker, J. A. (2002). Smart people or smart contexts? Cognition, ability, and talent development in an age of situated approaches to knowing and learning. *Educational Psychologist*, 37(3), 165–182.

Blanton, W. E., Moorman, G., and Trathen, W. (1998). Telecommunications and teacher education: A social constructivist review. *Review of Research in Education*, 23, 235–275.

Brown, J. S., and Duguid, P. (2000). *The Social Life of Information*. Cambridge, MA: Harvard Business School.

Brown, J. S., Collins, A., and Duguid, P. (1989). Situated cognition and the culture of learning. *Educational Researcher*, 18(1), 32–42.

Chung, W. L. D., and Chen, D. T. V. (2002). Learning within the context of communities of practices: A Reconceptualization of tools, rules, and roles of the activity system. *Educational Media International*, 39(3/4), 247.

Cole, M. (1996). *Cultural Psychology: A Once and Future Discipline*. Cambridge, MA: Harvard University Press.

———. (1998). Can cultural psychology help us think about diversity? *Mind, Culture, and Activity*, 5, 291–304.

Cole, M., and Engeström, Y. (1993). A cultural-historical approach to distributed cognition. In G. Salomon (Ed.), *Distributed Cognition: Psychological and Educational Considerations*, pp. 1–46. Cambridge: Cambridge University Press.

Davydov, V. (1995). The influence of L. S. Vygotsky on education theory, research, and practice (S. Kerr, Trans.). *Educational Researcher*, 24(1), 12–21.

Engeström, Y. (1987). *Learning by Expanding: An Activity-Theoretical Approach to Development Research* (p. 174). Helsinki, Finland: Orienta-Konsultit.

Engeström, Y., Miettinen, R., and Punamäki, R. (1999). *Perspectives on Activity Theory*. New York: Cambridge University Press.

Fosnot, C. T. (1996). *Constructivism: Theory, Perspectives, and Practice*. New York: Teachers College Press.

Lave, J. (1988). *Cognition in Practice*. New York: Cambridge University Press.

Lave J., and Wenger, E. (1991). *Situated Learning: Legitimate Peripheral Participation*. Cambridge, MA: Cambridge University Press.

O'Donnel, A. M., and Levin, J. R. (2001). Educational psychology's healthy growing pains. *Educational Psychologists*, 36, 73–82.

Prawat, R. S., and Floden, R. E. (1994). Philosophical perspectives on constructivist views of learning. *Educational Psychology*, 4, 17–38.

Rogoff, B., and Lave, J. (1984). *Everyday Cognition: Its Development in Social Context*. Cambridge: Cambridge University Press.

Turner, J., and Meyer, D. (2000). Studying and understanding the instructional contexts of classrooms: Using our past to forge our future. *Educational Psychologists*, 32, 69–85.

Vygotsky, L. S. (1978). *Mind in Society: The Development of Higher Psychological Processes*. Cambridge, MA: Harvard University Press.

Wenger, E. (1998). *Communities of Practice: Learning, Meaning, and Identity* (p. 215). Cambridge, MA: Cambridge University Press.

Wertsch, J. V. (1985). *Vygotsky and the Social Formation of Mind*. Cambridge, MA: Harvard University Press.

Wertsch, J. V., and Rupert, L. J. (1993). The authority of cultural tools in a sociocultural approach to mediated agency. *Cognition and Instruction*, 11(3/4), 230.

CHAPTER 48

The Culture/Learning Connection: A Cultural Historical Approach to Understanding Learning and Development

YATTA KANU

INTRODUCTION

This article adds to the burgeoning collection of research that views learning and development as psychosocial and cultural processes, an emerging notion that challenges educational psychology's traditional assumption that the mind does not extend beyond the body and that learning and development are purely psychological processes. Based on research utilizing the cultural historical approach to understanding and characterizing patterns and regularities of engagement in learning among Native-Canadian (Aboriginal) students from low-income communities, the article invites educators and educational psychologists to reconsider the artificial boundary traditionally drawn between the individual and the social in the development of mind, and attend to learning and development through the lens of cultural socialization and its pervasive role in human learning and development. Too often cultural context is neglected in the study of development and education, particularly in studies on ethnic minorities like Native American, Native Canadian, Latino/a, and Black students from poor backgrounds, who have been historically underserved in public schools. I propose that an integration of cultural socialization processes into teaching and learning, based on an understanding of the places where people live their lives and how they are culturally socialized to participate in routine practices in these settings, will improve educational outcomes for racial and ethnic minority youth.

The article begins with a brief discussion of the primacy of cultural mediation in the learning process, after which the focus shifts to the cultural historical approach which concerns understanding how individuals' or groups' patterns of participation in shared practices in their cultural communities/places contributes to their learning and development. Using the cultural historical approach to inquire into the influence of cultural participation/socialization on learning, I identify four valued Aboriginal cultural practices that appear to be socially meaningful and consequential in shaping pathways of learning and development for particular groups of Aboriginal students from low-income communities in western Canada.

THE CENTRALITY OF CULTURAL MEDIATION IN LEARNING AND DEVELOPMENT

Why does it matter that we undertake research that helps us better understand cultural socialization and its mediating influence on, and consequences for, student learning? It matters because social-cultural and cultural-historical psychology begins with the assumption of an intimate connection between the special environments that human beings inhabit and human psychological processes. In their work, James Wertsch and Michael Cole have explicated this link by explaining that the special quality of the human environment is that it is suffused with the achievements of prior generations in reified form. This notion is also found in the writings of cultural historical psychologists from many national traditions. John Dewey, for example, wrote that, from birth to death, we live in a world of persons and things which is in large measure what it is because of what has been done and transmitted from previous human activities. When this fact is ignored, experience is treated as if it were something that goes on exclusively inside an individuals' body and mind. According to Dewey, experience does not occur in a vacuum; there are resources outside an individual that give rise to experience (Dewey, 1938 and 1963). The early writings of Russian cultural psychologists also emphasize the cultural medium. They argue that the special mental quality of human beings is their need and ability to mediate their actions through artifacts previously shaped by prior human practice, and to arrange for the rediscovery and appropriation of these forms of mediation by subsequent generations (Cole and Wertsch, 2001). In this regard, Vygotsky (1981) wrote: "the central fact about human psychology is the fact of cultural mediation" (p. 166).

From the perspective of the centrality of cultural mediation in mind and mental development, the mind develops through an interweaving of biology and the appropriation of the cultural heritage. Higher mental functions are, by definition, culturally mediated, involving an indirect action in which previously used artifacts are incorporated as an aspect of current action (Cole and Wertsch, 2001).

This perspective has several implications for learning and cognition. First, cultural artifacts do not simply serve to facilitate mental processes; they fundamentally shape and transform them. Second, because artifacts are themselves culturally, historically, and institutionally situated, all psychological functions begin and, and to a large extent, remain culturally, historically, and institutionally situated. There is no universally appropriate form of cultural mediation. A third implication is that context and action are not independent of each other. As Cole and Wertsch put it, "objects and contexts arise together as part of a single bio-social-cultural process of development."

These implications suggest that mind can no longer be seen as located solely inside the head. Rather, higher psychological functions include the biological individual, the cultural mediational artifacts, and the culturally structured social and natural environments of which individuals are a part. The positions of Dewey, Vygotsky, Cole, and Wertsch, and others on the centrality of cultural artifacts in human mental processes has great resonance in recent movements in cognitive science, and the position undergirds much of the emerging science on distributed cognition and situated learning.

This primacy of cultural mediation in learning and development invites us as educators to provide opportunities for our most disadvantaged groups to draw on their cultural capital—what they bring from prior cultural socialization in their homes and communities—to support and enhance classroom learning for them. Understanding how individuals or groups historically engage in shared practices in their cultural communities may account for dispositions they may have in new circumstances such as classroom learning.

UNDERSTANDING LEARNING AND DEVELOPMENT THROUGH A CULTURAL HISTORICAL APPROACH

Research on understanding learners, learning, teaching, and thinking through the lens of psychosocial and cultural processes is often undertaken using the cultural learning styles approach. This approach attributes individual learning styles/traits categorically to ethnic group membership and, based on this, prescriptions are made for creating learning environments that complement the learning styles of different ethnic groups. Undoubtedly, the cultural learning styles approach has contributed positively to the attempt to leave behind the deficit-model thinking in which cultural ways that differ from the practices of dominant groups are judged to be less adequate without examining them from the perspective of the community's participants. The approach can also appeal to teachers who may have limited training, support, and resources to meet the challenges of cultural diversity in classrooms. Yet, the cultural learning styles approach does not sufficiently help us understand the relation of individual learning to the practices of cultural communities and it sometimes hinders effective assistance to student learning by producing overgeneralizations within which a single way of teaching and learning may be used with a particular group without accounting for individuals' past experiences with certain practices or without providing instruction that both extends those practices and introduces new and even unfamiliar ways of doing things. The approach also creates a false dichotomy between contexts and actions, viewing individuals as though their characteristics were unrelated to the cultural contexts in which they and their families have participated in recent generations (Gutierrez and Rogoff, 2003).

A cultural historical approach addresses these shortcomings by helping us understand how patterns/regularities in the engagement of shared and dynamic practices of different communities contribute to human learning and development. Rather than viewing an individual's learning style as a static, essentialized trait that is independent of tasks and contexts, constant over time and setting, and attributable to ethnic group membership, the focus in a cultural historical perspective shifts to individuals' histories of engagement in activities in their cultural communities. A central and distinguishing feature of the cultural historical approach is that the structure and development of human psychological processes emerge through participation in culturally mediated, historically developing, practical activities involving cultural practices in contexts (Gutierrez and Rogoff, 2003). The approach also appreciates that individuals participate in the practices of cultural communities in varying and overlapping ways, which change over their lifetime and according to changes in the community's organization and relationships with other communities. Of course, there are patterns and regularities in the ways groups draw on cultural artifacts to function and participate in the everyday practices of their respective communities but, as Gutierrez and Rogoff argue, the emergent goals and practices of participants are in constant tension with the relatively stable characteristics of these environments. It is this tension and conflict that accounts for and contributes to the variation and ongoing change in an individual's and community's practices.

Researchers and practitioners can examine people's usual ways of doing things and characterize the commonalities of experience of people who share cultural backgrounds.

To be able to characterize learners' repertoires of cultural practices and help them extend these practices or use them in new ways in the classroom, the researcher and practitioner need to understand both the community and the individual practices, and the nature and forms of cultural tools/artifacts used (e.g., social relations, belief systems, customary approaches to performing specific tasks). To facilitate this type of understanding, cultural historical psychologists suggest prolonged observations in multiple situations in communities, assuming various vantage points so as to understand not only the complexity of human activity but also the participant's familiarity of experience with cultural practices.

CULTURAL MEDIATORS OF LEARNING FOR NATIVE CANADIAN (ABORIGINAL) STUDENTS IN THE FORMAL SCHOOL SYSTEM

Using cultural historical theory as explicated above, I set out to investigate and understand aspects of Aboriginal cultural socialization and its mediating influence on the learning of urban Aboriginal students from low-income backgrounds in Manitoba, western Canada. In both Canada and the United States the persistent failure of Aboriginal/Native students in the public school system has been consistently explained in terms of the differences between the sociocultural environments of their homes and communities and those of the school. Particularly in the case of urban Aboriginal students who constitute the highest incidence of school failure and dropout in Canada, the lack of Aboriginal cultural knowledge among teachers—who are predominantly middle-class Euro-Canadians—has been identified as a significant factor in school failure, prompting calls for the inclusion of Aboriginal cultural perspectives across school curricula, classroom practices, and teacher preparation programs. For me, these calls raised the following questions: (1) What specific aspects of Aboriginal cultural experience/socialization influence and mediate learning on which teachers can draw to support and enhance classroom learning for Aboriginal students? (2) Would these cultural experiences be similar and supportive of classroom learning for all students from a particular Aboriginal group or should we base interventions on regularities discerned in individuals' histories of participation in and familiarity with cultural activities? (3) What are the histories of individuals' participation and engagement in activities in their cultural communities? (4) What are the patterns and variations of engagement of shared cultural practices among particular groups of Aboriginals? (5) How does such participation/engagement contribute to learning and development both in the community and in the school? These questions led me to a one year study conducted among Canadian Aboriginal students, undertaken to identify aspects of their cultural socialization (existing knowledge structures) that influenced/mediated how they received, negotiated, and responded to curriculum materials, teaching methods/strategies, and learning tasks in their high school social studies classroom. Knowledge of cultural mediators of Aboriginal student learning is critical to our understanding of how teachers could best adapt classroom materials and processes to enable Aboriginal students to have generous and positive access to their cultural heritage while also acquiring knowledge and confidence with the content and codes of the dominant cultures. Historically, Aboriginals have faced tremendous social inequities that are structured into the fiber of Canadian society and of schools. Consequently, Aboriginal students suffer from enduring gaps in academic achievement compared to their more affluent peers or peers who belong to dominant cultural groups. In this regard, Aboriginals share many similarities with other ethnic minorities, including students of European descent who experience persistent intergenerational poverty in both Canada and the United States.

RESEARCH METHODS AND PROCEDURES

The Aboriginal students who participated in this study came from the Ojibwe, Cree, and Metis groups (Metis are mixed descendants of European and Canadian Aboriginal groups). The study occurred at two sites simultaneously. One site consisted of Ojibwe and Cree communities in a large urban location in western Canada where my Ojibwe research assistant and I carried out prolonged observations (one visit per week over 46 weeks) of ten research participants' engagement in shared activities in their communities. The other research site was an alternative high school with a very large Aboriginal student population (90%) where the research participants attended school, and where we observed classroom materials and teaching/learning processes in a grade 9 social studies classroom once every week over the entire 2001 academic year.

Data for the study was collected in an integrated grade 9 social studies classroom with 80 percent Aboriginal students, 20 percent whites, and two teachers (one was Euro-Canadian and the other

African-Canadian) who had been identified as successful teachers of Aboriginal students and who had expressed a willingness to enhance their understanding of cross-cultural instruction.

A social studies classroom was chosen for the study because it derives its subject matter from the social science disciplines, and therefore offers opportunities for the use of a variety of curriculum materials, teaching strategies, and learning tasks which apply across a large number of subject areas. As well, I (the researcher) am a social studies instructor and was more likely to understand the curriculum goals, concepts, and the teaching/learning processes targeted in the social studies classroom.

Among the twenty-eight students in the class, ten volunteered to be followed and observed each week as they participated in different activities in their communities (five of these students were Ojibwe, three were Cree, and two were Metis of European-Ojibwe-Cree ancestry). They and their parents/relatives also participated in the research conversations we conducted.

Ethnography offers enhanced opportunities to understand research participants within their own settings, and the flexibility to follow and document events as they arise during the research, and so an ethnographic approach was used for the study. In line with ethnographic methodology, multiple data collection methods were used. These were:

Site observations. In this study, my interest was in the importance and benefit of knowing about the valued, shared practices and activities of the Aboriginal groups under study, the history and patterns of participation/engagement of the ten research participants in these activities, and the mediating influence of these prior knowledge structures on their classroom learning. Therefore, my research assistant and I spent countless hours observing activities and interactions in the two Aboriginal communities and in the grade 9 social studies classroom. In the communities, we observed and wrote down field notes on the participation of the ten student volunteers and their parents/relatives in activities such as patterns of verbal communication, nonverbal communication, and their intended meanings, approaches to task performance, norms regarding competition and interdependence, extent to which children are brought up to accomplish things on their own and arrive at their own independent decisions and opinions, how children and adolescents engage in play and past-time activities, ways of responding to persons in authority, and interpersonal relationships and interactions. The intent was for us to be able to characterize the cultural repertoires of our ten student volunteers and their dexterity in moving between approaches appropriate to varying activity settings. Over the year's duration of the research, we would have an account of each participant's and the community's value-laden experience, and be able to speak about the usual/customary/habitual approaches taken in known circumstances.

At the school site our classroom observations focused on the curriculum materials, teaching methods/strategies, and learning tasks used in the social studies lessons, and how our ten student volunteers used their prior cultural socialization to negotiate and cope with these classroom processes. Data collected from both sites were later used as material for research conversations with participants.

Research conversations. In the two Aboriginal communities, we had many informal conversations with our ten research participants and their relatives to help us better understand the practices we were studying and confirm or disconfirm our own beliefs and hypotheses about issues such as social relations, rules, division of labor, cultural tools and artifacts used, and certain actions and the rationales behind them. More formally, we held two sets of research conversations (each lasting one hour) with the students in the study. The first set of conversations was intended to get participants' initial responses to our research questions pertaining to (a) how the curriculum materials and the classroom activities, processes, and interactions facilitated or inhibited class participation and conceptual understanding for them; (b) the specific aspects of their prior cultural knowledge and socialization that contributed to enhance or inhibit class participation and conceptual understanding when these classroom materials and processes were used; (c) their preferred teaching and learning methods in the social studies classroom and how these were similar to or different from the dominant methods through which they learned in their cultural communities; and (d) questions intended to further illuminate the data collected at the community and classroom sites. The second set of conversations provided the researchers with the opportunity to probe specific responses in more detail and explore any new questions and ideas that emerged. These formal conversations were audio-recorded and later transcribed verbatim.

Students' journals. Aboriginal students participating in the study were asked to maintain a journal where they documented the cultural experiences that influenced/mediated how they received, negotiated, and responded to curriculum materials, teaching strategies, and learning tasks in the social studies classroom.

Important sections of the data from the multiple sources described above were highlighted and summarized. Doing so enabled the researchers to get an overview of what the data offered concerning the research questions. As well, the researchers were able to see whether the data gave rise to any new questions, points of view, and ideas. All data were coded and categorized, using both deductive and inductive methods. Coded data were read and organized according to themes emerging from the data. The themes were examined collaboratively with the participants in order to understand what certain data meant and how certain facts could be explained. Data analysis and interpretation, therefore, incorporated both emic and etic perspectives. Research narratives based on the data were constructed. The research narratives were returned to the research participants for comments, changes, and/or confirmation before being included in the final report. In the following discussions of our findings I have attempted to respect the participants' words/contributions by including them as quotes, where appropriate, to enrich the research narratives. Where participants are quoted in the report, pseudonyms have been used to protect their identities. Therefore, the ten students are referred to as Mike, Ned, Kem, Rich, Liz, Joe, Don, Andy, Tim, and Jon. The teachers are referred to as Mrs. B. and Mr. X.

FINDINGS AND DISCUSSIONS

Analysis of the data generated from the different research instruments revealed several findings related to the two main concerns of the study: (a) the participants' history of participation in and familiarity with activities in their cultural communities, and (b) the curriculum materials and teaching/learning processes and interactions used in the social studies classrooms, and the aspects of Aboriginal cultural socialization which enhanced or inhibited Aboriginal student participation and conceptual understanding when these materials, strategies, and learning tasks were employed.

The first significant finding was that all ten students that we followed for this study showed an impressive level of familiarity with the cultural practices and knowledge structures of their communities. To a large extent, they easily and consistently participated in activities with comfort, authority, and knowledge of their culture. Of course, some differences were observed among individual participants, as the following discussion shows. However, there were sufficient common elements among them that appeared to conflict with the values, culture, and processes that are dominant in the conventional classroom. These common elements in the data provided the bases for the construction of themes.

Part I of this report presents, in tabular form, the curriculum materials, learning tasks/activities, teaching methods/strategies, and learning goals observed in the social studies classroom during the research (Table 48.1).

Part II discusses the themes that emerged from our site observations and conversations with the research participants about the aspects of their prior cultural socialization, which helped or hindered their learning in the social studies classroom.

Part I

Table 48.1
Curriculum Materials, Teaching Methods/learning Tasks, and Learning Goals in a Grade 9 Social Studies Class.

Curriculum Materials	Teaching Methods/learning Tasks	Learning Goals
No prescribed textbooks were used. Materials were selected according to needs and interests of students, but of relevance to successful living in mainstream Canadian society. Materials used included the following:	.	
Stories with moral messages from the book "Chicken Soup for the Soul."	Reading of the stories by the teacher; teacher-led discussion of questions on the stories (questions ranged from recall to higher levels of thinking).	To develop students' listening and comprehension skills, to develop higher-level thinking, to provide student motivation through the moral lessons in the stories (e.g., perseverance, respect for self and others).
Concepts such as "stereotyping," "discrimination," "prejudice," "racism," "lazy" that depicted some of the lived experiences of many Aboriginal students. Concepts of more general relevance and application, for example, "supply and demand," "critical consumer decision-making factors," "advertising," "motives for purchasing goods and services," "human rights."	Small group discussion of concepts; two teachers and one teacher aide in the room provided support to students as they worked in groups; sharing of insights through verbal presentations; teacher input through further discussion, examples, probing questions (scaffolding), and notes.	For students to understand the ignorance and discrimination present in stereotyping; for students to recognize their own prejudices; for students to improve their discussion and public speaking skills; to relate curriculum to students' daily lives.
Pictures of accomplished Aboriginal people in respected professions.	Whole class teacher-led discussion through higher-level thinking questions that encouraged student participation (expression of ideas and opinions).	To make the curriculum relevant to the Aboriginal students (students see themselves in positive ways in the curriculum); students will be motivated by positive role-models.
"The Canadian Scrapbook: Looking back on Aboriginal early lives".	Independent and small group worksheet activities; scavenger hunt locating information from pages already identified by the teacher (scaffolding research work), individualized instruction by teachers, whole class discussion of student responses	For Aboriginal students to understand their rich history; for students to develop research skills.
Teacher's notes on transparencies and other visual aids.	Visual aids were used by the teacher to explain certain concepts. Notes provided lesson summaries for students.	To support student learning through visual examples.

Part II: Themes Relating to Cultural Influences on Aboriginal Student Learning

Theme 1: Aboriginal Approaches to Learning.   Four indigenous approaches to learning that appeared to be common in the communities we observed were also found to have facilitated or hindered class participation and conceptual understanding for the students in our study. These were:

Learning through stories and anecdotes. Anecdotes and stories were sometimes observed to be used by adults, especially parents and elders, to convey important messages to the young and to each other in the communities we observed. This probably explains why all the students in the study agreed that the story reading method adopted by their social studies teacher was very effective in helping them understand the concepts and messages contained in each story. The research conversations revealed the following cultural reasons for the effectiveness of the storytelling method:

- In indigenous Aboriginal culture traditional stories, legends, songs, and many other forms of knowledge are passed on among generations by constant retelling (through stories) by elders and leaders who carry the knowledge of these spoken forms in their memories. As one student research participant put it,

   . . . My grandmother knows these stories inside out. My parents also know them and I learn the stories from them all. We all know the songs that go with each story. (Don)

- Children develop a sense of morality by observing parents and elders modeling certain behaviors, and through stories, anecdotes, and legends they hear from parents and elders.

   We learn what is right and wrong from these stories. For example, many stories of hunting my grandpa has told me are about being honest about the number of catches each person had on a group hunting trip . . . (Jon)

- Stories and anecdotes offer important ways for individuals to express themselves safely (e.g., convey messages of chastisement without directly preaching the message or specifically moralizing or blaming the culprit). From the research conversations we learned that Aboriginal peoples' stories are shared with the expectation that the listeners will make their own meaning, and that they will be challenged to learn something from the stories. Stories, therefore, appear to contain layers of meaning that listeners decode according to their readiness to receive certain teachings.

   . . . You just get the message as you listen to the story and you loosen up and improve your behavior, if you want to . . . (Ned)

Learning through observation and imitation. A second learning approach, which appeared to have a strong basis in the Aboriginal cultures we studied, was observational learning. Probing questions during our research conversations revealed a close link between learning by watching and doing and some traditional child-rearing practices, which have survived in many Aboriginal families. From our observations and the research conversations, it appeared that Cree and Ojibwe children have developed a learning style characterized by observation and imitation as children and adults in the extended family participate in every day activities. Joe, a student in the study elaborated on this approach to learning:

. . . When they (parents, grand parents, or teachers) actually show you and you see it in action, it's easier for you to grab. . . .

Kem, another student, linked this learning method to preparation for adult responsibility:

... Actually seeing how something is done, instead of reading how it's done, that's hard to remember. When you watch how it is done it automatically clicks in your head. It's like making bannock (an Aboriginal dough); you learn to make it by watching the older people and then making it by yourself.

By contrast, students in the study pointed out that the "talk approach" to much of school instruction actually inhibited classroom learning for them. In an effort to reconcile this data with the benefits of verbal instruction earlier touted by these participants during our discussion about storytelling, I asked them for clarification. Liz's comment below reflected those made by the rest of the students:

Do you remember how I said some teachers explain too much and too fast? That really confuses me. I get lost in the explanation. But Mr. X, he cuts it down to size, right to the chase, works the formula on the board which I watch step by step. I like that. . . .

It appears that while verbal instructional methods such as storytelling are an important cultural approach to learning for these students, the verbal saturation which characterize much of school instruction, especially when this instruction is fast-paced and delivered through a different language, is not conducive to academic success for some Aboriginal students.

This finding is significant because differences in approaches to learning have far-reaching consequences in the formal education of some Aboriginal students, particularly in view of the fact that the formal education system almost always favors those who are highly verbal.

Community support encourages learning. Learning through verbalization was also disparaged by the students for another reason—they felt lack of support in the integrated classroom, compared to the family and community support we observed. All but one Ojibwe participant pointed out that the teaching/learning method they found most uncomfortable was when they were called upon to make a verbal presentation in front of the class. The students revealed that they were intimidated by the direct criticism, which this method entailed in the formal (Western) school system. Jon's comment on this point is instructive:

It's like they are looking out for the mistakes you make and they pounce on you. Even the teachers sometimes make you feel dumb by the questions they ask after you have presented something. . . .

I probed further to see how learning would be different in their community and Ned said:

In the (Aboriginal) community, if you don't have the right answer you are not criticized directly and you ask for some help because you know the people that are around you, so you feel secure. Also, in the community you are doing it for the community or their approval, so everyone is supportive and pitches in to help or encourage you. In school you are doing it for your own education as an individual. . . .

These comments are consistent with our observations and informal conversations with two of the relatives of the student volunteers about parenting and social interaction in some Aboriginal cultures as entailing "non-interference" (meaning refraining from directly criticizing the individual).

For these Aboriginal students, silence seemed to be the best defense mechanism in an integrated classroom where they felt they were among white strangers whom they have been raised to believe are constantly critical of them. Chris's comment spoke to this point:

Yeah, that's why I prefer to remain silent in class. . . . It's just that I don't really know and trust people here. At home and in my community, I know and trust people, so I just blabber along without fear of making mistakes or being criticized. But when school starts, I don't talk, period, so they leave me alone . . .

The Ojibwe participant who said he was not uncomfortable with verbal classroom presentations is a clear indication that membership in a certain group does not predict behavior; it only makes certain types of behavior more probable. This shows that culture is not a unified monolithic whole, and while there may be distinctive learning patterns among cultures, variations do exist among individuals within groups.

Learning through scaffolding. When asked about the type of support they needed to learn most in social studies, the data indicated that all the students in the study required some form of scaffolding or temporary framework of support, at least until they were able to develop the skills to learn independently. Forms of scaffolding identified included: specific direction and guidance from the teacher through clear and concise explanations (Jon, Liz, Rich, Mike), concrete examples preferably from the students' own background (Jon, Ned, Andy), explicit steps to follow in the performance of a given task (all, except Ned), direct feedback from the teacher (Liz and Andy).

(Data from the classroom observations showed that the two teachers and one teacher aide in the classroom provided some of these structures to enhance Aboriginal student learning).

These four forms of support appear to have direct foundations in child-rearing practices between the two Aboriginal groups we studied where children are socialized to accomplish tasks largely through the support, direct guidance, and feedback from parents and other significant adults. Don compared this classroom support to what obtained at home:

Mrs. B., Mr. X. and, Ms. T. always go round when we are working on our own, to explain more about what we are to do. It helps a lot, just like at home. . . .

Theme 2: Effective Oral Interaction Between Teacher and Aboriginal Students Assists Learning.   This theme emerged from our conversations about cultural and socioeconomic class differences in patterns of oral interactions between parents and children. In studies conducted on linguistic interactions among different cultural and socioeconomic groups researchers observed that middle-class parents tended to use discussion, playfulness, and questions when instructing their children (e.g., "Is that your coat on the floor") whereas working-class whites and African-American parents tended to be more overtly directive (e.g., "Pick up your coat from the floor and hang it in the closet.")

Our research suggests that some Aboriginal parents also communicate with their children mainly through the use of overt directives. Two of the research participants, for example, said:

They (parents) tell me directly what they expect me to do; they do not leave it up to me to figure out what they mean . . . (Liz)

Mr. X. (the African-Canadian teacher) tells you straight what he requires from you. I like that . . . (Don)

Since teachers in Canadian classrooms are mainly white and come from middle-class backgrounds, some Aboriginal students are less likely to understand what to do if the teacher uses indirect statements. Clarity is important to school success because students are judged by what they produce in class and on tests. Such a product, based as it is on the specific codes of a dominant culture (English or French in the case of Canada), is more readily produced when the directives of how to produce it are made explicit. The study data strongly suggested that effective parents and teachers of Aboriginal students offer clarity about what they demand, and they provide structures that help learners produce it. My conclusion here is not that Aboriginal students are incapable of learning through discussions or questions and indirect statements. Instead, I draw attention to the fact that teachers must be helped to recognize and attend to the particular strengths and needs that underserved groups may have in relation to new instructional strategies such as discussions in the classroom, while also questioning the role of schooling in the perpetuation of such linguistic inequities in society.

Theme 3: Concepts of Self.   This finding refers to notions of the self, how the self is constructed and understood, and how this construction mediates the learning process in different cultures. The research revealed that, in describing their identity, the Aboriginal students in the study were not comfortable with the term "self", with its implications of individualism, autonomy, and unity. Rather, they considered themselves as "subjects" whose identities were constructed and understood in terms of interdependence, communality, and interaction with the world around them more so than, say, Caucasian groups who tend to treat the self as a relatively self-contained agent. Because they viewed themselves less as a separate psychological unit and more as a part-function of the cultural forces from which they emerged, the students identified a cultural model of learning that is grounded in Aboriginal cultural values such as cooperation, collaboration, group effort, and group rewards. In school, these values would lend themselves well to group work and cooperative tasks and it was, therefore, not surprising that eight out of the ten research participants disclosed that they thrived better as learners in cooperative/collaborative/group work situations. However, they also pointed out that because group work and cooperative learning tasks in school were not usually organized effectively for productive work, group work had actually hindered rather than promoted learning for them. Several of them elaborated on this point, as the following quotes demonstrate:

You see, it's different in school than in the (Aboriginal) community. In the community everybody participates equally or almost. You have a bunch of people who carry an equal share of the task and they know it is for the good of the community. So everyone does their part and you learn from each other. In school no one in the group cares, really. Group members do not share their opinions or ideas. . . . (Don)

And they make a lot of noise during group work. . . . (Liz)

Yes, and if you have someone smarter than the other people in the group, then they are going to rely on that one person for all the ideas (Mike).

So I think what we need is better group work organization from them (the teachers). I like group work because you can talk to others. You can discuss your ideas if you don't understand something, like in the community. . . . But in class that does not happen in groups (Ned).

Our findings suggest that communal work is integral to life and each day in the Aboriginal communities we studied. Community members worked together, each taking on the responsibilities appropriate to their knowledge and abilities.

What is clear from these discussions is that attention needs to be paid to the contextual barriers that interfere with the deployment of cultural tools such as the cooperative, collaborative, and communal aspects of Aboriginal cultural socialization, which enhance student learning. Teachers do not generally seem to acknowledge group identity, insisting that all students are individuals with individual differences, thereby denying that group membership is an important part of some students.

Theme 4: Teacher's Interpersonal Style.   Under this theme are subsumed three subthemes which emerged to describe those dimensions of teacher interpersonal style that are effective in eliciting intellectual participation from the Aboriginal students in the study. In order of importance to the study participants, these dimensions were:

Respect. All the research participants identified "respect" as the most important dimension of the educator's (teacher, parent, or significant others) interpersonal style. Since research on cultural difference has found that different cultures may hold very different views of behaviors that express such feelings as respect, participants were asked to elaborate on what they meant by "respect" in the educator-learner interactions. For them, respect referred to the following teacher behaviors:

Not stereotyping me as the drunken, failed Indian whose image the teacher already has in mind (Ned).

Treating me like I already have something the teacher respects (Liz).

Not making me feel dumb in front of the whole class. Treat me like I know something which the teacher may not know . . . everybody knows something. . . . (Don)

It is as simple as valuing and understanding me as a person. Like, just teach the way you want to be treated. . . . You know, teach with respect for us as individuals and do not treat us like all Indians are the same. (Rich).

Previous research and our own observations support the students' assertions. Members of the two communities we observed frequently expressed positive opinions about each other and treated each other with unusual gentleness, patience, and respect (e.g., if some members of the community were late for a meeting, the others patiently waited for hours and showed no anger when the late-comers eventually arrived). Similarly, Haig-Brown et al's. (1997) research interviews with sixteen students of Aboriginal ancestry (Cree, Ojibwe, Metis, and Saulteaux) from Joe Duquette High School (an all Aboriginal school in western Canada), found that all the students identified "respect" as "the number one rule" for successful interactions among the teachers, staff, and students in the school. According to these researchers, respect is integral to traditional Aboriginal values. They wrote: "Respect encompasses the understanding that children are complete human beings given as gifts from the Great Spirit on loan to adults who share with them the responsibility for preparing them for life's journey" (p. 46). The researchers also quoted what a member of the school's Parent Council said about "respect" during an interview: "You are born as equal and you are born with respect . . . every individual has it (respect) and you don't have to earn it" (p. 46).

Strictness. Although the practice of "non-interference" (meaning not attempting to control the behavior of others by direct intervention) has been documented as a prominent characteristic of parenting and social interaction in many Aboriginal cultures, the image of the teacher as a strict disciplinarian who corrects and guides learners toward appropriate behaviors emerged as the second most important characteristic of the teacher's interpersonal style, suggesting that how Aboriginals practice the cultural value of non-interference could be changing according to what is valued in the dominant culture surrounding them. As the pressure to succeed in mainstream Canadian society has mounted, some Aboriginal parents appear to be abandoning the attitude of non-interference in favor of more direct interventions in the behaviors of their children to increase their chances of success in the society. With one exception (a Metis student in the study who was being raised by his Cree grandmother), participants seemed to expect their teachers to be strict, intolerant of nonsense, and act like the authority figures they are. Otherwise the message is sent that this adult has no authority and the students react accordingly. As the following quotations show, the Aboriginal students in this study firmly believed in this strict image of the teacher:

I think Mrs. B., I don't know what it is, but she should be tougher with us. After all she is the teacher, she has the authority. . . . (Jon).

I agree with Jon. She needs to be stricter to keep the class more in order. Some people call her down and treat her anyhow . . . whatever, and she just stands there. . . . (Mike).

Some of the things kids do in her class, I know I can never get away with at home. I know my boundaries and how far I can take my family, especially my dad. If I go past that boundary I know I am in trouble . . . probably get grounded for days or something, without any argument. I was surprised at first at what she (Mrs. B.) was tolerating from them. . . . (Ned).

Ned's surprise could have also come from the fact that in his Ojibwe community, we observed that elders and parents, as respected teachers, often conveyed to the young the acceptable rules of behavior and the values to be honored through subtle verbal and nonverbal communication. Such a teacher is a role model whose own behavior and attitudes are absorbed by the children.

However, as pointed out earlier, the image of the teacher as a strict individual wielding authority in the classroom did not seem to hold for one of our Metis participants, suggesting diversity in how the cultural values and traditions of Aboriginal peoples are engaged. In response to Ned's comments about behavioral boundaries he had to observe at home, this Metis student said:

Jeez, I can never live like that. My grandmother lets me do what I want. I go and come as I like, no questions asked. Sometimes, I go for two days . . . as long as I stay out of trouble. (Chris).

Chris's comment is consistent with our finding that among some Cree community members the principle of noninterference is still predominant. The child's will is respected, and adults do not interfere in the choices made by the child. The imposition of the adult's will on the child is considered inappropriate except, of course, in instances where the child may encounter harm. From our research conversations, we learned that this noninterference, nondirective approach determined a basis for a future lifestyle. Children matured rapidly and became adept at determining their own actions and making their own decisions, while being sensitive to the expectations of the collective and to elders.

The contrast between this laissez-faire approach and the regimentation of the classroom experience, including the exertion of the teacher's authority, constitute a discontinuity between the school and the home environment. This cultural conflict has been cited in several documents as a threat to the Aboriginal child's identity in the formal education system and a major cause of school failure.

Personal warmth. The data revealed that nine out of the ten participants in the study expected their teachers to treat them with emotional warmth and have personalized relationships with them. This finding is consistent with Haig-Brown et al's. (1997) report that teachers at Joe Duquette High School referred to their students as "extended families" and students referred to their teachers as "friends," "second parents," and "sensitive."

Warmth as a teacher attribute emerged during our conversation about the effectiveness of the individualized instruction, which we observed each student regularly receiving from the two teachers and one teacher aide present during each lesson. Ned's comment on this point was typical and instructive:

When she (Mrs. B.) is teaching from in front of the room, she is kind of far from you and she is usually talking to everyone, not to any of us in particular except if she is addressing a question to someone specifically. But when we are working on our own and all three of the teachers go round and help us individually, that helps a lot.

Wishing to find out more about how this personal contact/closeness, as opposed to the professional distance teachers typically maintain in the classroom, enhanced Aboriginal student learning I asked Ned to elaborate on his comment and he said:

Well, I mean, the close contact means personal attention. When they (teachers) come close to you, sometimes they bend down to your seat level and you tell them your specific problem and they explain and help you. When you get the point right, sometimes they pat you on the back. They are also more friendly one on one. . . .

Individualized instruction has been found to have a positive effect on student academic achievement in general. For these Aboriginal students in particular, individualized instruction appears to carry added benefit because of its significance in communicating the warmth which they perceived as important in interactions between them and their teachers. Joe expressed this feeling best in his closing comment on this aspect of our conversation:

When they (the teachers) are that close and personal you get the feeling they care. . . .

These data do not suggest that all "respectful," "strict," and "warm" teachers are good teachers of Aboriginal students. They do, however, suggest that there are different notions among different cultural groups about which characteristics make for a good teacher. It is, therefore, impossible to create a model of the good teacher without taking issues of cultural and community contexts into account.

CONCLUDING REMARKS

This was a small-scale exploratory research, undertaken to identify aspects of Aboriginal cultural socialization which mediate/influence the learning of some students of Aboriginal ancestry in the Canadian formal school system. Four examples of such cultural mediators have been identified as significant in providing place-conscious education for two groups of Aboriginal students. Research is still inconclusive about many claims relating to specific or predominant cultural practices and classroom learning, highlighting the difficulty in arriving at any final "formula" for helping a cultural group perform better in an educational setting. However, taken together, these examples signal a vibrant counterpoint to the dominant system of education, which fails to connect meaningfully to the lives of learners and the communities from which they come. The examples are, therefore, suggestive of a badly needed conversation about the relationship between the places we call schools and the places where students live their lives.

The last two decades have seen profound changes in educational psychology that have placed psychosocial and cultural processes squarely at the center of learning and development. We are witnessing a resolution of the antimony traditionally heard in discussions about the primacy of individual psychogenesis versus sociogenesis of mind, in favor of the recognition that learning and development arise through the interweaving of individual biopsychological processes and the appropriation of cultural heritage. This new view adds a political dimension to the conversation as it moves cognitive and educational study from the individual level which hides the effects of race, socioeconomic status, and culture, to the level where learning and development are understood within cultural and larger sociopolitical contexts and their effects. The new position calls for research into what different groups bring to processes of learning and development and how this interfaces with the culture and practices of the school. In this paper, I have provided an example of such research, and argued that the design of any study intended to inquire into how cultural processes mediate and influence learning and development must focus on understanding individuals' or groups' histories of participation in activities in their cultural communities instead of simply attributing general traits of individuals categorically to ethnic group membership.

TERMS FOR READERS

Individual psychogenesis—The view that learning and development are individual mental functions that originate in the mind, unaffected and unmediated by the outside world.

Sociogenesis—The view that the development of mental functions are influenced and mediated by factors such as social interactions, and the contexts and environments surrounding the individual.

REFERENCES

Cole, M., and Wertsch, J. V. (2001). *Beyond Individual-Social Antimony in Discussions About Piaget and Vygotsky*. Retrieved November 22, 2003, from http:/www.massey.ac.nz/~alock//virtual/colevyg.htm.

Dewy, J. (1938/1963). *Experience and Education*. New York: Macmillan.

Gutierrez, K. D., and Rogoff, B. (2003). Cultural ways of learning: Individual traits or repertoires of practice. *Educational Researcher*, 32(5), 19–25.

Haig-Brown, C., Hodgson-Smith, K. L., Regnier, R., and Archibald, J. (1997). *Making the Spirit Dance within: Joe Duquette High School and an Aboriginal Community*. Toronto,ON: James Lorimer.

Vygotsky, L. S. (1981). The genesis of higher mental functions. In J. V. Wertsch (Ed.), *The Concept of Activity in Soviet Psychology*, pp. 144–188. Armonk, NY: Sharpe.

CHAPTER 49

Endorsing an Angel: Peggy Claude-Pierre, the Media and Psychology

MICHELLE STACK

From 1993 to 2002, there were at least five different talk shows on which Claude-Pierre was a guest, approximately 300 newspaper articles[1] about her and Montreux, six programs that aired television feature pieces, and six women's magazines that published pieces on Claude-Pierre and Montreux, as well as articles in *USA Today*, *Maclean's*, and *People Magazine*. In addition, there was media coverage in Germany and Australia on patients from those countries admitted to Montreux.[2]

Two investigations into allegations against Claude-Pierre and her Montreux clinic have been conducted. The second investigation concluded that patients had been exposed to substantial health and safety risks because of Montreux's treatment. Allegations included force-feeding, forcible confinement, verbal abuse, improper nutrition, lack of basic first aid know-how, and absence of suicide prevention knowledge among staff. In December 1999, the Health officer for the Capital Health Region in Victoria, British Columbia revoked Montreux's license to operate. Montreux fought the decision but in 2002 agreed to hand in its license to operate a residential treatment facility. It continues to offer outpatient services and training for therapists.[3]

MONTREUX IN CONTEXT

In 1983, singer/songwriter Karen Carpenter died of cardiac arrest after years of self-starvation. Also in 1983, Jane Fonda revealed that she was bulimic (Brumberg, 1989). In the same year, eating disorders, particularly anorexia nervosa, became a matter of great public interest. The media expressed a growing concern over this new epidemic affecting mainly young, intelligent, middle- to upper-class girls (Gordon, 2000). Simultaneous with media interest, medical interest in eating disorders intensified (Gordon, 2000).

A year after Carpenter's death, doctors told Peggy Claude-Pierre that her fifteen-year-old daughter had anorexia. Nine months later, her younger daughter, Nicole, was diagnosed with the same illness. In her book, *The Secret Language of Eating Disorders* Claude-Pierre states, "I made myself the platform for Nicole's survival. Anything else I may have needed—including finishing my doctorate, which I wanted to do so desperately—I had to put aside." Claude-Pierre did not, nor does she now, have a doctorate but was working on her bachelor's degree in psychology; however, this information persists through much of the media coverage.[4]

Claude-Pierre opened an outpatient counseling practice in 1988. It was not until 1993, however, that with media attention, Claude-Pierre began a rapid ascent from a locally known therapist to an internationally sought after "expert" in the treatment of people with eating disorders, mostly teens and those in their early twenties.

MEDIA ATTENTION

In February 1993, reportedly at the behest of Claude-Pierre's patients, she received her first media coverage in a local women's magazine, *Focus on Women*. Kerry Slavens, the author, states, "As for Peggy, she's casually dressed in jeans and a shirt. There's no white coats here; no psychobabble or force-feeding, just friendly talk and subtle encouragement." In this same article and a subsequent one a month later, *Focus on Women* decried the death of services and highlighted the relief women felt once they began receiving treatment from Claude-Pierre. Similar to other journalists I interviewed, Slavens relies on being an eyewitness to understand the truth of what she saw.[5] The "before" and "after" pictures of Montreux patients provide visual testimony on which virtually all media coverage about Montreux focused. Some media provided word-pictures of emaciated patients; nonetheless, the need to "show" photographs or footage of the miracles is essential to being a journalist, that is, a legitimate eyewitness. This *Focus on Women* piece, and every piece thereafter, detailed Claude-Pierre's experience in helping her two daughters overcome anorexia, and how she had used her background in psychology to do so.

A month later, Claude-Pierre received province-wide attention in a tabloid newspaper, *The Vancouver Province*. Wendy McLellan[6] the health reporter at the time for the *Vancouver Province*, explained to me that she spent fifteen hours with Montreux's founder, which resulted in a two-page feature on Claude-Pierre. McLellan too believes that it made "common sense" that Claude-Pierre's method would be more effective than the methods traditionally employed by the medical system. McLellan appears to be challenging the establishment. She believes Claude-Pierre's patients were those who had been failed by the traditional system, but who were able and willing to pay the US$1,000 a day.

McLellan's report was picked up on a wire service by the staff of the *Maury Povich Show* and thereafter began its rapid ascent to the interconnected American talk show circuit, news programming, print, radio, and publishing industries. Ten months after McLellan's feature, Peggy Claude-Pierre appeared as a guest on *The Maury Povich Show*, an American talk show alongside a mother who had lost one of her twin daughters to an eating disorder. It was Povich who connected Claude-Pierre with a patient from the United Kingdom, Samantha Kendall, who had been featured on one of his prior episodes. Kendall thereby became Claude-Pierre's first patient outside of North America, providing her with international media attention. In July 1994, Montreux was turned down for B.C. government funding due to a lack of professional staff, as well as issues around a lack of confidentiality and the health and safety of clients. This rejection was not widely reported by the local media nor mentioned by any of the American media soon to arrive at the clinic.

THE MIRACLE SPREADS

A mother who was considering sending her anorexic daughter to Montreux asked Alan Goldberg, a friend and producer for ABC's *20/20*, to investigate the truth of Claude-Pierre's claims (Personal communication, August 3, 1999). I spoke with Goldberg a number of times, first in 1999 after allegations had been leveled at Montreux and a hearing process had begun to determine whether its license should be revoked. We talked again in 2001, more than a year after the license had been revoked. Despite these events Goldberg maintained a commitment to what he regarded as the truth of Montreux and dismissed those who disagreed with him as jealous or as disgruntled employees. He knew he had witnessed something out of the ordinary and that it made a powerful human-interest story. In our first interview, Goldberg provides the **framing** for the Montreux story:

I'm trained to be skeptical. On the first day I was blown away. Granted, all anecdotal. There was no scientific analysis or studies. I think you know that in Canada it is a socialized medicine system. They like to think that medicine is untainted by politics—baloney—especially in socialized medical systems. Montreux contends that doctors are jealous. Montreux has saved the lives of patients they were less successful with (Personal communication, August 3, 1999).

For Goldberg, psychological and medical care is clearly based on the ability to pay, and hence universal health care systems that do not treat it as such are suspect. Goldberg became further convinced that he was watching a woman who was selfless in her devotion to patients in a way not present in institutions:

Her level of compassion for kids, devotion to her own daughters and then the stray puppies that ended up at Montreux is remarkable. It was that it is a mom and pop operation that I found endearing. It is not affiliated with any major hospitals or universities. They bought a house and for a long time lived in debt to fix kids. It is a sacrifice to do that. A saint is willing to give up many things to help others. This is true with Peggy (Personal communication, August 3, 1999).

We now have someone who fits the American Dream—an enterprising person who provides care as a charity to the desperate. Goldberg convinced *20/20* management to devote an entire hour to Montreux, something rarely done at the time (Personal communication, August 3, 1999). It was the airing of this program that created a massive demand for the clinic's services. In less than two years from opening, Montreux thereby became known to over twenty million viewers of *20/20* as a place of "last resort" and of "salvation" for the most ill of anorexics (*20/20* Transcripts, December 2, 1994). The program used a great amount of before and after footage with emotional testimonials from young patients who stated they would be dead without Montreux and Peggy Claude-Pierre. The program concluded with ABC correspondent Lynn Sherr telling Barbara Walters that *20/20* had spoken with a number of families and patients, finding "no evidence of failure whatsoever" (*20/20* Transcripts, December 2, 1994: pp. 14). The only word of caution came from a medical doctor, Timothy Johnson. Hugh Downs asked Johnson if experts are embracing Claude-Pierre's approach:

Dr. Timothy Johnson, ABC News Medical Editor: Well, the first question, I would say no. I think the real experts in this field are very humble about how little they know and how much they don't know, and they try to incorporate many different approaches in their treatment. As to her work, I think they would applaud it. They would be amazed at the commitment and the dedication she brings to it. I think they would be very envious of her resources, having five staff people per patient and being able to have them in a place like that for nine to twelve months.

Barbara Walters did not ask Johnson to elaborate. For example, what did he mean when he said the "real experts" are humble? Was he implying Claude-Pierre does not know what she is doing? Did Johnson talk to anyone who treated people with eating disorders? Why did they choose not to feature someone on the program that might have a different opinion than Claude-Pierre? Instead of exploring this, Walters simply asked Sherr to talk more about the type of children and adults who become anorexic. Sherr at this point made use of Johnson's statements not only to provide legitimacy to Claude-Pierre's miracles but also to demonstrate the superiority of Claude-Pierre, given that she is also a mother.

Well, don't forget Peggy Claude-Pierre was a parent when she figured this all out. She was studying psychology, but she was a parent. She learned it on her own and she kind of stumbled into this intensity, the thing that *Time* was talking about that the other physicians are applauding. So could a person do it at home? Probably not. She's writing a textbook. She hopes to get the word out. Maybe other clinics will open up so that other doctors, other hospitals will use some of the same techniques (*20/20* Transcripts, December 2, 1994).

20/20 won a number of awards for its representation of Montreux and anorexia, including the Peabody. The Peabody was the most prestigious honor but, Goldberg explained to me that his office wall was full of other certificates and prizes including: the British Medical Association film and video competition; the Santa Clara County Psychological Association award for a significant contribution to the field of psychology by the media; and the Gabriel for inspiring stories about compassion by Catholic Broadcasters (Personal communication, July 10, 2001).

A representative of British Medical Association later explained to me (Personal email communication, December 5, 2001) that the award provided to *20/20* is no longer in existence, and that *20/20* had received the "lowest" category of their four awards. In any event, Goldberg was proud of these awards and other accolades received. For example, he told me of how King Juan Carlos of Spain upon seeing *20/20* wished to set-up a similar program in that country. Furthermore, he noted that Hilary Clinton conveyed to Sherr that she thought the *20/20* program was excellent (Personal communication, July 10, 2001). These accolades had further fortified the view in Goldberg's mind that his program "got it right." Those like Michael Strober, a well-known psychologist and director of the University of California (UCLA), Los Angeles Eating Disorder program, who complained about *20/20*'s positive coverage of Montreux were basing their complaints in jealousy, not on the "truth."

THE DOMINO EFFECT: MEDIA AFTER *20/20*

The *20/20* broadcast precipitated a domino effect precipitating further media and professional attention from Australia, Britain, Canada, and the United States. Perhaps the most significant media coverage following the *20/20* program was Claude-Pierre's appearance on the *Oprah Winfrey Show* in 1996, and again in 1997. Prior to being on *Oprah,* Claude-Pierre spoke about anorexia as merely a symptom of what she called Confirmed Negativity Condition (CNC). Oprah provided a large audience to further promote this theory, with the visual illustration of the aforementioned three-year-old boy, Doug, who appeared on the show as one of Claude-Pierre's patients.

Oprah perpetuated the pre-1997 media-created dichotomy—Claude-Pierre the compassionate saviour versus the heartless and ineffective doctors and psychologists. Oprah emotionally shared: "Well, I think that what you [Claude-Pierre] do–I'm going to not cry-but I think that what you do is really like an angel on earth, you know?" (*Oprah Winfrey Show* Transcripts; p. 27) She used the language of medicine by talking about "cases" and "the prescription," but like Goldberg she expressed her frustration that doctors didn't unconditionally love people back to health.

CLAUDE-PIERRE'S BOOK AND 20/20'S ESTABLISHED TRUTH

The subsequent release of Claude-Pierre's book, *The Secret Language of Eating Disorders,* created two streams of coverage: the continued positive coverage that cited the book as evidence of the miracle cure, and pieces by reporters who were covering the story for the first time and questioned the validity of the cure. To be sure, academics were also critical of Claude-Pierre prior to her book launch. From 1993 to the latter part of 1997, however, their voices were concentrated in professional discussions and journals rather than in the popular media. More prominent in the media were endorsements from professionals and patients who extolled the power of Claude-Pierre. Many of these endorsements, including two on the back of Claude-Pierre's book were from medical doctors, each had a daughter who was being treated at Montreux. Neither doctor/father has a background in eating disorders, but instead their testimonials highlight the emotional tension and relief of a parent who has found a miracle cure for his dying daughter, and a doctor who knows it is real.

In 1997, Claude-Pierre was invited to a Women's Health conference at the University of Connecticut and a press release explained her "proven" approach:

STORRS, Conn.—Eating disorders expert Peggy Claude-Pierre, who has been profiled on, *20-20* and *Oprah* and is the author of the new book *The Secret Language of Eating Disorders*, will be the keynote speaker at the University of Connecticut's seventh Women's Health Update Conference. She began counseling in 1983 when both her daughters, Kristen and Nicole, were gripped by anorexia. Claude-Pierre could not find physicians who could adequately treat her girls and decided to take matters into her own hands. Her success led to her working with other patients afflicted with eating disorders. She established an outpatient practice in 1988 and a clinic in 1993. The clinic has a treatment success rate of more than 90 percent (University of Connecticut, 1997).

This press release is of interest on a number of counts. First, the reference to *20/20* and *Oprah* served as an imprimatur, and second, Claude-Pierre's success was assumed and the treatment success of 90 percent was claimed without a qualifier as to where this information had been obtained and how it was established. The university assumes that 90 percent is the "truth." Given that there had been neither outcome studies nor independent assessments, one can only assume that this information must have come to the university via the release that Random House had put out with Claude-Pierre's book. Presumably, that release contained what Claude-Pierre told her publisher and other media about her work.

By October 1997, articles had started to be published questioning Claude-Pierre's success rates, as well there were critical discussions concerning her methods among professionals belonging to the Academy of Eating Disorders. Yet Brigham Young University (BYU) hosted a conference on obesity and eating disorders at which Claude-Pierre was an invited plenary speaker. The BYU press release (Larson, October 7, 1997) referred to Claude-Pierre's 99 percent success rate and asserted that she had been so successful that doctors from around the world were seeking her assistance. The press release, like that from the University of Connecticut, referred to Claude-Pierre's appearances on *Oprah* and *20/20*.

Coverage about Claude-Pierre and Montreux also appeared in *The American Psychological Association Monitor*, widely available on the Internet. In the article, titled: Innovative Anorexia Clinic Offers Remarkable Success (Clay, March 1997), Clay writes:

Although Claude-Pierre never returned to her academic studies, the lessons she learned from her daughters' struggles became the basis of her life's work. Her staff of 15 specially trained care-workers including her daughters and a former patient who weighed just 49 pounds. In these comfortable surroundings, patients undergo a medically supervised, five-step process designed to parallel human development (March 1997).

In this sample excerpt, the language of psychology is used to make credible the process of recovery "five-steps . . . designed to parallel human development." The article does go on to say some are skeptical: "'I'm open to the possibility that programs like Claude-Pierre's work, but her approach hasn't been proven,' said Kelly D. Browell, PhD, a psychology professor at Yale University." However, the article concludes on a note that appears to question why anyone would be so trivial as to question Claude-Pierre: "When my children got better, I never wanted to see an anorexic again," Claude-Pierre was quoted as declaring. "Then I wanted to stop once I'd cured the cases in front of me. I hoped the line-up would stop. It didn't." The numbers of care-workers and patients change from story to story, even when the number is provided for the same period.

An American psychologist, whom I interviewed, Dr. D (pseudonym) spoke of how she had cried while watching *20/20*. She had treated patients with eating disorders for over twenty years and written numerous books and journal articles about treatment approaches. Watching *20/20*, she thought that finally help was available for those who did not seem to receive what they needed from traditional care. Dr. D met Claude-Pierre at an academic conference. Dr. D was immediately struck by the dissonance between the visual power of *20/20*'s presentation of Claude-Pierre versus what seemed to be more of a religious aura to the Montreux founder when she met her face-to-face. Patients in the audience gave emotional testimonials and Claude-Pierre's presentation appeared to be more based on this incandescent quality rather than on delivering the kind of low-key speech usually expected at an academic conference. Dr. D chided herself, however, for being so cynical about a woman who appeared so selfless, a woman who *20/20* had stated had achieved remarkable success and who was not doing her work for money but out of compassion.

Reportedly, it was the images from the *20/20* documentary that stuck with Dr. D until she was confronted with the cognitive dissonance between this imagery and information that was provided by a producer at NBC's *Dateline*. That producer's allegations against Claude-Pierre convinced Dr. D that Claude-Pierre had lied about her credentials, treatment of patients, and a number of other issues. Dr. D was distraught, she had seen Claude-Pierre as "her guru" brought to her by *20/20*, a program she was confident was a reputable newsmagazine and therefore "must have done their research." (Personal communication, December 1, 2000).

Despite the research examining the different paradigm under which journalists determine the legitimacy of research, certain professionals I spoke with indicated that their early support for Montreux was based on their being confident, as was Dr. D that "a reputable program like *20/20* would do their homework." Goldberg maintains that *20/20* did "do their homework": they saw patients get better, they talked to Claude-Pierre, and they witnessed "miracles."

HOW DID MEDIA DETERMINE THAT MONTREUX WAS REMARKABLE?

A theme of importance for professionals and academics is the difference in journalistic versus academic evaluative discourse. McLellan, the reporter for the *Vancouver Province*, determined that a doctor she spoke with who specialized in the treatment of people with eating disorders was not critical of Montreux: "If he had said to me, 'Oh my god, you know this person is totally insane and is risking the futures of these kids,' that would have been a whole different wake-up call." Inasmuch as this doctor did not say, "This woman's insane," McLellan reasoned that Montreux was having success where others had failed.

McLellan is confident that her information is a responsible portrayal of what Claude-Pierre was doing: "It is a feature on a woman that was doing something new." For this study, thinking it would be helpful to know more about how McLellan came to her knowledge, I asked if she had read Claude-Pierre's book or other books about eating disorders and documents concerning Montreux. McLellan responded:

I never read it. If had to read a book on every subject I wrote about, I'd be insane. I did a huge four-page story on genetically altered foods. I read two books to write that story. I don't know, if you read it you'd probably think I was positive about organic or something. [It] depends what's going on in your own head. You try and be objective, but again we don't know anything about genetically altered foods (Personal communication, November 10. 2000).

The reader will note frequent use of the pronoun "we." A common-sense understanding is that if the reporter did not know about an issue, then "we" as a society also did not know and the know-nothings include those people who may have a great deal of understanding and experience but since they are not part of the "we as reporters" group, are therefore irrelevant. Knowledge is again something based on one's "nose for news" or "professional" ability to smell, hear, and see the truth. Knowledge is not that which comes from critical reviews of relevant literature, debate, or grappling with uncertainty, but from one's direct experience in and of the world.

From my interviews, it became clear that pre-1997 reporters had read nothing to very little about eating disorders beyond their peers' accounts of the illnesses, yet they were confident that they were helping build knowledge and therefore were providing a public education function. When asked if there was enough evidence to write a piece about Montreux and its success, McLellan, who sees herself as building knowledge, expressed her opinion of the absurdity in waiting to tell what you know. "You could say that about any story—pollution—not enough evidence. You have to wait for the final results to see if separation is really good for Quebec. I think that there may have been positive stories written about her [Claude-Pierre] because she was doing something new and there was no success in hospitals either." Again, McLellan, the health-reporter, is confident in explaining the absence of "no" success in hospitals and is thus setting up Montreux as an alternative in which common sense dictated that recovery would prevail.

In 1999, ABC's Goldberg explained to me that "If you press Peggy on the 100% she will back off on it. Her success rate is probably closer to 80% or 90%." From his armchair research, however, Goldberg understood the failure rate in other facilities to be over 75%; thus his sense that the success rate at Montreux was 80% to 90% was extremely newsworthy. While in an interview in 2001, Goldberg seemed more cautious about providing a success rate but, he still was comfortable in relying on his senses to maintain his belief that Montreux, at least when he "discovered" it, had a "magic to it." He was further convinced of Claude-Pierre's success, given that she told him that no client had died at her facility. This seemed remarkable to Goldberg who had read that the mortality rate for people with anorexia was high. He was not aware that studies around mortality demonstrate that deaths generally did not occur in hospital or treatment centers where an anorexic was monitored, but rather when patients were out of hospital and at risk for complications caused by prolonged starvation or suicide (Crisp et al., 1992).

Two of the women that 20/20 focused on as success stories have since died. After the death of Samantha Kendall, Goldberg stated she had left before treatment was completed and therefore could not be considered a Montreux failure because she had refused to finish the program. The second death was that of Donna Brooks. Goldberg believed that Montreux had in fact helped her. Seeing himself as witnessing Brook's improvement, Goldberg focused on this past improvement rather than on the reality that she had died, weighing as little at death as she did before arriving at Montreux (Personal communication, July 10, 2001).

Research, available at the time when 20/20 and other media were preparing stories about Montreux, strongly indicated that a person could not be considered to be "recovered" while still in a residential program, given it was an unnatural setting (Garfinkel, 1986). Goldberg, though, saw "recovery" and provided the visual proof of this to viewers. His interpretive framework did not enable him to see discrepant facts in his miracle cure framework. He later found out that a third patient portrayed on 20/20 required intensive care after leaving Montreux, but he stated that Montreux still had helped her, articulating his "knowledge" that maybe there are some who just can't be helped. A lack of definitive information was taken by McLellan and Goldberg as either implicit support or at the least not explicit opposition.

Like Goldberg, Slavens and her editor at the time, Leslie Campbell, state that their support for Claude-Pierre was partly due to Montreux's juxtaposition to a medical system perceived as arrogant and resistant to sharing information about medicine's inability to help people with little-understood illnesses. These journalists believed that Claude-Pierre had found something "new" to help those with anorexia. All believed that they had been diligent in collecting extensive data to demonstrate the truth of their story—Claude-Pierre was a revolutionary who could cure even those in the most dire circumstances. When I asked McLellan about the criticism that Claude-Pierre's theories were not new but developed in the 1960s by Hilde Bruch[7], she responded, "Interesting. Never by themselves. Interesting, it just happened she was the vortex . . . because everything was changing at that point." Again that which exists is that which reporters know rather than what may actually exist. For her part, McLellan shifted the focus, explaining that her piece was about building knowledge and about Claude-Pierre, not about treatment for people with eating disorders.

It was about Peggy Claude-Pierre and what she was doing. And I've written many stories since about what we don't have here that is available in other jurisdictions. Knowledge grows. [It's] like anything, when you are the one to write about it first. Start off—become more knowledgeable. You can't know everything at the beginning. Grow—knowledge builds (Personal communication, November 10, 2001).

Again the focus is on merely transferring that which one hears or sees as "fact"; the journalist's responsibility is to ensure that the source of the information is reliable and to provide information in a manner that is easy for the journalists to understand. Klaidman (1990) argues that often investigative journalists collect "exquisite detail" to support a "strongly held hypothesis." A problem arises when journalists consciously or subconsciously reject information. For example, two reporters from *The Washington Post* with no background in science or medicine determined that a National Cancer Institute Phase Drug trial was killing hundreds of patients. They did not seem to understand that most of the patients were already terminally ill, and therefore, their deaths were not necessarily due to the drug, but that the drug had not created the hoped-for cure.

CONCLUSION

20/20, *Oprah*, *Cosmopolitan Magazine*, *The Maury Povich Show*, *The Montel William Show*, as well as numerous newspapers, magazines, and radio programs did not revisit their positive portrayals of Montreux, even after two investigations, patient deaths, and evidence from Montreux's own case files of serious abuse and neglect of patients. However, it is not only the media that is guilty of withholding information that does not fit into the desired construct. Some psychologists and academics continued to promote Claude-Pierre without reference to evidence contrary to that gleaned through media and Claude-Pierre. For example, The Southern State University of Connecticut offered a one-day workshop in 2001 taught by Claude-Pierre; the promotion for the workshop states, "In spite of its outstanding success rate, the treatment methodology has not been endorsed by the mainstream medical profession and her clinic license was revoked." There is no reference in this promotion to patients who have died, to the nature of the allegations by not only the medical establishment but also by careworkers who came to work at Montreux because of their interests in alternative care. Also overlooked in the university's promotion of Claude-Pierre was a patient who stated she was drugged and shown on television despite her wishes, or another patient who states she was taken off a diet designed by a doctor because Claude-Pierre said it would make her fat. How the university has ascertained the success rate is unknown given there has never been an outcome study done to determine recovery amongst Montreux's patients.[8]

The fact that the critics who went to the media to criticize Montreux and Claude-Pierre were all white middle-aged males speaking about an illness in which 90 percent of those that suffer are female may have impacted on how journalists received their critique. Ironically, Claude-Pierre's model is represented as alternative to the coldness of the male *medical model*, yet in some ways more patriarchal than the majority of hospital programs that give cursory mention of gender. Claude-Pierre ascertains eating disorders have nothing to do with society or gender, but that they are symptomatic of a condition that children are born with, a condition that strikes the upper classes more frequently than the poor. It is this focus on the pathological individual rather than society that was attractive to the media and perhaps the professionals that became ardent supporters of Claude-Pierre.

Media coverage about Montreux points to the dominance of a cultural pedagogy in which the media defines the nature of a psychological pathology and the preferred cure. It is a pedagogy that is connected to the willingness of mental health professionals playing giving legitimacy to this role. A critical educational psychology must disrupt the dominant cultural pedagogy that represents children as problems who can be cured with a quality psychological product.

Media coverage about Montreux does raise issues not only of research literacy but also of media illiteracy on the part of both journalists who believed what other journalists reported as TRUTH, as well as professionals who saw journalistic research as a process similar to that applied in academic and applied research environments. Professionals were an integral part of solidifying the legitimization process by providing testimonials as to the effectiveness of Montreux, testimonials which were often based on media advertising Claude-Pierre's seemingly remarkable success with even the most ill.

Mental health professionals supporting or becoming psychological gurus through media attention is not new;[9] nor is their ability to influence professionals, families and ultimately the lives of children and youth deemed by their caregivers to require specialized services. To criticize the media for how they came to believe in Montreux is not to say that credentialed psychology has a great piece of the truth pie. It too silences diverse voices, and with growing corporate involvement in psychology and psychiatry, the issue of independent exploration may also become problematic as it has for journalists who do wish to be critical of the media conglomerate for which they work. It is to say that mental health professionals need to take the role of media seriously not only in its ability to persuade young people, but also in its power to influence the thinking and decisions the people charged with determining what is best for them.

NOTES

1. I attended the twenty-six day licensing hearing, visited the Montreux clinic, conducted a qualitative content analysis of over 300 media pieces, licensing transcripts and 1300 pages of court documents concerning Montreux, and conducted twenty-nine semi-structured interviews with the founder of Montreux and its staff, mental and medical professionals, and journalists.

2. Nexus, as well as the Canadian Database, CBCA were used to locate articles. In addition, media materials were provided by interview participants.

3. Pseudonyms are used for mental health professionals and ex-staff and managers at Montreux. Ethics approval was sought and received from the University of Toronto to use the real names for the founders of the clinic, Peggy Claude-Pierre and David Harris, as well as, the name of the Medical Health Officer and members of the media. These individuals agreed to have their names used.

4. 20/20 stated Claude-Pierre was "working on her doctorate." The *Maury Povich Show* referred to her as Dr. Claude-Pierre. A number of other media outlets, following these established "facts" also referred to her as doctor, or as working on her doctorate.

5. I interviewed Kerry Slavens on November 15, 2000. All quotes are based on transcripts from this interview.

6. Quotes from McClellan are from the transcripts of an interview I conducted with her on November 10, 2000.

7. Hilde Bruch was considered to be in the forefront of developing latter twentiethh Century theories of and treatments for anorexia.

8. I did email the person in charge of the program and leave a phone message, but did not receive a reply.

9. Sutton (1996) and Pollak (1997) found that Bruno Bettleheim, for example, started off having weekly dialogues with mothers, but soon was quoted in the academic literature, media, and women's magazines speaking on everything from Autism to protesters of the Vietnam War having an Oedipal Complex.

REFERENCES

Brumberg, J. J. (1998). *The Body Project: An Intimate History of American Girls*. New York: Vintage Books.

Clay, R. (1997). *Innovative anorexia clinic offers remarkable success*. APA Monitor March.

Crisp, A. H., J. S. Callender, et al. (1992). Long-term mortality in anorexia nervosa: A 20 year follow-up of the St. George's and Aberdeen cohorts. *British Journal of Psychiatry* 159: 325-333.

Gordon, R. A. (2000). *Eating Disorders: Anatomy of a Social Epidemic*. Oxford: Blackwell Publishers Ltd.

Klaidman, S. (1990). Roles and responsibilities of journalists. In Atkin and B. Atkin (Eds.), *Mass Communication and Public Health: Communicating Health Information*. Thousand Oaks, CA: Sage Publications.

Larson, T. (1997). *BYU hosts conference on obesity and eating disorders*. The Daily Universe. Provo.

Sutton, N. (1996). *Bettelheim: A life and legacy*. New York, Basic Books.

CHAPTER 50

The Buddha View: ReVIEWing Educational Psychology's Practices and Perspectives

PATRICIA A. WHANG

Tracing the growth and development of the field of educational psychology unearths its largely Eurocentric and patriarchical roots. Consider, for example, the table of contents of a recent book, *Educational Psychology: A Century of Contributions* (2003). Fifteen of the nineteen chapters of this book are profiles of individuals who have made seminal contributions to the field. More specifically, thirteen of the chapters document the achievements of Caucasian men, all of whom are American except for Binet, who was French; Vygotsky, who was Russian; and Piaget, who was Swiss. Maria Montessori and Ann Brown are the only two women profiled and they were Italian and British, respectively. Calling attention to the token representation of women, the absence of people of color, and the invisibility of educational psychologists of non-European or American descent in this book is not meant to diminish the accomplishments of the individuals profiled. Rather, the point is to contextualize the importance of questioning how the contributions made by educational psychologists have been constrained by the largely male and Euro-American perspectives, values, and traditions held by influential members of the field.

This question resonates with me because I am an educational psychologist who is intentionally positioned on the margins of the field. That is, as an Asian American woman holding a Psychological Foundations position in a teacher education department, I have struggled to commit my time and energy to the traditional pursuits of educational psychologists, as reflected, for example, in the types of articles that get published in the field's most prestigious journals. This has not always been the case. As a graduate student I received my doctoral degree in educational psychology from UC Berkeley and was a student of Arthur Jensen, the prolific and controversial researcher of intelligence. I was well prepared to continue deploying the experimental methods, quantitative statistical tools, and theoretical perspectives that I had acquired in graduate school and I did so for a few years. Despite my growing involvement in the field, I felt a gnawing dissatisfaction with my intellectual pursuits and yearned to commit my time and energy to endeavors that I was passionate about and that held personal meaning. For example, as a person of color I see the need to contribute to a more just, dignified, and sustainable world. My scholarly efforts to make such a contribution ultimately necessitated trespassing the traditional boundaries of educational psychology and exploring what other disciplines had to offer in terms of purposes, methods, and theoretical perspectives.

It is important to point out that others have questioned the impact and import of the work of educational psychologists. Earlier, Jackson (1969, 1981) offered an unsettling commentary that seems to have fallen on deaf ears. Unfortunately his points carry no less potency today than they did in years past. In his quest to engage educational psychologists in an honest appraisal of what they have to offer teachers, Jackson (1969) urged an imagining of "what would happen if all of the knowledge in our field were suddenly eliminated from minds and books. . . . How far back toward caveman status would such a catastrophe put us?" (p. 70). Even with the advantage of more than thirty years to add to the stock of offerings, total elimination of the contributions made by educational psychologists would probably not substantially change the teaching and learning that takes place in schools. Jackson also encouraged educational psychologists to imagine standing before an audience of teachers reading the table of contents of its most prestigious journals, as evidence of disciplinary preoccupations and of the ways they are laboring to benefit schools and schooling. He feared that these earnest efforts would be drowned out by the laughter of those they are meant to serve. Moreover, a quick perusal of recent issues of the disciplinary journals affords evidence of the continued concern and debate over the direction, focus, and relevance of the field. I resurrect Jackson's provocations and draw attention to current disciplinary concerns to reinforce the point that the work of educational psychologists might profit from a broadening of its sources of influence.

LOOKING BACKWARD BEFORE CHARTING A FORWARD COURSE

ReVIEWing the historical context that situated the emergence of educational psychology as a discipline provides a basis for critically considering how historical conditions have influenced the gestation and subsequent development of the field. More specifically, the efficiency reform movement and the drastic improvements in the quality of life resulting from scientific and technological advances will be used as a means of understanding why certain positions and perspectives have been fortified to such a great extent. Also, this history will be used to foreground what has been omitted and committed as a result of the developmental directions the discipline has followed. Then, Buddhist teachings will be used to demonstrate how unexplored and untapped perspectives offer a beneficial broadening or grounds for reconsideration of current disciplinary perspectives, practices, and values. It is important to point out that in forwarding a consideration of the potential influences afforded by Buddhist teachings, I am not advocating a religious or faith-based solution. Profiting from Buddhist teachings requires neither belief in or reverence for a supernatural power or being nor blind faith in a system of beliefs, values, or practices. Rather, Buddhist teachers advocate approaching teachings with open-minded skepticism and a willingness to test the teachings with respect to how they impact the quality of one's life.

My choice of Buddhism as a perspective from which to reVIEW aspects of educational psychology is purely incidental. In fact, I am not advocating a consideration of Buddhist teachings from the position of someone raised as a Buddhist or trained as a Buddhist scholar. In fact, my introduction to Buddhist teachings occurred by happenstance. On a whim, I happened to purchase the book *An Open Heart* by the Dalai Lama and was immediately struck by the ways in which his teachings were consistent with theoretical positions that stress the need for developing vigilant awareness, critical questioning, open-minded reflection, and ethical action. Perhaps what has resonated with me the most is that Buddhism has offered me a basis for thinking about, engaging in, and evaluating my professional activities from a more holistic and coherent manner that is ultimately about working toward freeing onself, and eventually others, from those habits, perspectives, and actions that result in suffering. Briefly, a central tenant of Buddhism is that all sentient beings have in common the desire to minimize suffering and maximize happiness. More specifically, the teachings help us understand the causes of suffering, the possibility of ceasing that suffering, and the path or means of achieving less suffering and more happiness. In short, I have found that Buddhist teachings expand how I think and do my work as an educational psychologist. I offer the following in hopes of intriguing others to consider the power and potential in a more widely influenced educational psychology.

Making Efficient Disciplinary Progress

In the United States, the field of educational psychology was begot during a time of great ferment and change. The largely agrarian society was giving way to industrialism. That is, labor evolved from nineteenth-century craft guilds, where master craftsmen taught apprentices the total production process, to large factories, where labor was required to perform specialized and routinized tasks in the name of effective and efficient mass production. In this new era, interest in efficiency spilled over to the burgeoning schools, which subsequently fashioned themselves after the production-minded factories.

It was in this context that disciplinary ancestors were nurturing the growth of educational psychology in a space between scientific psychology and the more applied field of education. Pivotal negotiations of this space occurred as two American males, Edward Lee Thorndike and John Dewey, vied for the attention and the allegiance of educational psychologists, with Thorndike eventually prevailing. Conjuring up both of these disciplinary ancestors should remind us that although disciplinary space has largely solidified around a particular vision, the fundamental assumptions about preferred goals and methods have been contested and are not immutable. Nevertheless, it was the experimenter and quantifier who set the template for what it means to be an educational psychologist, which in turn resulted in many educational psychologists' preferring to stepping into laboratories in search of generalizable principles of learning and instruction, rather than into classrooms and the complex world of schools. More specifically, Thorndike insisted that whatever behavior constituted a child's response to a particular stimulus was a reflection of the content of that child's learning. This conception of learning permitted the quantification of responses and paved the way for the scientific study of learning and the mathematization and mechanization of human experience. Tools were developed that allowed quantified responses or data to be compared, tabulated, ordered, correlated, or judged for probability. When communicated to educators, the results of these statistical manipulations were assumed to offer an improved basis for determining the effectiveness of teaching and learning.

Thorndike was in the right place at the right time, given that the societal preoccupation with efficiency lent credence to the perspectives and practices that he represented. In fact, Thorndike's concept of mind, his experimental conception of psychology, and his faith in statistical research and measurement legitimated what is referred to as the social efficiency reform movement. Efficiency-minded administrators found the research produced by educational psychology to be an acceptable source of insights and knowledge that could be used for improving teaching and learning.

Although educational psychology seemed to take up and profit from the societal preoccupation with efficiency, it should be noted that, in doing so, educational psychologists tended to cultivate a preference for particular practices and perspectives, to the neglect of others. That is, the perspectives adopted by educational psychologists contrasted sharply with, for example, those put forth by Dewey, who actively promoted the understanding that schools perform important social functions and that making this world a better place requires considering both educational and social changes. Educational psychologists, however, were unconcerned about the purpose of education or about education's social role and tended to think in terms of what was rather than what could be. In other words, educational psychologists have historically worked without an explicit vision or larger purposes to guide the differences that their work should make; hence there is little evidence of any moral obligation to address issues of power, democracy, inequality, ethics, or politics. In sum, although supporting society's efficiency impulse seems to have bolstered the perceived usefulness of educational psychology, perhaps it is now important to consider how aligning the discipline with an efficient enterprise has occluded or excluded other practices or perspectives.

Reviewing Efficient Disciplinary Progress

To be efficient is to act or produce with minimum waste, expense, or effort. An interesting counterpoint to an emphasis on efficiency is the Buddhist concept or practice of mindfulness. To be mindFUL is to be fully present and fully attuned to the current moment in a way that is open, curious, flexible, and nonjudgmental. As the Vietnamese Buddhist monk Thich Nhat Hanh points out, mindfulness practice involves cultivating greater awareness of and openness to our body, feelings, mind, and objects of our mind. Mindfulness does not represent a mind full of preconceptions, assumptions, or unruly thoughts or feelings that feed into reflexive or habitual responses.

For example, rather than reflexively acting out our feelings of agitation, the cultivation of mindfulness provides us with the tools and wherewithal to recognize the clenching of our fists, the rise in our body's temperature, and the angry cascade of thoughts as agitation. Without feeding our agitation by thinking about the ways in which it is justified, we openly accept our current state, but work to recognize it as wholesome, unwholesome, or neutral. If we recognize the agitation as unwholesome because the actions that stem from our agitation do more to escalate ill feelings than bring about a positive resolution to the problem, then we have created a wedge in what once was a reflexive response to a strong emotional state. In this space we have created between our emotional state and the mindless responses that the state provokes, we have the opportunity to consciously work with our body, emotions, and thoughts to respond more constructively. Cultivating sustained mindful energy and attention requires effortful practice, because responding to the world habitually or reflexively is so effortless. As such, Buddhist teachings on mindfulness provide insights and tools essential to ceasing those behaviors, thoughts, or emotions that contribute to suffering, whether that suffering be our own or others.

Engaging in habitual or reflexive responses to the world is an effective way of maintaining the status quo. Consider how, for example, any field of study follows a developmental course influenced by the people who have invested their identities and livelihood in particular traditions and perspectives. These negotiated traditions help define what ideas are worthy of consideration, which theoretical perspectives have currency, and what methodological approaches are acceptable or preferable. As mentioned earlier, educational psychology has strongly solidified its practices and perspectives around those championed by Thorndike.

Changing or expanding preferred practices or traditions may be difficult given that those who are invested in the field give shape to it. That is, one's reputation as a scholar and researcher depends on one's investments' paying off. Ironically, the greater the success one experiences the greater one's opportunity to define what counts or matters because of the role peer reviews play in hiring, promotion, publishing, and grant funding decisions. This could promote the tendency to function as if one's commitments are the best or the soundest, and may encourage a lack of openness, curiosity, and flexibility toward new, alternative, or contradictory perspectives or practices.

As a countervailing force to this tendency, mindfulness offers techniques and strategies for bringing greater awareness to the actions, feelings, and thoughts that we engage in mindlessly. This awareness provides a basis for considering the implications of our actions. Essentially, approaching one's work mindfully should force a broader consideration of the import and implications of one's work and make problematic, for example, the reflexive desire to act in ways that are ultimately self-protective or self-promoting. Serious consideration of the importance of working mindfully seems warranted given that the work of educational psychologists has the potential to directly impact the lives of others.

Finding a Way to Progress Scientifically

In addition to changes in labor and production, people living during the early 1900s were experiencing vast improvements in the quality of their lives as a result of scientific and technological advances. Given the successful contributions the sciences were making to the transformation of society, it is perhaps unremarkable that ancestral forefathers saw fit to bind the field of educational psychology to these same scientific methods, practices, and perspectives. Educational psychologists were buoyed by the optimistic hope that following the precedents set by the natural sciences, research could provide a means of efficiently and uniformly improving schools and schooling. In fact, educational psychologists did not travel the path toward the scientific alone. Given the stature of the sciences during the nineteenth century, academic respectability was considered attainable by aligning with the traditionally powerful disciplines. In fact, even today, the relative standing of a discipline within academic circles continues to be judged by the objectivity, power, and rigor of the discipline's methods and the closeness with which it aligns with those fields using "hard" methods.

The nascent field of educational psychology was caught in the odd predicament of possibly compromising the scientific development of psychology if it emerged with an applied emphasis. This predicament is said to have resulted in efforts to minimize the appearance that educational psychology was more practically focused than scientific. The desire to approximate experimental conditions lent credence to Thorndike's studying learning in a psychological laboratory with animals. Moreover, there was disciplinary reluctance to get involved with educational issues, such as educational reform, that reached beyond classrooms and into society. Ironically, those studies that have the greatest claim to validity and reliability may be the most trivial or the least practical because the results have been obtained by means that negate the complexity that inherently characterizes schools and classrooms.

Moreover, as a result of assuming the stance of the neutral and objective scientist wielding scientific tools and procedures, distance has been created between researcher and researched. Creating such distance absolves researchers of the need to include those being researched in question posing, data collection, or analysis. In fact, by holding tightly to positivistic methods, educational psychologists have been able to position themselves as experts within the educational community who produce a specialized form of knowledge that is typically more valued than the knowledge produced by practitioners, thus conferring upon educational psychologists the authority to inform teachers' practices and perspectives within their classrooms. Essentially, the desire to professionalize the discipline required academic social scientists to distinguish themselves from amateur theorists. This required social scientists to establish themselves as professionals, who unlike amateurs, had knowledge and methods that could offer objective, uncontestable, and correct solutions. The distinction between professionals and amateurs was made by establishing doctoral training programs, professional societies, esoteric jargon, and specialized publications. Thus, upholding Thorndike's scientific ideal was interpreted as progress for a field that prior to the turn of century was both jargon and methodless. The disciplinary progress evolved from a body of scholarly work accessible to any educated person, to a literature complicated by the method sections and method books we have grown accustomed to.

It is important to note that schools of education seemed to accept, and perhaps implicitly contribute to, educational psychology's belief in the utility of attaining scientific certainty by relying heavily on laboratory experiments and on quantification. That is, being bound to the scientific was probably seen as essential for a field striving to raise its status from that of a trade taught to high school graduates in what were referred to as normal schools, to that of a full-fledged academic field of study in colleges and universities. In fact, the legitimacy of teacher preparation programs was questioned in academic circles because the ways normal schools structured their courses were grounded experientially rather than scientifically. Educational psychology courses were developed with the hope of upgrading the status of teacher education by providing a scientific means for infusing scholarship and rigor into professional programs.

Stepping back to reflect on the historical conditions that contextualized the growth and development of the field may lead to the conclusion that current disciplinary commitments reflect the ways that the profession has responded to the need to establish itself as a legitimate and useful discipline. Now that the field of educational psychology is established, it might profit from the infusion of ideas that spur a consideration of new practices or perspectives. To this end, Buddhist teachings on compassion will be used to push thinking about the scientific progress of educational psychology. A consideration of compassion is important because when Thorndike stepped into a laboratory to study learning, he began the long tradition of treating children, teachers, parents, and schools as data sources.

Reviewing Educational Psychology's Scientific Progress

The word *compassion* has been defined by the Dalai Lama as the wish that others be free of suffering. Cultivating mindfulness is important to furthering our ability to be compassionate, because being fully present or mentally aware affords opportunities to discern the presence of suffering in others as well as some of the ways in which our impulses are shielding us from having to confront or address that suffering. Moreover, mindfulness helps clarify the relationship between our own self-interests and the suffering or happiness experienced by others. For example, I might be able to buy a very inexpensive taco from a fast-food restaurant, but it is important to reckon with the fact that the people picking the tomatoes for that taco are being exploited as a result. If compassion is about caring so deeply about others that we take responsibility for and do everything in our power to ease their suffering, then we might decide that a more wholesome response is to forego the taco. Essentially, coupling compassion with mindfulness is important because compassion challenges us to look beyond our own self-interests and to understand the ways in which lives are interconnected.

Unfortunately, it is necessary to cultivate compassion, because although we tend to form close attachments to those near to us, we have to learn how to have compassion for people outside our immediate circles. As the Dalai Lama has explained, our compassion toward strangers or mere acquaintances is limited, partial, prejudicial, and predicated upon how close we feel to them. With this in mind, it is interesting to consider the ramifications of the practice of maintaining distance between researcher and researched. Such distance can be problematic, because it allows the researcher to remain unaware and hence unconcerned by such aspects of lives as joys, triumphs, agony, or fear. This is beneficial if one desires to avoid being held accountable for responding compassionately. Furthermore, maintaining distance dilutes any sense of agency or responsibility, decreases the likelihood of alliances being formed, and can suppress the moral imagination or a consideration of what could be. This allows researchers to have their research needs met by taking what they want from the subjects of their studies, with little or no dialogue or interaction, and then leave fulfilled while the subject leaves unfulfilled and perhaps even feeling used. The suggestion is not to discontinue involving people in research. Rather, working from a desire to research compassionately one may decide to bridge the usual distance by engaging the researched in a more egalitarian and respectful manner. This can be achieved by affording opportunities to dialogue about the what, how, and why of the research to be conducted.

CONCLUSION

Educational psychologists are not studying rocks, chemicals, or the solar system. Rather the inquiry that educational psychologists engage in is hoped to have very real consequences in the lives of thinking, acting, and feeling people. Typically, the participants or beneficiaries of the disciplinary efforts of educational psychologists are children, who are developing an understanding of the world and their place in it. I have found that Buddhist teachings help me to work in ways that are responsive to the ethical responsibilities inherent in endeavors meant to positively benefit the lives of others. This has proved an effective counterbalance to disciplinary practices and perspectives that encourage pursuing expertise and knowledge. As the Dalai Lama has pointed out, knowledge is important, but even more important may be how we use it. Our use of what we know is influenced by the wisdom we bring to the situation. Wisdom, like mindfulness and compassion, is not a state that once achieved remains forever. Rather, wisdom, as understanding or insight into what is true, right, or lasting requires cultivation. Given the influence that our work can have on the lives of others, is it not imperative that we seek out perspectives that promote our ability to make wise decisions?

I am advocating the value of a discipline influenced by Buddhist teachings because it provides the means for making wise decisions. Buddhist teachings on suffering, its causes, the possibility of eliminating suffering, and the means for achieving the cessation of suffering have given me a touchstone from which to consider the import and impact of my practices and perspectives. Consider further the power and potential in achieving mindfulness through bare attention, non-judgmental awareness, and deep listening. What realities about their practices and perspectives would educational psychologists become aware of? Yes, vigilantly working to attain a mindful state might bring us face to face with the suffering of others, and if moved by Buddhist teachings we would be beholden to acknowledge our responsibility through acts of compassion. Responding compassionately requires understanding the nature of suffering and the wisdom to determine how we can contribute to the lessening of the suffering. It is true that even after looking into the face of suffering and understanding the ways in which our privileges and power are entangled with the oppression of others can result in inaction. But this greater clarity in seeing what one was previously unaware of may plant a seed of discomfort that makes one's complicity in perpetuating indignities difficult because the bliss that ignorance affords us has been stripped away. Simply, the importance of achieving compassion is that once injustices or suffering becomes visible, an impetus to remedy the situation exists. Given the work of educational psychologists has the power and potential to influence the lives of others, is it not essential that we seriously consider the wisdom in approaching that work mindfully and compassionately?

TERMS FOR READERS

Compassion—As pointed out by Thich Naht Hanh, *compassion* is the closest translation of the Sanskrit and Pali word *karuna*. The translation is not direct because compassion is derived from *com*, "together with," and *passion*, "to suffer." However, *karuna*, or the intention and capacity to relieve and transform suffering and lighten sorrow does not require that one also be suffering in order to respond.

Mindfulness—According to Thich Naht Hanh, the Sanskritt world for mindfulness means "remember," as in remembering to come back to the present moment and not, for example, get lost in the distraction of past or future events. Considering the Chinese character used for *mindfulness* is also instructive. The upper part means "now," and the lower part means "mind" or "heart."

Wholesome—To paraphrase the *American Heritage Dictionary*, something that is wholesome is conducive to sound health or well-being. Or, in other words, it promotes mental, oral, or social health.

REFERENCES

Jackson, P. W. (1969). Stalking beasts and swatting flies: Comments on educational psychology and teacher training. In J. Herbert and D. P. Ausubel (Eds.), *Psychology in Teacher Preparation* (pp. 65–76). Toronto: OISE.

———. (1981). The promise of educational psychology. In F. H. Farley and N. J. Gordon (Eds.), *Psychology and Education: The State of the Union* (pp. 389–405). Berkeley: McCutchan.

Lama, The Dalai (2001). *An Open Heart: Practicing Compassion in Everyday Life*. Boston: Little, Brown and Company.

Zimmerman, B. J., and Schunk, D. H. (2003). *Educational Psychology: A Century of Contributions*. Mahwah, NJ: L. Erlbaum Associates.

CHAPTER 51

Without Using the "S" Word: The Role of Spirituality in Culturally Responsive Teaching and Educational Psychology

ELIZABETH J. TISDELL

Spirituality is an important part of human experience. Bookstores are filled with many popular titles on the subject. Not surprisingly, most popular press books on spirituality focus on its individual dimensions: how to cultivate mindfulness; how to develop a better relationship with God or a Higher Power; how to draw on spirituality and meditation to reduce stress, and thus lead to a greater sense of health and well-being; even how to have a prosperous life. There are few discussions of spirituality that focus on its cultural aspects. Indeed, just as in psychology, where the traditional focus is on the individual with little attention to the cultural context that inform the life and development of that individual, most discussions of spirituality also focus on its more individual dimensions. But there is a cultural dimension to spirituality, and a spiritual dimension to culture. Thus far in the field of educational psychology, there has been little attention to spirituality in general, much less to its cultural dimensions.

The relative silence about spirituality is not particularly surprising in educational psychology. Indeed, the field has been dominated by behaviorists and clinically oriented cognitive psychologists, who have been grounded in positivism and the scientific method. Such a view of the world has traditionally seen spirituality either as wish fulfillment, or "background noise" that needs to be tuned out to make studies "scientific." In addition, the separation of church and state grounded in enlightenment period philosophy and in positivism might give further pause to educational psychologists about either considering the role of spirituality in cognitive and overall development, or doing research in this area.

Just as the field of educational psychology has been reticent about dealing with issues of spirituality, until recently they have been quite hesitant at acknowledging how structural power relations between dominant and nondominant groups based on sociostructural factors of race, ethnicity, gender, sexual orientation and class, affect one's view of the world. Traditionally, theories of human development, including cognitive development, in all areas of psychology were based on white, male, middle- to upper-middle-class participants. If a particular person didn't fit with the theory, he or she was assumed to be less developed, or less evolved, since most of these theories tended to ignore gender and cultural issues. This of course has changed in the last two decades, with the greater attention to gender, and to some extent cultural differences in the field of psychology (Hays, 2001). However, because educational psychology has focused largely on psychometrics, the attention to gender and culture has lagged somewhat behind other areas of psychology and education, although clearly there is more of a concern with power relations based on gender, race, class, and culture now than ever before, even in educational psychology.

Obviously the discourses in education that focus on dealing with gender, race, class, and sexual orientation have a great interest in the cultural context in education; indeed that is their purpose. But like the field of educational psychology, these discourses focused on power relations and how to alter them, and have mostly ignored the role of spirituality in the ongoing development of identity and in culturally responsive education. There is, however, a growing body of literature in education that talks about the role of spirituality and learning (Astin, 2004; Glazer, 1999; Palmer, 1998; Parks, 2000). Most of this literature, however, has not attended to how spirituality interconnects with culture. Therefore, the purpose of this chapter is to examine the role of spirituality in culturally responsive teaching, and its potential role in challenging power relations, and what it suggests for educational psychology. Much of this discussion is based on the results of qualitative research study of how spirituality informs teaching to challenge power relations of a group of 31 educators of different cultural groups, as well as my own experience as a white woman teaching in a graduate-level higher education setting of how to do it. The discussion of the study itself here is necessarily brief, but I have discussed the role of spirituality in culturally responsive teaching in depth elsewhere (see Tisdell, 2003). But before this discussion goes any further, it's important to consider what is meant by spirituality and how does it connect to culture.

DEFINING SPIRITUALITY AND ITS CONNECTION TO CULTURE

Most often in discussions of spirituality, it is argued that spirituality is about meaning making, a belief in a higher power, or higher purpose, the wholeness and the interconnectedness of all things, and that it is different from religion, although for many people it's interrelated. Many people also discuss it as related to developing a sense of greater authenticity. Indeed, most authors agree that this is some of what spirituality is about. But faith development theorist James Fowler (1981) notes that spirituality is also about how people construct knowledge through image, symbol, and unconscious processes. While Fowler has not discussed the connection of spirituality to culture, obviously image, symbol, and unconscious processes are often deeply cultural, and thus deeply connected to cultural identity.

As noted earlier, in most of the education and psychology literature, discussions of spirituality are focused more on an individual level—on what meaning individuals make of spirituality and spiritual experience, with little attention to the role of culture in the expression or understanding of spirituality. Some authors do, however, more explicitly discuss spirituality as a fundamental aspect of their being rooted in their cultural experience. To a large extent, these contributions and discussions have been made by people of color or those who are explicitly interested in cultural issues. Indeed, as hooks (2000) suggests, these authors are a part of the counterculture that are trying to "break mainstream cultural taboos that silence or erase our passion for spiritual practice" (p. 82) and the spiritual underpinning to cultural work.

In order to consider further how spirituality relates to culture, and to culturally responsive teaching, it is important to consider the phenomenon of developing and sustaining a positive cultural identity. Again the field of educational psychology has tended to ignore the process of *cultural* identity development, largely because its traditional focus has been on measurement, and of isolating and measuring a particular variable, usually devoid of the multiple cultural effects that shape an individual's identity. But in order to attend to culturally responsive teaching, it is important to understand the dynamics of cultural identity development. Those who have discussed race and ethnic identity models of development have built on the pioneering work of William Cross (1971), who initially posed a five-stage model of racial identity. According to this model, in addition to the positive views of their culture they may have inherited from their families, individuals from these cultural groups may have internalized (from the White dominant culture) some negative attitudes toward themselves. This results partially in the phenomenon of internalized oppression, an internalized but mostly unconscious belief in the superiority of those more representative of the dominant culture. The educational psychology might simply label such a person who has internalized oppression as someone with bad self-esteem due to a mother who was not loving enough, or other such individualist effects, rather than acknowledge that internalized oppression is a phenomenon that is a part of structural social relations based on race, class, ethnicity, and so on. But even most of those who do write about the sociocultural dimensions of internalized oppression have tended to ignore the role of spirituality in healing from oppression. Latino writer David Abalos (1998) lends insight here. He suggests that in order for particular cultural groups to be able to create and sustain positive social change on behalf of themselves and their own cultural communities, it is necessary that they deal with the phenomenon of internalized oppression. He argues it is necessary to claim and reclaim four aspects or "faces" of their cultural being: the personal face, the political face, the historical face, and the sacred face. This "sacred face" is related to the spirituality that is grounded in their own cultural community, by claiming and reclaiming images, symbols, ways of being and celebrating what is sacred to individuals and the community as a whole. Those who reclaim their sacred face and its connection to cultural identity often experience the process of working for transformation of themselves and their communities as a spiritual process. In Abalos's (1998) words,

The process of transformation takes place first of all in the individual's depths. . . . But each of us as a person has four faces: the personal, political, historical and sacred. . . . To cast out demons in our personal lives and in society means that we have freed our sacred face. (p. 35)

In the exploration of the four faces, Abalos has grounded the individual in not only a cultural, historical, and spiritual context (in his attention to the sacred face), but a personal context as well. His conceptualization has implications for the field of educational psychology in that it recognizes the multiple and interconnected aspects of an individual's being as related to a history, a culture, and a spirituality, all of which affects overall identity development.

Now, with the above as background and theoretical grounding, and given the fact that this discussion is about spirituality, it is important to summarize and to be as clear as possible about what is meant by the term *spirituality*, particularly as it relates to culture and education, as it is used here. As noted elsewhere (Tisdell, 2003), based on both the literature and the findings of the study discussed below, spirituality is about the following: (1) a connection to what is discussed as the Lifeforce, God, a higher power or purpose, Great Mystery; (2) a sense of wholeness, healing, and the interconnectedness of all things; (3) meaning-making; (4) the ongoing development of one's identity (including one's cultural identity), moving toward greater authenticity; (5) how people construct knowledge through largely unconscious and symbolic processes manifested in such things as image, symbol, and music, which are often cultural; (6) as different but, in some cases, related to religion; and (7) spiritual experiences that happen by surprise. Understanding how these dimensions of spirituality have played out in the lives of educators who conceive of this process of positive cultural identity development as a spiritual process can offer new direction to a culturally responsive educational psychology.

A SUMMARY OF THE STUDY

The qualitative research study itself was informed by a poststructural feminist research theoretical framework, which suggests that that the positionality (race, gender, class, sexual orientation) of researchers, teachers, and students affects how one gathers and accesses data, and how one constructs and views knowledge, in research and teaching. Thus, my own positionality as a white middle-class woman who grew up Catholic and has tried to negotiate a more relevant adult spirituality, in addition to the fact that I teach classes specifically about race, class, and gender issues, has influenced the data collection and analysis processes.

Purpose and Methodology

My primary purpose in this study was to find out how educators teaching about cultural issues in education, the social sciences, and the humanities either in higher education or in community-based settings interpret how their spirituality influences their work in their attempts to teach for social and cultural responsiveness, and how their spirituality has changed over time since their childhood. I was attempting not only to provide some data-based information about how their spirituality informs their work, I was also trying to examine the cultural aspects of spirituality. In essence, I was interested in looking at the often-ignored sociocultural dimensions of spirituality, and to explicitly make visible the spiritual experience of people of color, as well as the experience of white European Americans, which is the group that the spirituality literature in North America tends to primarily be about. There were thirty-one participants in the study, twenty-two women and nine men (six African American, four Latino, four Asian American, two Native American, one of East Indian descent, and fourteen European American). Twenty-three of the thirty-one taught in higher education settings, while eight taught in community-based settings.

The primary means of data collection was a.1.5–3-hour taped interview that focused on how their spirituality has developed over time, relates to their cultural identity and overall identity development, informs their education practice. Given the poststructural feminist theoretical framework, which attempts to avoid "othering" participants (Fine, 1998), I approached the interviews as a shared conversation, and looked at the process as an ongoing one where we were constructing knowledge together. Thus, if participants asked me a question, I briefly answered it. Many participants also provided written documents that addressed some of their social action pursuits or issues related to their spirituality. Data were analyzed according to the constant comparative method (Merriam, 1998), and several participants were contacted for member checks once data were analyzed to ensure accuracy of the analysis.

There were several findings to the study relating to the participants' conception of the role of spirituality in claiming a positive cultural identity. Three of these that are particularly related to educational psychology and to culturally responsive educational and psychological practice are discussed briefly below.

Unconscious and Cultural Knowledge Construction Processes

People construct knowledge in powerful ways through unconscious processes, and ritual, gesture, music, and art has enduring power. These aspects of knowledge production are nearly always connected to culture, and often have spiritual significance as well. Take the case of Anna Adams, an African American education professor, who has long since moved away from the African American Christian religious tradition of her childhood. But Anna discussed Aretha Franklin and her music as an important spiritual symbol for her that connects to her cultural identity and her spirituality, a spirituality that has become more important to her as she has gotten older. In reflecting on the connection of Aretha's music to her own cultural identity, Anna explained:

I grew up in a Black community doing and understanding and experiencing things of Black culture, so when I say Aretha takes me back, she takes me back to my childhood and the things that I understood then—things like music and dance, and the way of walking, the way of talking, the way of knowing, the interactions, the jive talk, the improvisations, you know, all those things that I learned coming up—the music of the church, the choir that I sang in, all of that. And because I was raised in that community with that knowledge her music takes me back even farther than I know, because I don't know where all of those things come from.

Obviously, for Anna, Aretha's music is a great source of inspiration because of its connection to her ancestors, her own spirituality, and its rootedness in her own cultural experience.

Julia Gutierrez also spoke of the journey of reclaiming a positive cultural identity as a spiritual experience, and the role of the cultural symbol of *La Virgen de Guadalupe* in that process. Julia has long since moved away from the Mexican Catholicism of her youth, but in reflecting back, she notes,

I think part of my journey is going back to my heritage, my Aztec and indigenous roots. . . . Ana Castillo (1994) gives a different picture of what *La Virgen* could represent in terms of powerful women. . . . But there's another side to it. . . . I don't always just go with "this is the way that it is" because I do question "was that a way for the Spaniards to . . . convert the Aztecs into Catholicism? Or is it really an Aztec goddess?". . . But I do believe it's a spirit—a spirit that kind of watches over me.

Further she discusses some of the affective significance she holds to this image of *La Virgen de Guadalupe* in her family and cultural history:

We have this ritual in my family—every time I go home, and when I 'm getting ready to leave, I ask for my parents' blessing, and so they'll take me into their room, and each one of them will bless me. . . . And I don't feel complete if I don't do that. . . . So my father will bless me, "te encomiendo a Dios Padre, y a *La Virgen de Guadalupe*," and ask my grandmother and *La Virgen* to watch over me, and so I feel like my Grandmother's watching over me!

For Julia the importance of the cultural symbol is in its significance to her ancestral connection, to her cultural roots, and the affective dimension associated with the family ritual of blessing.

Spirituality in Dealing with Internalized Oppression

Many of the participants discussed the role of spirituality in unlearning internalized oppression based on race or culture, sexual orientation, or gender. But many of them also talked specifically about the role of spirituality in that process. As noted above, the pressure to adopt the views from the dominant culture about one's identity group can result in the internalized but mostly unconscious belief in the inferiority of one's ethnic group, and/or to being exposed to little to no information about one's cultural group if one's parents, family, or immediate community overemphasized assimilation. Unlearning these internalized oppressions is often connected to spirituality, and for most people is a process. Elise Poitier, an African American woman, describes recognizing that she had to some degree internalized white standards of beauty, when as a young adult she moved from the Midwest to Atlanta and explained, "In Atlanta, my beauty was affirmed. I could walk down the street and see myself; there was a sense of connectedness . . . that I would consider a spiritual connection."

Tito, a Puerto Rican man, described the process of reclaiming his Puerto Rican identity as a spiritual process. As he explains,

I found out that I was Taino [the Indigenous people of Puerto Rico], African, and European. This made me happy. But I had to learn more about the history and stories of these cultures in order for me to be "whole.". . . But even after learning about that, I felt empty. . . . I then look into the sacred story of my ancestors.

For Tito, knowing about the spirituality of some of his ancestors was an important part of his healing process.

Penny, a Jewish woman, spoke very specifically to the phenomenon of internalized oppression.

Raised as an assimilated Jew in White Christian middle-class suburbs, I learned well how to blend in and belong as White. . . . I felt uncomfortable around people who looked and/or behaved in ways that were "too Jewish." When told I didn't "look Jewish," I replied "Thank you.". . . In brief, I had learned to internalize societal attitudes of disgust at those who were "too Jewish"; I had learned to hate who I was, and I did not even know it.

Penny began the process of reclaiming her Jewish heritage, her sacred face, by reading the works of Jewish women that filled her with stories that she related to. In summing up and reflecting on how this relates to her spirituality she noted,

My spirituality is all about how I relate to my world and others', how I make meaning of life. From Jewish prophetic tradition and mysticism (via the Kabbalah) comes the concept of "tikkun olam" or the repair and healing of the world. This aptly expresses my core motivation in life, towards social justice, towards creating a life that is meaningful and makes a difference. I believe I get this from my Jewishness/Judaism, which for me is a blend of culture and spirituality.

This blend of culture and spirituality embodied in the Jewish concept of "tikkun olam" not only motivates her activism, it has also motivated the healing of her own world, the healing of her own spirit, in confronting and dealing directly with her own internalized oppression.

Spirituality and Mediating Among Multiple Identities

As many participants discussed, we are not only people of a particular ethnic group, we also have a gender, a class or religious background, and a sexual orientation, and several participants discussed the role of spirituality in mediating among these multiple identities. Harriet, a forty-eight-year-old nurse and adult educator, is a case in point. Harriet is a community activist, a white woman from a rural Southern, working-class background who grew up in the Pentecostal Church, where she went to church four times per week. In considering the intersection of class, religious background, and culture, she reflected back, noting, "It [her religious upbringing] has to be understood in the context of being your culture. It's not your religion or spirituality, because it's everything you *are* and what you *do* and *how you live your life*. . . . It's your way of life!" While she didn't have much class consciousness growing up, in reflecting back, she noted, "Pentecostal folks are pretty poor people."

It was in this religious/cultural/class context where Harriet, who found meaning and identity in these intersections, began to wrestle with another important aspect of her identity: her sexual orientation. In her early twenties, she talked to many ministers and church people, who alternately made her feel guilty and hopeful, and one finally suggested to "leave it up to God." Harriet described a pivotal experience that happened about a year later, where she experienced what she believed was a healing after a sports injury, and explained that it helped her come to terms with her lesbian identity. "Why would God heal me, if I was this person that was condemned to hell?" God wouldn't do that for me, and I thought "OK, this is my sign that it's OK for me to be a lesbian."

While this particular experience was a significant turning point for Harriet, in terms of her own acceptance of her lesbian sexual identity, she knew she was not going to find public acceptance for it in the Pentecostal Church. Yet in her heart, the authenticity of her identity, confirmed through what she describes as this particularly significant spiritual experience, gave her the courage to embrace who she is and, over time, to ultimately develop a positive identity as a lesbian, and one that resulted in her considerable activism, not only around lesbian and gay issues, but around race, class, and gender issues. Over the years, she has developed a more positive spirituality that has helped her mediate among these identities that inform all her activism.

Harriet has lived in the same community her whole life. While communities never remain static and are always changing incrementally, the cultural context in which she was negotiating various aspects of her identity remained relatively stable—at least much more so than if she had moved to a different geographical area. But those who are immigrants to North America (or elsewhere) generally negotiate various aspects of their identity and their spirituality against the backdrop of a very different cultural context than that of their home countries. Aiysha is a Muslim woman of East Indian descent, born in East Africa, and after living in Africa, England, Canada, she immigrated to the United States in her late teens. Moving a number of times and having to negotiate being a member of a privileged group in some contexts but being a member of an oppressed or lower-status group in other contexts has made Aiysha negotiate her own shifting identity in a constantly shifting cultural context. These moves and identity shifts that are a part of her personal life experience, along with the fact that Aiysha is a professor with a subspecialty in multicultural issues, has forced her to think a lot about the development of her religious and cultural identity as an immigrant and a Muslim in the United States. In describing the connection between her ethnic identity and her religious identity, she noted,

Being of East Indian origin AND a Muslim, not only here in the U.S. but everywhere I've lived, has served as a double reinforcement of my otherness. In some cases, for me it's a question of privilege. For example, in Africa where we were, there's no doubt that the Indian population was part of the business population, whereas in London, I was definitely NOT part of the privileged class. In terms of societal structures, I identified a lot more with the lower classes, and came to the U.S. with a thick cockney accent.

In being both an ethnic minority and a religious minority but as one who is educated with a doctoral degree and has both education and class privilege in the United States, Aiysha has developed the ability to cross cultural borders to be able to speak to many different groups and in many different contexts fairly comfortably at this point in her adult life. But developing this ability has been a process that has taken time, as there had always been subtle pressures to blend in. She gave the example of how this had been manifested earlier in her life. In her Muslim community, occasions of joy are often marked with the application of henna. "In the past I would think very carefully of where I was going on the past two or three weeks, before putting on henna, I now do not hesitate to do it," she explained. At this point in her development, she does not try to blend in, but rather uses those occasions when people ask what she has on her hands as a point of education about Islam and about her East Indian ethnic heritage. She described how this shift has taken place over time, and reflected on being both Muslim and East Indian:

Before it was just a matter of fact for me. Now, it's still a matter of fact, but it's also a matter of pride. I've taken the attitude "This is WHO I AM. If you are going to know me and like me, you're going to know the whole of me, not just parts of me." So in a sense the dichotomization of my identity that I described at the beginning, I'm beginning to take that and create a whole from it in the way that I interact.

Aiysha attributes the shift that's taken place over time to formal education that has partly focused on the negotiation of cultural and religious difference, positive personal experiences where she was deliberately in religious and culturally pluralistic situations that allowed her to experiment with being more overt with these aspects of her identity, and to the experience of becoming a parent. But this sense of "the whole" is related to her spirituality, which is tremendously important to her. Like Harriet, and nearly all the participants in the study, Aiysha has drawn on her spirituality and her growing sense of her "authentic" and more centered self to mediate among these multiple identities.

CONCLUSIONS: TOWARD A CULTURALLY RESPONSIVE EDUCATIONAL PSYCHOLOGY PRACTICE

So what does this suggest for culturally responsive teaching and educational psychology practice? It seems that for all participants in this study, the claiming of the "sacred face" was key to developing a positive cultural identity. Participants discussed the spiritual search for wholeness, by both embracing their own cultural identity by dealing with their own internalized oppression and through the experience of crossing cultural borders, and finding what was of spiritual value that was more prevalent in cultures other than their own. Neither spirituality nor cultural context were "background noise" to their ongoing identity development as has been traditionally conceptualized in educational psychology. Rather, both were interconnected and absolutely central to the reclaiming of their cultural identity through dealing with their internalized oppression.

While space limitations don't allow for further discussion of these findings which are discussed in depth elsewhere (Tisdell, 2003), there are some specific implications for practice. These educators also attempted to draw on their own spirituality in their own teaching by developing opportunities for students "to claim their sacred face" in developing culturally responsive educational practices, not so much by talking directly about spirituality but in ways they conducted their classes. On the basis of their responses and my own experience of attempting to do this, some general guidelines for the implications of practice include the following seven principles or elements of a spiritually grounded and culturally responsive teaching and educational psychology practice:

1. An emphasis on authenticity of teachers and students (both spiritual and cultural)
2. An environment that allows for the exploration of:
   • the cognitive (through readings and discussion of ideas)
   • the affective and relational (through connection with other people and of ideas to life experience)
   • the symbolic (through artform—poetry, art, music, drama)
3. Readings that reflect the cultures of the members of the class, and the cultural pluralism of the geographical area relevant to the course content
4. Exploration of individual and communal dimensions of cultural and other dimensions of identity
5. Collaborative work that envisions and presents manifestations of multiple dimensions of learning and strategies for change
6. Celebration of learning and provision for closure to the course
7. Recognition of the limitations of the classroom, and that transformation is an ongoing process that takes time

Clearly, every educator or educational psychologist needs to determine for herself or himself how he or she can implement such principles in practice, in light of her or his educational context and cultural identity. In the remainder of this discussion, I will very briefly explore how I do this in teaching teachers in graduate higher-education settings as a white woman concerned about cultural issues, and as one who believes it is possible to attend to spirituality, although I tend to be somewhat implicit in my attention to it.

An important aspect of learning is creating a space. Thus for my classes that deal with cultural issues, or adult learning, I bring symbols of the elements of the world—earth, wind, fire, and water, because learning takes place in the context of our life experience in the world, and these symbols can serve as a reminder of that, and implicitly takes learning to what the heart of spirituality is about—the interconnectedness of all things. I am also trying to set up an environment where students will explore the meaning that they map to symbol, so that learning through symbol, and affect, as well as the obvious academic readings can be a part of the learning environment right from the beginning. I also begin each class with a brief check-in of joys and difficulties that have been a part of the learning lives they've had since the last time we met. This five-minute activity is an attempt to create a learning community that honors the life experiences of the learners.

I usually begin my own classes that focus on cultural issues with an assignment where learners write aspects of their own cultural story. Stories touch our hearts and put a human face on the world of ideas. Thus learners' initial assignment will include story readings, and a written assignment of analyzing aspects of their own story (with some guidelines) related to the content., such as how their own awareness of their cultural identity developed. In particular, they describe their culture of origin in terms of their race, ethnicity, religion, and class background; the cultural mix of the communities in which they grew up; what messages they received about themselves and "others" through both the overt curriculum and the hidden curriculum in schools and in other institutions; who important cultural role models were for them. In essence, in this initial assignment, I am attempting to pose questions that might help them think about how their cultural consciousness developed, and the role of social structures in shaping their identity and their thinking. I try to model this by sharing some of my own story. In particular, as a white woman trying to deal with cultural issues, I discuss pivotal points in my own ongoing understanding of what it means to be white, as a system of privilege, and how it interacts with my Irish Catholic female cultural upbringing, and how I am still very much working on this. Sometimes I share a poem, or a song, that has been meaningful. My intent is to encourage students to do the same in their own writing: to use critical analysis and their creativity in analyzing their own stories relative to the larger society.

I rarely use the term *spirituality* in my classes. But at a point in the class, I ask them to bring or create a symbol of their cultural identity. Often, their use of art, poetry, music, and other artform and use of this cultural symbol touches on the spiritual for some people, and encourages it to be present in the classroom. Others don't map to such activities in that way, but whether or not one experiences something as "spiritual" depends on the learner. Furthermore, learners also generally do a collaborative teaching presentation on a particular subject. They use multiple modes of knowledge production in their presentations. They often incorporate the spiritual and cultural, as well as the affective and analytical in these presentations, that is grounded in their own cultural experience, and suggestions for social change. This ensures its cultural responsiveness. In closing, we often make use of some of what they created throughout the course in a final activity that hints at a ritual through use of song, poetry, dance, art, and ideas from significant reading in stating our intent of next steps for action; after all, there are limits to what can be accomplished in any given education context, including in higher education where I teach.

In conclusion, it is clear that it is time for the field of educational psychology to continue to move forward from its historically positivist underpinnings that paid little attention to gender or culture, to not only attend to these issues but to consider how culture interconnects with spirituality. Furthermore, a culturally responsive educational psychology and teaching practice that attends to spirituality by drawing on the role of imagination, and how people construct knowledge through image and symbol, which is always expressed through culture, can facilitate continued development and continued healing, both individually and in the larger world. It is a way of drawing on spirituality, and engaging the "sacred face," without ever necessarily using the "s" (spirituality) word. By helping learners engage in multiple dimensions of knowing by attending to the individual, the cultural, political, the historical, and sacred faces that affect their own and others' ongoing identity development, there is a greater chance that education will become transformative, both personally and collectively. It is not, however, learning based strictly on the rationalistic and individualistic assumptions of Descartes, "I think, therefore I am." Rather, as my colleague Derise Tolliver of DePaul University says, it is based on the collective insights of the African proverb and spiritual traditions that offer some collective wisdom for the building and sustaining of community and the work of social transformation: "I AM because WE ARE: WE ARE, therefore I AM." Perhaps, drawing on this collective wisdom helps all of us begin to claim a sacred face, and can also contribute to a more culturally responsive and holistic view of teaching and educational psychology.

REFERENCES

Abalos, D. (1998). *La Communidad Latina in the United States*. Westport, CT: Praeger.

Astin, A. (2004). Why spirituality deserves a central place in liberal education. *Liberal Education*, 90 (2), 34–41.

Cross, W. (1971). Toward a psychology of black liberation. The Negro-to-Black convergence experience. *Black World*, 20(9), 13–27.

Fine, M. (1998). Working the hyphens. In N. Denzin and Y. Lincoln (Eds.), *The Landscape of Qualitative Research* (pp. 130–155). Newbury Park, CA: Sage.

Fowler, J. (1981). *Stages of Faith: The Psychology of Human Development and the Quest for Meaning*. San Francisco: Harper and Row.

Glazer, S. (Ed.). (1999). *The Heart of Learning: Spirituality in Education*. New York: Putnam.

Hays, P. (2001). *Addressing Cultural Complexities in Practice: A Framework for Clinicians and Counselors*. Washington, DC: APA Press.

hooks, b. (2000). *All About Love*. New York: William Morrow.

Merriam, S. B. (1998). *Qualitative Research and Case Study Applications in Education*. San Francisco: Jossey-Bass Publishers.

Palmer, P. (1998). *The Courage to Teach*. San Francisco: Jossey-Bass.

Parks, S. (2000). *Big Questions, Worthy Dreams*. San Francisco: Jossey-Bass.

Tisdell, E. (2003). *Exploring Spirituality and Culture in Adult and Higher Education*. San Francisco: Jossey-Bass.

CHAPTER 52

Beyond Readiness: New Questions about Cultural Understandings and Developmental Appropriateness

LISE BIRD CLAIBORNE

When is a student "ready" to learn? The notion that teachers should try to gauge each student's readiness for learning was once a central concern of educators, one that educational psychologists were well placed to comment on. Although this concern is less likely to be voiced aloud these days, theories of human development are still seen as relevant to classroom learning and are discussed in most educational psychology textbooks. In this chapter I look at expectations that a child of a certain age "should" be able to accomplish particular tasks. Questions can be raised about these expectations that have implications for work in schools. The field of educational psychology will be defined broadly as both an academic discipline and as the domain of teachers and school psychologists who work with students experiencing learning or behavioral difficulties (see Bird, 1999b). The questions raised here have no simple answers, but they may provide new insights for readers' own reflections on their own and others' development.

The notion of readiness refers to the idea that each student's capability is to some extent determined by his or her level of development. As children mature, they are expected to improve in all aspects of their learning, progressing day by day in a straightforward, linear march. The timetable of improvements might include an expectation that a six-year-old should be able to master the basics of reading or that a nine-year-old should become efficient in multiplication. Because not all children learn at the same rate, there is the further assumption that most children will fit into the performance expected in their age group, while a minority of students will progress more slowly or quickly than others.

It may be useful to begin with a sporting metaphor to describe the notion of developmental readiness. Imagine the teacher as both a coach and a race official for the student who is a runner in a long-distance race. The ideal teacher runs alongside the runner, shouting encouragements and also handing over crucial materials at just the right time. The teacher-coach must judge the right moment to hand over a cup of water or sports drink. If the teacher is too early in handing over the drink, the student may not be able to swallow, while if the teacher is too slow the student may collapse from dehydration. At the end of the race the teacher also becomes the official who declares who has won the race, who has completed it competently for his or her age group, and who might need extra help to become a good runner. The teacher's job is to try to gauge the readiness of the student to receive the next input from the teacher, the "right moment" in which the student will be receptive to knowledge that will stretch him or her—not too little nor too much—to new learning.

The foundation for these expectations of what a child can learn at a particular age is in theories about human development. These can be useful, but they also have problematic assumptions. These will be outlined below, before some alternatives are considered.

THE DEVELOPING CHILD

These days most educational psychology textbooks do not presume to tell teachers how to spot the right moment for a child to learn a particular skill or piece of knowledge. However, most contemporary educational psychology textbooks have chapters on development, emphasizing theorists such as Jean Piaget, Lev Vygotsky, Erik Erikson, Urie Bronfenbrenner, and Lawrence Kohlberg. (More detailed descriptions of these theorists can be found in textbooks on human development.) The idea of "readiness" was probably cemented in place with the use of Piaget's theory in the training of several generations of teachers from the mid–twentieth century. Piaget developed an account of the child's cognitive progress that had its origins in a biological account of human intellectual functioning. He considered that the child's logic—the way of seeing and being in the world—shifts as the child grows older. He outlined four big qualitative shifts, referring to these as the stages of sensorimotor, preoperational, concrete, and formal operational thinking.

Originally a biologist, Piaget was interested in the unfolding competencies of all children over time as an interaction between the child's physiology and the surrounding environment. He was not interested in schemes to "accelerate" the speed at which the child would acquire various concepts, because he thought there were many interconnected processes that had to improve together to make changes. Advancement on one set of skills would not, in his theoretical account, be likely to accelerate the child's whole cognitive structuring (called schemes) in a particular stage. So training in learning to measure the amount of water in different-sized glasses would not, in his view, improve the child's overall competence at a concrete operational task such as understanding that the volume of water in a glass does not change just because it is poured into a different-shaped container.

Piaget's theory was a contrast to earlier views of development that relied more heavily on notions of biological maturation. Arnold Gesell (e.g. Gesell & Ilg, 1949) argued that development followed a maturational timetable set by genetic factors. Piaget focused more on the interaction between maturational factors and their shaping by the child's physical and, to a lesser extent social, milieu. His idea of readiness was based on the maturational unfolding of the child's skills over time due to a genetic timetable, but with environmental factors intertwined at every point.

Much research since the 1980s has attempted to test the limits of Piaget's theory. It now seems that children may achieve Piagetian developmental tasks such as object permanence at a much earlier age than previously envisioned (e.g. Baillargeon & DeVos, 1991). There has also been considerable critique of the notion of stages in Piaget's theory. So, while generations of students still memorize the Piagetian stage sequence, these are less likely to be the basis of contemporary developmental research. Knowledge of Piaget's views of changes in thinking could be helpful for teachers and educational psychologists for particular purposes, such as in working with a refugee child whose background and skills are unknown. The child's performance on a Piagetian task might give important clues about the kinds of experience and education the child has had so far. But it would probably not be helpful in a comparison of that child to the "average" child of the same age in their new classroom, because a single measure might not give a wide enough view of all the child understands.

The work of Lev Vygotsky has in many ways succeeded that of Piaget in popularity. In education, Vygotsky's notion of the zone of proximal development ('ZPD') has become a central notion, especially in the popularization of the term *scaffolding*. The ZPD is defined as the individual child's sphere of competent action with others that stretches the possibilities beyond what the child can do alone. An example of the zone might be the difference between what a particular child of a certain age could do with a set of blocks and what the child could accomplish with hints from an older child or adult helping the child. In this theory readiness can be seen as finding activities within the ZPD for the child, in other words, expanding the child's competence by a certain amount, not too small nor too great, to be effective.

CRITICISMS OF DEVELOPMENT: IMPLICATIONS FOR EDUCATIONAL PSYCHOLOGY

Most theories of human development share three assumptions that have implications for the concept of readiness to learn: (1) that processes and achievements are *universal* in all children, regardless of circumstance or culture; (2) that the *individual* person is the main unit of concern; and (3) that development is *progressive*, or that each child improves over time through a set sequence of positive changes. These assumptions about development have been taken to task by a number of critical writers. These criticisms have interesting implications for people interested in the ways that children's learning changes over time.

The first problem is the idea that children's development can be described with reference to universal principles. Developmental psychology has been criticized for its practices of normative regulation through notions such as "timetables" and "milestones" for talking and walking, or its emphasis on "age-appropriate" behaviors. These expectations, which have come from particular dominant middle-class cultural perspectives in Europe and the United States, may unintentionally create strong normative pressures for children living in many other cultures to "act their age." Every culture may have its own unique views of the timetable of milestones a child is expected to achieve as they grow older. For example, Goodnow et al. (1984) showed how differently Anglo- and Lebanese Australian mothers viewed the appropriate ages for children to act independently on such tasks as answering the phone or walking to a local store alone. However, in our current era of vigilance about crime and terrorism in countries such as the United States or Israel, "appropriate" ages for independent moves by a child might be increasing. In that case, the age of "readiness" may be largely shaped by social factors.

An example of mismatched cultural expectations could involve an educational psychologist working with an indigenous Australian child living in a tribal area in a central desert. If that psychologist expected the child to classify family members into a "family tree" pattern along the lines of some of Piaget's work, such testing could create a *colonizing* scrutiny of the child's actions. In other words, that minority child's reality would be measured against a standard set by the dominant culture (i.e., educated, middle-class, Euro-American researchers). Furthermore, such tests have in the past been used as a means for *regulating* what is considered acceptable or normal in the classroom. An example might be a classroom exercise that involves drawing or writing about family members, when there is a social norm (expectation) that most families consist of two married parents and their children (even if the nuclear family is no longer the statistical majority). A child whose parents are recently separated or who is from an alternative family structure might not feel confident about describing his or her own family in class. That child's silence could be an example of the subtle ways that our behavior is regulated by certain (hidden) expectations about what is considered "normal." This does not mean that all testing is bad; instead it suggests that we need to keep in mind the wider context involved in the creation of tests (and our own involvement with tests) and the way they might be used to mark a child's progress.

How does this apply to the notion of readiness? A problem with universal ideas about human development is that one way of learning or doing things is seen as normal, or natural, which implies that any other way is automatically less valid. This happens through a logical device known as a *dualism*. In western thinking since the Greek philosopher Aristotle, there has been a tendency to understand the world by dividing ideas into two opposing camps. In other words, knowledge about anything is divided in two (e.g. good versus bad, strong versus weak), with nothing in between. The idea that forms of development can be cleanly divided into the "normal" and "abnormal," or "natural" and "unnatural" or artificial, is based on a dualism that oversimplifies the diversity of development.

Beliefs about "natural" forms of development have been debated for well over a century. For example, Lewis Terman, the popularizer of the standardized intelligence test, did not think that children should be "pushed" to develop, as that would be like "pruning a tree to hasten its fruit" (Terman, 1905, p. 147; his talents were obviously not in horticulture!). He considered that talents should emerge at their own pace (i.e., when the child was "ready" to display them), and he was critical of school practices that might accelerate the child's formal acquisition of knowledge ahead of the "natural" unfolding of the child's learning. Terman later became famous for conducting one of the first large studies of "gifted children," children he considered to be naturally faster in the development of their learning for their age group. His emphasis on development proceeding at a "natural" pace was based on an assumption that the pace was greatly determined by genetic inheritance. More recently in the field of the gifted and talented there has been wider acknowledgement of the special supports that many talented people have had in their lives (e.g., Bloom, 1985) as well as of the diversity of pathways that people with talent may take (see Mistry & Rogoff, 1985). So the whole notion that there is one universal path of development, that some children fly ahead while others trudge behind, lacks sensitivity to the diversity of cultural expressions of development.

A second problem with theories of development is that they tend to have a narrow focus on the *individual* person. This may be a reflection of a particular Euro-American cultural viewpoint. There have been a number of critiques in psychology about the individualism of U.S. culture (e.g., Sampson, 1984; Scheman, 1983). Rather than focus on interconnections between people and collective aspects of culture, Americans have been described as focusing on the individual as an independent person. This focus downplays the importance of wider social forces such as families and the ways that each person's achievements may be intertwined with the efforts of others. These criticisms have been around a long time; John Dewey expressed worry about American individualism in the 1920s (Dewey, 1962). Some cultures have a more collective focus on group processes in development. In my own teaching of human development in Aotearoa, New Zealand, Samoan students have commented on the strangeness of studying infancy as a specific period in life, without considering the ways that infant and mother or caregiver may be together most of the time (see also Bradley, 1989).

A third problem in developmental theories is the notion that there is only one straightforward path of *progressive improvement* from immaturity to maturity, from infancy to adulthood. At the turn of the twentieth century, this view was linked with a stereotypical view of Darwin's theory of evolution (Morss, 1990), which supposedly created a single ladder of all species, with lowly ferns near the bottom and an ascension upwards through reptiles, birds, and mammals to human beings at the top. In fact, Darwin was more interested in a widely branched family tree of species without assuming that some species were better than others because they had lasted longer (see Gould, 1977). In this stereotypic view, infants are seen as lacking the skills of children, children as lacking the skills of adolescents, and teens lacking the full maturity of adults. John Morss (1990) suggested that Darwin's evolutionary theory has been used to give enormous scientific credibility to the idea that each individual human advances in development over time, from an earlier state that is somehow lacking to a satisfactory maturity.

Stereotyped views of evolution were also used to support the view, earlier in the twentieth century, that gifted children might somehow be the best of what evolution could offer, while children (e.g., with disabilities) who took longer to learn the same ideas might be at an evolutionary disadvantage (Gould, 1977). Elsewhere I have written about both the gendered and cultural biases in contemporary notions of "competence," particularly academic competence, connected with some of these ideas about development (Bird, 1999a). The whole notion that some children are "slower" than others is based on overuse of a single, linear scale to compare children. That linear scale (or ladder) is a misuse of Darwin's evolutionary ideas that were intended to apply only to species, not to individuals.

More recently, Morss (1996) has suggested that one of the ideas underlying the belief that human development has a linear path aimed toward constant progress is its inherent *modernism*. Much has been written about the way beliefs about the world as "modern" are part of our focus on the future, that leads to a valuing of new technologies as the way to overcome problems, of progress at any cost, along with a denigration of "tradition" and any lessening of consumer purchasing. There is a large body of literature criticizing modernism as a discourse with implications for the planet (e.g., Hall et al., 1992). French historian Michel Foucault (1977) used the term *discourse* to refer to the way a particular construction of reality shapes the views recognizable in a society, although the discourse's operations are likely to be subtle and hidden from our perceptions. For example, both Erica Burman (1994) and Valerie Walkerdine (1984) have written about ways that developmental psychology is involved in the regulation of the ways that individual children and families can "be," through the kinds of decisions made by early childhood teachers or family service professionals who draw on the language of developmental theories in reproducing a certain kind of reality with all its consequences. Discourses indicate the ways that the power of language and established habits maintain a certain "obvious" view of reality that seems "natural" and hence difficult to question. We become constrained by such ways of viewing the world, even if we try to identify and resist the discourses that make up our lives, because they are made up of so many little everyday practices, speech, and actions. "The modern" is an example of a discourse that seems ubiquitous even today. Though I can write critically about modernism, I also find it difficult not to get taken in by such views because they are so pervasive and subtle. For example, I might try to get students to avoid racist comments by urging them to take a more "up-to-date, modern" view of teaching, just as I might find myself complementing someone on their "modern" kitchen renovation. This particularly "Western" perspective on change (that everything is getting bigger and better) can be contrasted with a view—perhaps more central in many traditional cultures—that the child is interesting, valuable, and basically alright as she or he is, at any given moment, not just in the sense of a future potential.

In my view there is considerable healthy questioning of modernism in education, particularly in the special education or disability studies field. A focus on speedy learning traps us into a focus on each individual's path of progress as though each student were a unified, knowable quantity—if only the perceptive educational psychologist could determine that child's level of functioning. Doubts about speed have important implications for the notion of readiness. Instead of the teacher (or school psychologist) attempting to track where a child is on some linear scale of development, in order to push them along to advance as quickly as possible, the teacher might instead be still listening to the unique sounds and watching the ways the child moves in the group of students. The five-year-old who does not yet speak might no longer be described as having abnormalities in development, but as having many ways of communicating and being in the world that are a joy to her parents or caregivers. In other words, that child may be fully appreciated "as she is," and as being on an unusual yet nonetheless satisfying trajectory through life, even if it does not look like the path predicted in a developmental textbook. In my experience, teachers and psychologists do appreciate children's uniqueness, but I think there are also likely to be contradictory expectations that the child will improve at a particular pace, to develop, to *fit in* to a display of speech often found in a "typical five-year-old."

READINESS IN CONTEMPORARY PRACTICE

I do not want to downplay the importance of the concept of readiness for practitioners. I have been involved in teaching and supporting child therapists in training. As one senior clinician said to me, "It's important for clinical trainees to know what "normal" is so that when a disturbed child comes to them they can know what to do." I felt uncomfortable being the arbiter of what is "normal" in child development, because there may be so many different cultural views about what is acceptable.

At present I am interviewing small groups of educational psychologists in the field in New Zealand. Such professionals work in a variety of settings, as external consultants for schools or within schools, but their government-mandated focus is on students identified with the most pressing learning or emotional difficulties. (For an overview of special education provisions and their place in the wider education system see New Zealand Ministry of Education, 2004). Instead of using the word *normal* to indicate the child's fit into a standard classroom, most psychologists used the word *regular*. This simple difference in terminology suggests a focus on the wider situation rather than on an individual child. Rather than concentrate on changing the acting-out or slower-reading child to "fit" the classroom, these psychologists spend much of their time coordinating the links across various groups, such as the extended family, social workers, child and youth services, teachers, principals, teaching assistants, special resource teachers for learning and behavioral difficulties, and perhaps the police. What particular groups will be involved depends on the particular issues for the student, such as whether their current difficulties are described as "behavioral" or disability-related. So the focus is not on changing the child to be more "normal" to fit the "standard" (unchanged) classroom, but on stretching the understandings and expectations of all involved with the student. This idea of a two-way process in which the student better fits the school and the school accommodates to better serve the student is called *inclusion*. However, inclusion is an ideal that can be elusive in practice. I would like to take these professionals' views on board in next presenting some alternative ways to think about the students' development and their "readiness" for learning.

ALTERNATIVE CONCEPTIONS OF DEVELOPMENT AND READINESS

We have looked at criticisms of modernism in developmental theories, with its assumption that there will be forward progress over time in the student's development. Critics have presented some alternative perspectives beyond the modern, which collectively could be called "postmodern." (Here "post" refers to questioning of modernism rather than to a later, more advanced stage.) A postmodern perspective on development that questions the universal, linear, individual path of development might emphasize a multiplicity of possible paths for a life-course full of interconnections with other people.

There are alternative perspectives on development that eschew universal principles in favor of principles defined flexibly depending on their context, and which include room for local cultural concerns. In a our search for an approach to human development that would be sensitive to the multiple perspectives that can be found in Aotearoa, New Zealand, including indigenous cultural views, Wendy Drewery and I (Drewery and Bird, 2004) emphasized a number of developmental principles framed as dualisms that could be used by professionals and questioned at the same time. We built on some of the traditional dualisms that have been considered in developmental theory. For example, "nature" (genetic inheritance) was contrasted with "nurture" (everything else), universal features were contrasted with the local and particular, and the idea of development as change that is continuous and almost imperceptible was contrasted with the view that change is abrupt and noticeable ("discontinuous"). In addition to these, we contrasted single causal descriptions of development (such as saying a child's attention problems were due to a particular gene) to multiple, multidirectional influences (e.g., considering a variety of factors such as genes, nutrition, parenting expectations, and cultural norms about activity levels for each gender). We also contrasted the linear view of maturation as knowable in advance with a view of development that emphasizes a plurality of outcomes and that acknowledges that we may show different kinds of maturity (and be different kinds of people) in different situations. We argued that this approach, presenting dualisms and then questioning and reflecting on them, is more likely to be sensitive to a range of cultural understandings.

An example of how this might work in practice could be useful here. In my own work as an academic educational psychologist, I attend an annual examiner's meeting at which graduate students' final grades are determined. Over the years there has been an encouraging shift in our deliberations. At first there were serious discussions about whether students are "able" or not, whether they have reached the peak of their development as thinkers, as though they could all be compared as being on a single ladder of development from average to gifted. Later, after considerable comment by several staff, there was more complex discussion about mitigating circumstances, about different cultural priorities in the use of time, and about different kinds of motivation. Lately this has gone further, to include humorous references to the regulations that require us to determine the "quality of mind" of students. I think this indicates a wider cultural shift away from the belief in a single, universal ladder of developmental (and evolutionary) progress in which some people end up right at the top and most others a few rungs further down.

I would like to add one more theoretical alternative here, in my search for new perspectives on human development. Recently Roy (2003) argued that educators could explore new creative possibilities by using the work of postmodern philosopher Gilles Deleuze and his collaborator, the political psychoanalyst Felix Guattari. For me there are tremendous possibilities for "development" in this approach. Within the framework of these theoretical ideas, the student is no longer seen as an individual completely knowable or identifiable in terms of family background, test scores, "developmental level," ethnicity, gender, impairment, or typical behavior or appearance. Instead, all the different aspects of personhood (ontology) are seen as fragments that may be combined in various ways to make a diverse collection or "assemblage" (Delueze and Guattari, 1987), depending on the desires emergent in a particular culture and era and locality. An example might be the kind of desire teachers may have for the productive, cheerful, rational student who participates confidently in classroom activities; this desire may emerge in various industrial-ized countries as a specific hope about "good students" and "successful education." In different countries there may be different desires; for example, the good student sought may be one who demonstrates quiet obedience and respect for elders. (Of course there is great diversity among teachers in every country about these values.)

Another metaphor may be useful here, although it is difficult to pin down concrete examples that follow from Deleuze's philosophy. Instead of the teacher standing beside the road while the runner goes by, there might be a grouping that links the forward movement of all the runners moving in a mob with the bodies of those on the sidelines urging them on. Instead of focusing on the right moment of "readiness" to hand over the sports drink for a single runner, another collection might form around thirst, water, movement, a human reliance on moisture that links us all (literally, genetically) to tortoises and camels living in the desert, to children "being Roadrunner," on and on in an appreciation for water, which is the core of life.

The idea of an assemblage can also be applied to the classroom. There might be linkages across various students in a classroom, for example, in terms of sets of eyes bent studiously over papers on a desk, linked with eyes of all kinds of office workers in jobs requiring similar, literate concentration, and further outwards to the technologies of desks and chairs, to spines that work in particular ways in humans (and related species), a loose grouping that unites a host of disparate things for that moment of concentration. Deleuze might refer to that moment as centered on a desire, rather than in terms of knowledge or skills that some students might lack while others might have in abundance.

Deleuze's view of desire is wide and positive, having possibilities for new beginnings. For me, this very unusual theory offers a view of the "inclusive" classroom that is quite different to that which is based on a grouping of individual bodies that can be placed on a ladder that ascends from "slow learner" to "average" to "gifted." All the eyes focusing well would instead, in a Deleuzian view, be on the same "line of flight" or trajectory toward a certain kind of work, while those drifting off into reverie, or having trouble focusing, might be on a different creative path.

A concrete example could be useful here. A child with autism provides some challenges to developmental theories and expectations about the path to maturity. The "autistic" child staring in fascination at leaves of a tree moving against the window and then at the pattern on the paper on his desk might be part of that "good student" assemblage for a time, as all the eyes in the room are linked to papers on desks, and through to the textbooks writers and all those knowledges that link together; but then eyes move off, the assemblage reshaping into something different. For me, this is not just a fanciful way of talking about differences and education, but also a radically new way of thinking about students' competencies and capacities. It is based on a particular line of philosophical thinking that considers that what a body is capable of is not what the body is made of but what it can do at any particular time. For me, personally, there is sometimes a feeling of despair, as I see a child with autism "lost" on some other planet, laughing to himself at who knows what, showing excitement all of a sudden, "cause unknown." On one occasion I searched in some panic for a boy who had wandered off from a group visiting a house. I rushed out the front door and looked up and down the street, but there was no sign of him. Then I heard some noise on the top floor of the house and went upstairs to find him standing stock still, seemingly staring "at nothing." Then a wise and special educator suggested to me, "it's the clock: I think he's staring at the clock." Why would someone who does not speak or "tell time" look at a clock for several minutes? If I turn to Piaget or Vygotsky I am left only with some lack in the child's development of knowledge. But there are other possibilities, linking clocks/time/ticking noises, the little machine that we all stare at (collection of eyes pointed to the display), and then all of a sudden we speed up, picking things up and running for the door (hands, legs, speed, tick, tick, such a precise little sound, like the refrigerator slowing down on a hot day, like the car engine when it is turned off)—in other words, perhaps, making for the moment a larger, more encompassing assemblage that includes a range of things across different bodies and other objects. To consider clocks, time, and rushing movement is to begin to bring together an interesting collection that could include the work ethic, the industrial revolution, the globalization of the world economy, and the teacher accountability movement; in other words a range of linked items from the very small object to larger social forces.

WHERE TO FOR READINESS?

I do not mean to imply here that a focus on development is wrong, because in most cases a single teacher may be working with a number of students and attempting to give each child tasks that "stretch" them beyond the skills and ideas already accomplished. It is the larger cultural "script" about appropriate times and ages that I think we could reflect on more tentatively and with greater openness.

So what does this mean for a perspective on developmental readiness? Most teachers have probably already experienced some sense of "postmodern" fragmentation in dealing with students who might differ from day to day depending on all kinds of things outside the school's doors. Janey, a middle-class Puerto Rican ten-year-old who was so involved in reading a book about insects yesterday, may be listless, lost in some unknowable thoughts today, while fourteen-year-old Damien, from a poor German/English background, may show intense enthusiasms about sports that are never seen in his math classes. Instead of seeing these children as bodies moving up and down daily on a hierarchy of school success (dipping more over time toward the "dropout" end), their passions, desires, and knowledges could be part of a larger assemblage beyond an individual body. Janey instead is hooked into the collective world of insects and forest ecology, while Damien is linked with the eyes and twitching hands and feet of soccer players on the field or on a videogame screen.

Let's return to the teacher, assisting the student in a footrace from the sidelines, on standby with the water or orange juice, trying to find just the right moment of "readiness" in the runner's progress to pass on what was needed to speed the runner's progress. Given some of the issues raised by postmodern and cultural questions about development, this imaginary teacher might leave the runners and see herself choreographing a village fair or school sports day in which there are multiple activities going on at the same time, with all kinds of different goals and achievements. Instead of focusing on an individual on a solitary path of development, the teacher might instead be part of a team of adults that includes parents and caregivers, extended family, social workers, ministers, educational psychologists, medical staff, youth aid workers and perhaps many others who know these particular students and their siblings. All these adults might be there on the school playground among students of all ages—such as might be painted by Pieter Breughel, the sixteenth-century Dutch painter of crowded village scenes. This may be a picture of school life you already have in mind, quite in keeping with the hectic nature of life these days, rather than the soft-focus lens aiming toward the single teacher and student working together.

Of course at the end of the day teachers and school psychologists must write reports commenting on the progress of individual students, perhaps suggesting interventions to students and their parents and caregivers. This reality of individual scrutiny, often with comparison to some linear timeline of developmental appropriateness, cannot be waved away so easily. It is difficult to know what Deleuze and Guattari might have said to educational psychologists, but their work is—if anything—unashamedly pragmatic and cognizant of the constraints people operate under. One possibility is that in the writing of the report, or in the filing of the case notes on a difficult student, there is much more than a positive statement about a student's potential. There could also be greater openness, and acceptance of the mysterious unknowability of all the lines of flight that might characterize the different developmental paths people happen along. Writing that report could be seen in a negative light, as taking all those flying fragments, those fragile possibilities, and turning them into rigid concrete. Deleuze and Guattari might then point to new lines of flight taking off from that very moment, whole new collections of interconnected possibilities emerging under, through, beside the concrete as the student looks at another student, and the teacher, and smiles. It's really just the beginning of the story, but one often very difficult for any of us to see.

ACKNOWLEDGMENT

I would like to thank Carol Hamilton for helpful comments on an earlier draft of this chapter.

REFERENCES

Baillargeon, R., and DeVos, J. (1991). Object permanence in young infants: Further evidence. *Child Development*, 62, 1227–1246.

Bird, L. (1999a). Feminist questions about children's competence. *Educational and Child Psychology*, 16(2), 17–26.

———. (1999b). Towards a more critical educational psychology. *Annual Review of Critical Psychology*, 1(1), 21–33.

Bloom, B. S. (Ed.). (1985). *Developing Talent in Young People*. New York: Ballantine.

Bradley, B. (1989). *Visions of Infancy*. Cambridge: Polity Press.

Burman, E. (1994). *Deconstructing Developmental Psychology*. London: Routledge.

Deleuze, G., and Guattari, F. (1987). *A Thousand Plateaus: Capitalism and Schizophrenia* (B. Massumi, Trans.). London: Athlone.

Dewey, J. (1962). *Individualism Old and New*. New York: Capricorn.

Drewery, W., and Bird, L. (2004). *Human Development in Aotearoa 2*. Sydney: McGraw-Hill.

Foucault, M. (1977). *Discipline and Punish: The Birth of the Prison* (A. Sheridan, Trans.). New York: Pantheon.

Gesell, A., & Ilg, F. L. (1949). *Child Development*. New York: Harper and Row.

Goodnow, J. J., Cashmore, J., Cotttons, S., and Knight, R. (1984). Mothers' developmental timetables in two cultural groups. *International Journal of Psychology*, 19, 193–205.

Gould, S. J. (1977). *Ontogeny and phylogeny*. Cambridge, MA: Belknap/Harvard University Press.

Hall, S., Held, D., and McGrew, T. (1992). *Modernity and Its Futures*. Cambridge: Polity/Open University.

Mistry, J., & Rogoff, B. (1985). A cultural perspective on the development of talent. In F. D. Horowitz and M. O'Brien (Eds.). *The Gifted and Talented: Developmental Perspectives* (pp. 125–148). Washington, DC: American Psychological Association.

Morss, J. R. (1990). *The Biologising of Childhood: Developmental Psychology and the Darwinian Myth*. Hove: Erlbaum.

New Zealand Ministry of Education. (2004). A summary of Special Education Services. Retrieved March 1, 2006, from http://www.minedu.govt.nz/index.cfm?layout=document&documentid=7325&indexid=7954&indexparentid=6871

Roy, K. (2003). *Teachers in Nomadic Spaces*. New York: Peter Lang.

Sampson, E. E. (1984). Deconstructing psychology's subject. *The Journal of Mind and Behavior*, 4(2), 135–164.

Scheman, N. (1983). Individualism and the objects of psychology. In S. Harding and M. B. Hintikka (Eds.), *Discovering Reality: Feminist Perspectives on Epistemology, Metaphysics, Methodology, and Philosophy of Science* (pp. 225–244). Boston: D. Reidel.

Terman, L. (1905). A study in precocity and prematuration. *American Journal of Psychology*, 16 (2), 145–183.

Walkerdine, V. (1984). Developmental psychology and the child-centred pedagogy. In J. Henriques, W. Hollway, C. Urwin, C. Venn, and V. Walkerdine (Eds.), *Changing the Subject: Psychology, Social Regulation and Subjectivity*. London: Routledge.

CHAPTER 53

Foundations of Reconceptualized Teaching and Learning

RAYMOND A. HORN JR.

The educational and psychological foundations of reconceptualized teaching and learning are grounded in the traditions of postpositivist thinking as exemplified by poststructuralism, postmodernism, critical theory, critical pedagogy, cultural studies, critical pragmatism, cultural studies, and postformalism. In addition, aspects of cognitive science and psychology are part of the foundation of a reconceptualized teaching and learning. The purpose of this chapter will be to synoptically describe the positivist foundation of traditional education and psychology, highlight the essential foundations of reconceptualized teaching and learning, and discuss how this postpositivist foundation has influenced the reconceptual view of teaching and learning.

POSITIVISTIC FOUNDATIONS OF TRADITIONAL TEACHING AND LEARNING

In the traditional perspective, which currently dominates education through No Child Left Behind (NLCB), the determination of valid knowledge, appropriate inquiry methodology, and effective knowledge acquisition is grounded in the traditions of Cartesian dualism, empiricism, and positivism. Generally, these rationalist traditions promote the assumption that physical and human phenomenon can be objectively studied and manipulated with a great degree of certainty when rational thinking and science are used to uncover the causes and effects that underlie the phenomena.

Initially, in a rationalist attempt to reconcile faith and reason, Rene Descartes theorized that the subjective reality of the mind and the objective reality of matter were forever separate. Building upon Descartes' theory, the classical empiricists promoted the idea that true or objective knowledge can only be uncovered through sensory experience. The radical dualism of Descartes separated knowledge into a binary classification of a priori knowledge, or knowledge of innate ideas that is acquired through the mind's employment of reason, and a posteriori knowledge, or knowledge of the objective world that is acquired through observation. Cartesian dualism further resulted in the bifurcation of knowledge and human activity into oppositional categories, such as "fact/value, objective/subjective, rational/irrational, analytic/synthetic, scheme/content, theory/practice, ends/means, description/prescription, and logic/rhetoric that have long characterized modern, analytic, and scientific thought" (Cherryholmes, 1999, p. 42).

Later empiricists theorized that the only significant knowledge was the knowledge of the objective world that could only be gotten through one's senses. British empiricists such as John Locke concluded that the mind is a blank slate upon which experience writes, thus further valuing the objective over the subjective as posed by Cartesian dualism. The empiricist position was strengthened by the work of scientists such as Isaac Newton and Francis Bacon, who extended the ability to objectively measure natural phenomenon through the invention of scientific instruments and constructed scientific procedures that further facilitated the acquisition of objective knowledge about the material world.

In the United States, this empirical view is currently promoted in the definition of scientifically based research in NCLB. NCLB explicitly states that scientifically based research is that which employs systematic, empirical methods that draw on observation or experiment. This emphasis on empirical research values formal knowledge of this type over knowledge that is not empirically derived, thus perpetuating such epistemological binaries as objective/subjective, rational/irrational, and theory/practice. Besides the NCLB mandate, educational preparation and practice that distinguishes between expert and practitioner or scholarly and practitioner knowledge is also grounded in the empirical tradition.

Two significant aspects of Newtonian/empirical thinking are determinism and reductionism. Determinism is the belief that all actions or effects are determined or caused by a preceding event or condition. Therefore, by using scientific methods, an individual can identify the causes of a phenomenon and by controlling those causes can predict with certainty the outcome or effect. Determinism promotes a linear view of activity from cause to effect, not from effect to cause. This activity sequence is important when deterministic thinking is applied to human activity. In deterministic thinking, "we do not need to try to discover what . . . plans, purposes, intentions, or the other prerequisites of autonomous man really are in order to get on with a scientific analysis of behavior" (Skinner, 1971, pp. 12–13). In other words, the affective nature of the individual (i.e., feelings, thoughts, desires) is not a necessary area of investigation. As Skinner later hypothesized, individuals are not free, purposeful, and responsible, but objects that are motivated by causative agents or environmental stimuli and reinforcement.

Deterministic thinking denies the need to understand the larger context of a complex phenomenon that includes human subjectivity. This kind of thinking is also reductionistic in its proposition that, by reducing the whole to its parts for scientific study, an individual can attain true knowledge about contextually complex phenomenon. Therefore, deterministically, the understanding of reality is a deductive process. Empiricists readily apply deterministic thinking that successfully uncovers natural laws on a macrophysical level to human activity that contains a subjective component. This belief is based on two assumptions. "The first is the belief that the *aims*, *concepts*, and *methods* of the natural sciences are also applicable in social scientific inquiries. The second is the belief that the model of *explanation* employed in the natural sciences provides the logical standards by which the explanations of the social sciences can be assessed" (Carr and Kemmis, 1986, p. 62). In other words, like nature, value-neutral immutable laws govern society, and the same scientific processes can be used to understand both.

Once again, in the United States, mandates such as NCLB represent deterministic and reductionist thinking when they identify the only appropriate inquiry methods as those that seek to understand educational phenomena in a cause-and-effect context in which the complex nature of the phenomena are reduced to decontextualized variables. Of course, the further assumption is that the only valid knowledge is knowledge that is derived through this reductionist process, and that there is a high probability of a cause-and-effect relationship.

During the seventeenth and eighteenth centuries, known as the Age of Enlightenment, scientific inquiry became the preeminent means to uncovering knowledge. In the modern era, from this time through the twentieth century, Cartesian–Newtonian thought became the dominant foundation of

Western political, economic, social, and cultural activity. Beginning with the theory of Auguste Comte (1798–1857), empirical–rational views of reality coalesced into a philosophical theory or doctrine called positivism. The essential belief of positivism, grounded in empirical thinking, is that only scientific knowledge is valid, and that other knowledge represented by nonscientific methods of inquiry, religion, metaphysics, and other nonpositivistic ways of viewing reality are at best suspect but most likely inaccurate.

In the early twentieth century, proponents of positivism attempted to boost the view of science as the only way that leads to true knowledge. Through the verification principle, the Logical Positivists connected all meaning to empirical verification. This resulted in the view that if empirical verification was lacking, then meaning was erroneous. This view led to the belief that only experimental quantitative methods could lead to true objective knowledge.

Related to this argument is the modernistic view of the value-neutral nature of scientifically generated knowledge. Since scientific procedures are objective, positivists argue that scientific procedures, scientific knowledge, and individuals who employ these procedures are not influenced by political, economic, cultural, or ideological factors. In addition, positivists argued that scientific thinking should be applied to political decision making, thus creating the potential for positivism, specifically scientific thinking, to be used as a social control measure.

The characteristics of knowledge acquisition within the empirical, positivistic, and modernist perspective align with the view that expert-derived scientific knowledge can be accepted with certainty, is value-neutral, can be discovered by an individual who is scientifically skilled, and can be transmitted by experts to others. In the United States, the educational research infrastructure that is being constructed through NCLB is grounded in this view of knowledge acquisition. Federally funded organizations such as the U.S. Department of Education's Institute of Education Sciences (IES) and the What Works Clearinghouse (WWC) function to promote empirical research and educational decision making that is exclusively based upon this view of knowledge and inquiry. The IES and the WWC have been established to promote scientific evidence, in the positivist tradition, as the only trusted source of knowledge for educational policy and practice.

During the early twentieth century, modernistic thinking in the form of technical rationality became entrenched in American education. The term modernism is associated with the time period "where the motivation to be rational, logical, scientific, and utility-maximizing in seeking progress, profits, accountability, and value-added outcomes produces behavior where solutions precede the search for problems, which they, our previously identified solutions, can answer" (Cherryholmes, 1999, p. 88).

The modernistic social efficiency movement that promoted the scientific management of education introduced the technical rationality of the business community into American education. During this movement, the structure of education became hierarchical and hegemonic in order to better promote the specialization and bureaucracy found in the business community. The implementation of technical rationality created a need for control of every aspect of the educational process, the standardization of every task, planning and control by management departments instead of individuals, detailed record keeping, specialized roles in and precise execution of curriculum and instruction, and assessment procedures that guaranteed performance and accountability to the curricular and instructional decisions of the planners.

In the early 1920s, as a backlash to the Progressive influence in education, the essentialist movement promoted the teacher as the manager of the classroom to ensure more student discipline and work. In this context, just as theory and practice were separated, teachers became practitioners separate from others who as experts and scholars would generate the theory and policy that teachers would implement. Also, during this time period, the progressive influence of John Dewey gave way to the educational ideas of the behavioral psychologists led by Edward Thorndike. The increasing influence of Thorndike situated the empirically driven field of psychology as the dominant influence in education to the present, and solidified the separation of theory and practice and scholars and practitioners.

Historically and currently, the dualistic aspect of technical rationality is evident in the quantitative versus qualitative binary in educational research, in the separation of expert and practitioner knowledge, in the measurement of intelligence to categorize students, and in the sorting of students into mainstream and special-education categories. Likewise, the technical rational emphasis on scientific validation and predictability is evident in the extensive use of standardized testing and other measurement tools such as grade point average and the Carnegie unit. Cause-and-effect determinism guides the use of behaviorally oriented classroom management systems, the use of extrinsic rewards as motivational devices, programmed instruction, and teacher-proof materials in an attempt to technically control the variables that affect student learning. In addition, the regulation and restriction of practitioner and student input into their teaching and learning is representative of a deterministic disregard for human subjectivity.

Also, the modernistic emphasis on reductionism is evident in the separation of knowledge into discrete and separate disciplines as well as in the promotion of teaching as a disciplinary rather than interdisciplinary activity. There is a reductionist perspective in the specialization of roles and knowledge within a rigid and hegemonic hierarchical organizational structure. In describing a modernistic bureaucracy, Cleo H. Cherryholmes (1999) provides an apt description of the culture of a technical rational educational system, a system "that is rational and hierarchical; that has clear lines of authority, fragmented tasks, and a body of expert knowledge and skills in the hands of administrators and staff; and where systematic reforms can be implemented and evaluated" (p. 85).

Within a technical rational environment, educational culture mirrors the hierarchical structure. The separation of stakeholders into well-bounded different groups (i.e., administrators, teachers, students) as well as the role delineation of individuals within these groups (i.e., superintendents, principals, assistant principals; department chairs, grade-level distinctions, and teacher specialties; student grade levels, tracks within grades, and vocational preparation groups, such as college, business, or vocational preparation) facilitates the development of balkanized and individualized cultures within the school. Finally, the dominance of technical rationality is facilitated by how all of these components are interconnected and mutually reinforce a technical rationality perspective.

In modernistic technical rational school systems, the rigid differentiation of roles along with individualized and balkanized culture results in educational communities that sharply mirror the nature of community found in industry and business. Community vision and mission are bound to corporate goals, and the reproduction of the corporate culture is an essential activity that mediates all other community activity. Individuals within the technical rational community tend to be motivated to work together primarily because of self-interest with idealistic and spiritual motivators subsumed by the eventual need to comply with the goals of the organization. Ironically, many educational institutions have idealistically grounded vision and mission statements constructed by a representation of the different stakeholders. However, their implementation tends to be pragmatically shaped by less than idealistic external pressures, and often become subverted by the reproductive activity of the technical rational culture. Contractual relationships are the norm and guide stakeholder activity within the community. Seldom is stakeholder activity the result of a shared covenant whose motivational power transcends all stakeholder groups, and whose principles or spiritual focus binds them in common purpose and activity.

POSTSTRUCTURAL AND POSTMODERN FOUNDATIONS OF RECONCEPTUALIZED TEACHING AND LEARNING

In contrast to the positivism of modernistic education, poststructural and postmodern thinking have provided analytical strategies and methods that facilitate the critical interrogation of modernistic education. A critical interrogation of education is an essential activity if the complexity of education is to be engaged. Poststructural and postmodern analysis not only uncover the inconsistencies, flaws, contradictions, and exclusions found in education, but also facilitate an awareness of educational complexity as opposed to the simplistic reductionism of traditional understandings of education.

While structuralism created an awareness of wholeness and the systemic relationship between the individual parts of a phenomenon such as education, poststructuralism has enhanced the structuralist methods that are used to analyze the multiple and hidden meanings found in language and discourse practices, and subsequent human activity and organizations. The structuralist and poststructuralist understanding that the meanings that are created through discourse are relational provides the understanding that the construction of meaning is influenced by other entities. In relation to education, this means that the discrete parts of an educational system cannot be understood by isolating them and by denying their interconnection with the larger systemic context. Another important contribution to the reconceptual process is the recognition that institutional structures limit and control the choices that people have in constructing meaning.

Michel Foucault has provided an understanding of the impact of historical power arrangements on the nature of discourse. Through the practice of countermemory the relationship between past and present is better understood through Foucault's critical reading of how the past and present inform each other. Recognizing that historical periods and geographic locations are dominated by discourses, poststructural analysis allows an interrogation of authority and of how that power is arranged by that authority.

Another poststructural contribution to understanding human activity is Jacques Derrida's concept of deconstruction. In this concept, when subjected to critical analysis, all texts deconstruct, or disclose the inconsistencies, flaws, internal differences, repressed contradictions, and exclusions in their fundamental premise. These and other poststructural methods of analysis are important strategies that can be used in the reconceptualization of teaching and learning.

Postmodernism refers to an intellectual and cultural critique of modernist society, and challenges the existence of any foundational knowledge that individuals would go to in order to find truth (i.e., religion, political ideology, scientific theories). Postmodernists argue that all social reality, human constructions represented through language, discourse, and symbolic imagery, employ analytical processes that problematize foundational knowledge. As antifoundationalists, they believe that without a foundation or a center to attach oneself, the meanings created by individuals are seen as essentially relative to the individual and the cultural influences on the individual.

CRITICAL THEORY, CRITICAL PEDAGOGY, AND CULTURAL STUDIES AS FOUNDATIONS OF RECONCEPTUALIZED TEACHING AND LEARNING

Historically related to the philosophies of Hegel and Marx, critical theory is not a uniform or unified approach in the critique of social and political phenomenon, but rather a changing and evolving critique in light of new insights, problems, and social circumstances. Critical theory originally referred to the theoretical work of the Frankfurt School, which consisted of scholars such as Max Horkheimer, Theodor Adorno, Herbert Marcuse, and later Jurgen Habermas. Their ideas became a significant part of the theoretical base of the New Left in America during the 1960s. In their critique of Marxist theory, they laid the groundwork for an understanding of the diverse forms of oppression such as race, gender, class, sexual, cultural, religious, colonial, and ability-related concerns. Contemporary forms of critical theory generally coalesce in their desire to promote critical enlightenment or the awareness of competing power interests between groups and individuals; critical emancipation or the attempt by individuals to gain power over their lives;

the rejection of Marxian economic determinism or the recognition that there are multiple forms of oppression; a critique of technical rationality; critical immanence or going beyond egocentrism and ethnocentricism to build new forms of social relationships; and a reconceptualized critical theory of power that interrogates hegemonic relationships, ideological positions, and linguistic/discursive power (Kincheloe, 2004). Integral to critical theory is the necessity to uncover the oppressive nature of one's own actions through critical self-reflection.

One recent application of critical theory to an investigation of the production of culture has resulted in cultural studies. The field of cultural studies involves the critical awareness and investigation of high and popular culture as contested sites in the reproduction of ideological, economic, and social interests, and in the oppressive consequences of this reproductive activity. An analysis of how culture is produced, distributed, and consumed creates an awareness of the oppressive nature of the hidden curriculum that pervades all human activity. In order to understand how power and domination play out in a society's culture, proponents of cultural studies apply an eclectic array of inquiry methods in the critical analysis of mass media and popular culture. Through the use of these methods, individuals who engage in cultural studies critically interrogate the actions of mass media and corporate structures that silence the voices of subordinate groups and individuals.

In the 1970s, critical theorists began the reconceptualization of education as another site of political struggle in the reproduction of ideological interests. Grounded in the radical pedagogy of Paulo Freire, critical scholars pioneered the idea of critical pedagogy, or the view of education as an empowering activity that would facilitate individuals to resist the oppressive social, political, and economic structures encountered in their lives. In advancing the idea of critical pedagogy, the purpose of education was redirected to the emancipatory goals of Freire and to the Deweyian promotion of a participatory democracy. Pedagogy was no longer merely about teaching, but was transformed into a critical project with the additional goals of creating critical awareness through a critical literacy and promoting resistance to oppression. Therefore, this radicalized pedagogy is grounded in the promotion of social justice, an ethic of caring, and participatory democracy. To accomplish this goal, critical pedagogy employs a diversity of knowledge bases and research methods such as African American studies, feminist perspectives, indigenous knowledge, critical theory, poststructural analysis, postmodern deconstruction, phenomenology, semiotics, discourse analysis, psychoanalysis, critical hermeneutics, and queer theory. Through the use of these eclectic epistemologies and methodologies, the inherent complexity of education can be better understood.

CRITICAL PRAGMATISM AS A FOUNDATION OF RECONCEPTUALIZED TEACHING AND LEARNING

Building upon Deweyian pragmatism, postpositivist inquiry, and critical theory, critical pragmatism promotes the pragmatic examination of the consequences of our actions through critical and postpositivist lenses of critique. Understanding that our consequences are "socially constructed within contexts that are political, economic, cultural, ethnic, socially stratified, linguistically diverse, and gendered" (Cherryholmes, 1999, p. 36), critical pragmatists are concerned about the consequences of their actions in relation to "the context of power, ideology, and history" (p. 37). Cherryholmes describes critical pragmatism as fallibilistic, contextual, contingent, and holistic. In other words, critical pragmatists understand that consequences may include unanticipated and unappealing outcomes, that how things will work out depends on the different context of each situation or locale, that there is no assurance that things will work out because of the changing context, and that we cannot view a situation as its parts but instead must engage the whole context. In addition, critical pragmatists must critique their own positionality so that all of the possible consequences become apparent.

Within a critical pragmatic perspective, technical definitions of participatory research that limit the questions that educators and students can pose about their problems and the potential consequences of their actions are replaced by emancipatory and pragmatic concepts such teachers as researchers, students as researchers, and administrators as moral leaders. In these new roles, educators and students engage in problem posing and problem solving with the understanding that the knowledge that they produce and critique is pragmatically relevant to their teaching and learning, to their own personal experience, and to the communities in which they live.

POSTFORMALISM AS A FOUNDATION OF RECONCEPTUALIZED TEACHING AND LEARNING

In opposition to the highly structured and formulistic thinking of technical rational education, postformal thinking reconceptualizes teaching and learning as creative activity whose purpose is to facilitate teacher and student engagement of the complexity of the educational process. Two questions need to be answered in order to understand the postformal nature of a reconceptualized teaching and learning. How is postformal thinking different from formal thinking? What is the role of postformal thinking (Kincheloe et al., 1999) in reconceptualized teaching and learning?

First, it must be recognized that formal and postformal thinking are fundamentally different ways of viewing natural and human phenomenon. As previously described, formal thinking is characteristically reductionist in its attempt to exclusively reduce inherently complex social phenomena into discrete parts whose cause-and-effect relationships can be determined and predicted through an objective scientific process that is value free. In addition, knowledge is viewed as information that exists apart from human cognition and therefore requires the expertise of individuals who through their technical training can discover knowledge and pass it along to others. This reliance on experts creates a social hierarchy that through its controlling organizational structure fosters arrangements of power that have the potential to be oppressive and marginalizing to individuals who are lower in the hierarchy or have views that differ from those who control the structure. Another outcome is the promotion of specialized roles, standardized processes, and generalized application of specific knowledge, skills, and values to all individuals and schools without a regard for the contextual differences of individuals, schools, and communities. In this formal context, theory and practice, as well as scholars and practitioners, become separate entities connected only within the rules established by those in control. Uncertainty is rendered undesirable, uncontrolled variables must be statistically controlled, and complexity is problematic if it cannot be reduced to parts that can be scientifically managed.

In opposition to this formal view, postformal thinking views human phenomena holistically. All human activity, including the production of knowledge, is viewed ecologically and systemically in that understanding one aspect of this activity requires a concomitant understanding that the activity under investigation is dynamically interconnected and interrelated to all other parts of the human activity system. The significance of this holistic view is that to gain a deep and broad understanding of the activity in question and the consequences of our conclusions about the activity, a simultaneous engagement of the whole system in which the activity is embedded is required. Postformal thinking recognizes the value of reductionist analysis as one technique in knowledge production but further requires this analysis to be critically interrogated within the larger systemic context. Just as in the investigation of natural phenomena, such as weather systems, the investigation of social phenomena requires a commitment to recognize and engage the systemic complexity of which the phenomenon is a part.

The holistic orientation of postformal thinking recognizes that there are patterns of human activity that once detected can expand our understanding of social problems within this activity. Some superficial patterns are easily detected but offer only a limited understanding of the problem and the consequences of our solutions. In this case, because of our narrow understanding, the solutions that are employed may have a minimal positive effect or even exacerbate the problem. However, through a postformal inquiry into the problem, deep and hidden patterns are uncovered that more substantially increase our understanding and create the potential for more effective action. By detecting and engaging these deep and hidden patterns in which the problem is nested, we are now becoming aware of the greater complexity of the problem and can construct solutions that will accommodate this larger context. The use of postformal strategies in pattern detection allows relationships between seemingly unconnected phenomena to become apparent. For instance, a formal investigation into ineffective education in an urban setting will focus on easily detected patterns involving curriculum, instruction, assessment, funding, resource allocation, teacher quality, inadequate facilities, and other easily detected conditions. However, a postformal inquiry will uncover how these conditions are connected to pervasive economic, political, social, and cultural policies and actions that result in patterns of social organization and behavior that are manifested in specific patterns of resegregation, systemic poverty, a lack of health care for segments of the population, pervasive crime, discriminatory economic policies, political and economically directed media representations of schools and individuals, and educational policies designed to achieve outcomes that benefit those who are in control at the expense of those with little power. In relation to the problems of urban education, an awareness of this more complex relationship of seemingly unconnected individuals, policies, and actions allows us to understand that a reductionist focus on standards and personal accountability will not alleviate the problems of urban education, and in actuality mask the complicity of others, who are outside of the urban education context, in this problem. In this case, the problems of urban education are seen as directly connected to larger patterns of economic, political, cultural, and social policies. In turn, this systemic awareness requires those who seek solutions to move beyond an understanding that results in solutions that are enervating and ineffective because of their simplicity, and to engage their greater awareness of the complexity of the problem by formulating equally complex solutions.

The detection of these less obvious patterns requires an ongoing expansion of our awareness of the context and contextual connectivity of any social problem. As just explained, a situation such as the problems of urban education exists within the urban context; however, this context is both unique and connected to other contexts. To understand what this means requires a postformal understanding of contextualization. When individuals postformally inquire into the context of a situation, they engage issues such as place, culture, and power arrangements. Our understanding of a situation is dependent upon our understanding of the context of the situation. For instance, urban, suburban, and rural places are different. The social and cultural norms, roles, and values of a place mediate and inform what people know and how people act within the context of their place. The meaning that they construct of the purpose and functioning of education is dependent upon the social and cultural characteristics of the place in which they live. Therefore, if education is to be an important, effective, and valued part of their lives, it must reflect the context of the place in which it occurs and the uniqueness of the individuals in that place. This postformal understanding is in opposition to the standardization and generalization of educational curriculum, instruction, assessment, and classroom management that is characteristic of formal thinking. A relevant educational psychology must accommodate the unique characteristics of the individuals and the place in which education occurs. Rigid educational strategies based upon generalized behavioral, developmental, and cognitive psychological research that essentializes educators and students cannot provide authentic, relevant, and effective education. In addition, there must be a postformal recognition that besides scientific knowledge other types of knowledge must be valued. Knowledge that is indigenous to the local place and culture as well as knowledge derived from faith and metaphysics is valued as an important aspect of the educational context. Likewise, reason and emotion are no longer separated as binary constructs, but viewed as interrelated expressions of the human experience. Knowledge mediated by emotion is valued as much as knowledge that is mediated by reason in the context of a postformally aware educational environment.

A postformal understanding of contextualization also includes an understanding of how power arrangements shape our lives. What we know, what we are expected to know, who we are, and who we are to become are all meanings that are informed and mediated by how power is arranged within the place that we live. As previously discussed, reconceptualized teaching and learning is inherently critical in nature. This criticality is also foundational to postformal thinking. When examining context to uncover hidden patterns of social activity, postformalists seek to understand how power is arranged within a place, and consequently how that arrangement empowers, silences, or oppresses those in that place. In any place, whether it be a city, a school, or a classroom, the arrangement of power is a context that needs to be critically interrogated. One aspect of this interrogation involves an examination of the educational psychology, which is the foundation of what happens in the educational setting. Postformalists recognize that traditional educational practice and its psychological foundation promotes specific power arrangements that seek to establish or perpetuate hierarchies of control. A reconceptualized educational psychology utilizes postformal strategies to critically interrogate educational practice and its psychological foundation with the explicit intent to promote a socially just and caring educational experience, and to facilitate the development of critically aware individuals who will participate in the promotion of a democratic society. This outcome cannot occur without an ongoing attention to the context of power.

Related to the postformal attention to context is recognition of the necessity to explore the origins of the meanings that we hold. In a postformally aware educational environment, individuals understand the necessity to critically probe the origins of what we know, the process of our knowing, our attitudes, and our values. Postformalists understand that social and historical forces mediate all our personal knowledge and the collective patterns of which we are a part. Simply, these social and historical forces are a significant contribution to our construction of the present. An understanding of the origins of what we believe occurs through processes of critical reflection and reflexion. An understanding of the connections of the past, present, and future is the outcome of our critical thinking about why the things that are around us and influence us are the way that they are. In addition, critical reflexion is when we turn our critical gaze inward and interrogate the origins of our own beliefs, actions, and the thought processes that we use. An essential aspect of this etymological inquiry is the ability to ask questions—questions that will uncover problems and aspects of problems that are undetectable without this critical interrogation.

A final way in which postformal thinking differs from formal thinking is in the inquiry process. Formal thinking requires adherence to the scientific method, which is too often narrowly defined as quantitative research. The insistence of postformal thinkers to continuously expand the complexity of a situation through the exploration of origins, context, and patterns requires the use of any research epistemology or methodology that can lead to a better understanding of the complexity of a situation. Because of this purpose, postformal inquiry utilizes an eclectic array of research knowledge and methods. Poststructural and postmodern methods are situationally applicable along with both quantitative and qualitative strategies. As postformal researchers, individuals function as bricoleurs who utilize these diverse methods and strategies to creatively uncover the contexts and patterns that are necessary to engage the complexity of educational phenomenon. Unlike formal researchers who focus on the acquisition and analysis of knowledge within the constraints of the rules of positivistic research, postformal researchers use their creativity in the employment of individual research methods and in the mixing of methodologies to enhance the potential of the inquiry process. In addition, this allows the postformal researcher to go beyond a simplistic cause-and-effect understanding of a phenomenon, and to allow this research process to synergistically construct more complex meaning.

In conclusion, those individuals who utilize postformal thinking to reconceptualized teaching and learning are neither scholars nor practitioners but are scholar-practitioners. Unlike the artificial positivist separation of experts/scholars and practitioners, postformal inquiry requires the integration of scholarship and practice. The effective engagement of complexity requires both the formal knowledge of scholarship and the experiential knowledge of the practitioner. By drawing from both sources, the postformal inquirer is able to become critically aware and literate, and from this position perform a critical reading of any phenomenon. Additionally, in the tradition of critical pragmatism, scholar-practitioners are also well positioned to take the social actions necessary to promote social justice, an ethic of caring, and participatory democracy.

REFERENCES

Carr, W., and Kemmis, S. (1986). *Becoming Critical: Education, Knowledge and Action Research*. Philadelphia: Falmer Press.

Cherryholmes, C. (1999). *Reading Pragmatism*. New York: Teachers College Press.

Kincheloe, J. L., Steinberg, S. R., and Hinchey, P. (Eds.). (1999). *The Post-formal Reader: Cognition and Education*. New York: Garland Press.

Skinner, B. F. (1971). *Beyond Freedom and Dignity*. New York: Alfred A. Knopf.

CHAPTER 54

The Diverse Purposes of Teaching and Learning

RAYMOND A. HORN JR.

Unlike the current federal proposition, as seen in No Child Left Behind (NCLB), that teaching and learning is a complicated process that can be controlled through the identification and implementation of curriculum, instruction, and assessment formulas and prescriptions, teaching and learning is more than complicated, it is complex. There is a significant difference between complicated and complex. Complicated infers that due to a plethora of variables, simple solutions to a problem will not be found, and, therefore, extensive validated research is necessary to uncover solutions and enact implementation processes that will bring the problem under control and eventually to an acceptable resolution. In seeing problems as complicated, individuals of this perspective believe that the variables contributing to the problem can be identified, organized into groups, and controlled through standardized procedures that are applicable to all individuals and environments. In this context, the federal government has identified one research paradigm, quantitative research, that is based on inferential statistical longitudinal studies, as the research method that can effectively identify the salient variables that contribute to specific educational problems. Once identified by research experts, other experts can construct programs and processes that will remedy a specific educational problem. For instance, if children are not doing well on internationally competitive standardized tests in mathematics, math programs can be expertly developed and subsequently required for all math instruction. To ensure compliance with the expert-derived programs, curriculum, instruction, and assessment is packaged as a teacher-proof, scripted educational activity. One outcome of this control is that good teaching and effective learning are now defined by the teachers' ability to not deviate from the package, and the students' ability to learn within the constraints of the package. However, this scenario along with its consequences is quite different when educational problems are viewed as complex.

Likewise, complexity also infers that due to a plethora of variables, simple solutions will not be found, and that extensive validated research is necessary to uncover solutions and enact implementation processes that will bring the problem under control and eventually to an acceptable resolution. However, individuals who see problems as complex additionally recognize that there is a larger context and hidden patterns that greatly expand the dynamic interrelatedness of the variables to the point where selected research methods and individuals cannot understand the whole complex phenomenon. Individuals who view education as complex believe that without expanding the inquiry process to include a diverse variety of research methods and individuals, any attempted solution will fail, or even exacerbate the problem. Another important difference between complicated and complex is the understanding that things change—often quickly change. In recognizing change as a factor that enhances the complexity of a situation, research-driven solutions are seen as part of an ongoing process, not as an endpoint that can be unrelentingly generalized to different individuals in different environments. Change requires flexible response. For instance, any teacher knows that each school year brings different variables into the mix— different students, different funding levels, and different societal and cultural contexts that place different requirements on the school and teacher. Last year's math curriculum, lessons, and assessments now need to be modified to meet the special and diverse needs of this year's students. Because of these changing variables, teaching effectiveness and student achievement are in a state of constant redefinition.

How do these distinctively different orientations toward educational problem solving relate to the different purposes of education? First, how one defines research, validity, the production of knowledge, the roles of stakeholders in the problem-solving process, and what constitutes an acceptable outcome is directly dependent upon one's purpose. Certain research methods, definitions of validity, methods in producing knowledge, and the organization of the activity of the stakeholders will produce results or outcomes that are quite different from the outcomes of other methods. Therefore, the purposes that individuals want to achieve dictate the processes and organizational arrangements of power that will lead to the desired outcome. The desired outcome focuses their purposeful behavior. Therefore, when educational problems need to be engaged, in order to fully understand the problem and the effects of the proposed solution, it is necessary to explore the full context of the problem and the purposes of the groups who propose very different solutions. Adding purpose to the mix increases the complexity of the problem, and, in turn, creates the opportunity to more effectively understand the problem and the effects of the proposed solution. Critically understanding how multiple and different views concerning the purpose of education affect the definition and resolution of educational problems represents a reconceptualized view of education.

FUNCTIONAL PURPOSES OF EDUCATION

One purpose of schools is to ensure individuals are able to function effectively in society. Today's schools are asked to perform multiple functions that are unrelated to the traditional purposes of reading, writing, and arithmetic. Besides promoting basic skills, the educational purposes of schools include learning knowledge provided by other disciplines such as the social sciences, science, language arts, music, art, physical education, health education, technology, vocational training, and others. Add to the list extracurricular activities such as the fine arts and sports, and one can easily see how complex the functional purpose of contemporary education has become. In addition, purpose has been expanded to meet the needs of special students such as the gifted, the disabled, and the mentally challenged. Of course, citizenship development is an additional purpose along with the promotion of values (e.g., character education, sportsmanship, environmental protection), and social behavior (e.g., student assistance programs, counseling, and psychological services).

The attempt by schools to meet these functional purposes is complicated by society's demand that schools must be sensitive to the poverty, gender, race, ethnic, sexual preference, lifestyle preference, and other aspects of diversity that are brought into the school by the children. To achieve these multiple and often diverse purposes, schools are further required to work in concert with governmental and community organizations and agencies. All of these many functional purposes add to the complexity of problems that occur in the classroom and school. However, a reconceptualized view of education requires a deeper analysis of how these functional purposes are contextualized. A reconceptual view requires a critical interrogation of how groups with quite different philosophical and political purposes in mind attempt to control, shape, and possibly eliminate some of these functional purposes to promote their own agenda.

PHILOSOPHICAL AND PSYCHOLOGICAL PURPOSES

To understand the effect of philosophical purposes on how schools attempt to meet this plethora of functional purposes requires a more complex interrogation of questions such as "What is appropriate knowledge?" "How is knowledge produced?" "How should the school be organized to achieve its functional purposes?" "Who should be the focus of school activity?"

All of these questions are good questions because in the attempt to answer them one's understanding of education and its problems gains complexity. For instance, the function of health education can be quite different if it is grounded in an idealistic, realistic, pragmatic, or existential view. Idealists and realists believe that truth, reality, and knowledge are fixed entities external to students, either in the form of virtues or ideals, or, in the case of realists, natural laws. In both cases, students can be brought to discover this knowledge through the guidance of experts who use the objectivist methods that are acceptable to their philosophical paradigms. However, a pragmatic view opens the door to a constructivist understanding of truth, reality, and knowledge. In this view, students are seen as co-constructors of knowledge, thereby leading to quite different views on curriculum, instruction, and assessment. An existentialist view would focus on the individual student as the sole creator of truth, reality, and knowledge and would attempt to facilitate the students' understanding of the nature of health within their own individual context. Basically, the philosophy that is the foundation for one's view of reality will mediate and inform one's decision making concerning the functional purposes of schools.

In the context of psychological theory, the functional purposes could be again influenced by these different ways of understanding human behavior. If a behavioral, developmental, cognitive, or humanistic perspective dominates the purposes of the school, then curriculum, instruction, assessment, and classroom management will differ. In addition, different philosophical and psychological stances will answer the previous questions quite differently. However, related to the different philosophical and psychological purposes and much more important in understanding the complexity of educational activity are political and ideological purposes.

POLITICAL AND IDEOLOGICAL PURPOSES

Individuals with similar worldviews (i.e., idealists, realists, pragmatists, existentialists, conservatives, liberals, and radicals) understand that one of the most important social institutions is education. Formal education, whether public or private, is the fundamental activity in which future generations acquire knowledge, skills, attitudes, and values that complement or contradict the worldview that is promoted in family, religious, or social contexts. Therefore, if the public education process appears to not align with views that are elsewhere promoted, than those whose views are not being reinforced see the need to gain control over public education. Historically, this battle over control of education has been fought in local (i.e., school boards), state (i.e., state departments of education), and national (i.e., federal education initiatives such as funding requirements, proclamations, and federal laws) contexts. The recent NCLB act requires educational compliance to very specific educational practices, which are grounded in specific philosophies, psychologies, and ideologies, and are enforced through the disbursement of federal funds for state and local education. In other words, if states and local schools do not comply, then they do not receive federal funds for education.

Individuals with similar ideological positions form interest groups whose purpose is to promote their beliefs through public and private education. Private or parochial schools can be established that overtly promote a specific agenda of knowledge, skills, attitudes, and values. However, the cost of this strategy to an individual is not offset by taxpayer dollars but requires an outlay of tuition beyond any taxes that the individual is required to pay. Therefore, the idea of vouchers, in which tax money is returned to the individual to offset the cost of private education, becomes a viable strategy that appeals to supporters of private schools, whose purpose is to promote a specific worldview. Another option would be to diminish the effectiveness of public schools. With public schools viewed as inferior to private schools, a stronger case can be made for the promotion of private schools. A final strategy would be for proponents of private schools to gain control of the schools and reconstruct them to accommodate a specific ideological position or economic advantage.

However, the very idea of a public school is incongruent with some ideological positions. For instance, historically, conservatives have argued against government involvement in the lives of individuals, and have acted to either directly diminish the size of government or to use government to enact policies that will require less government in the future. Individuals who take this position recognize that one of the largest governmental intrusions into the lives of individuals is public education. Therefore, a credible goal would be to undermine public education through policies and required practices that ensure the demise of the effectiveness of public education in the eyes of the public. In this way, the general public would become more receptive to policies that diminish public control over education through governmental agencies, and subsequently embrace the privatization of education.

This sort of political activity is ideologically focused; however, there are other nonideological interests who also engage in this sort of educational political activity. Some of these interests are economically based, such as specific corporations or the business community in general. If the scarce resources allocated for public education can be reallocated for functional purposes that create more profit for business and industry, the financial bottom-line is maximized. Also, the schools house a significant population of consumers, who can become the target of marketing efforts, either as immediate purchasers of goods and services or as the objects of efforts to inculcate consumer attitudes and practices through which businesses will reap future benefits. In addition, the failure of business policy and practice and federal economic policy can be masked and redirected by placing the blame on the schools. Finally, some groups simply desire to gain political control over others through the domination of the schools.

Whatever the reason for the political activity, the important understanding is that if one ideology or other interest is in control, then the teaching and learning that occurs will be very different from the nature of the teaching and learning promoted by a different interest group. There is a discernable pattern of alignment between political, philosophical, and psychological views on the purpose and conduct of education. As discussed throughout this encyclopedia, specific philosophies and ideologies will recognize and require specific educational psychology pedagogical strategies, and deny the use of others that may result in outcomes that contradict the intent of the philosophy or ideology that desires dominance.

THE PURPOSE OF RECONCEPTUALIZED TEACHING AND LEARNING

As promoted by this encyclopedia, a reconceptualization of education and psychology has a quite different purpose. Grounded in radical ideology, this reconceptualization poses additional questions about education. Individuals holding a reconceptualized view also ask questions such as "What is appropriate knowledge?" "How is knowledge produced?" "How should the school be organized to achieve its functional purposes?" "Who should be the focus of school activity?"

However, a reconceptualized position inquires into the critical consequences of how these questions are answered. This critical inquiry expands the context of these questions to include "How is power arranged in relation to how these questions are answered?" "Which individuals, cultures, and perspectives are being excluded, silenced, or marginalized?" "What are the consequences of these answers in relation to social justice, caring, and participatory democracy?" The answers to these questions are significant in that they require critical reflection and reflexion that leads to a critical consciousness. Once critically aware of the consequences of specific educational policies and practices, critically conscious individuals are positioned to take informed and morally grounded action intended to result in educational policy and practice that is socially just, caring, and democratic. These individuals engage in a critical pragmatism that critically interrogates the potential consequences of a course of action, and then engage in a critical praxis of action, critical reflection, and subsequent action.

Returning to the issue of educational complexity, a reconceptualized view of teaching and learning desires to uncover and engage complexity through postformal inquiry. Only through a critical engagement with educational complexity can education achieve its multiple purposes of meeting the needs of all individuals and society in a socially just, caring, and democratic context. The achievement of this goal requires an understanding of the origins, the greater context, and the hidden patterns in which the answers to these questions are grounded. This broader and more substantive understanding is not possible without the use of an eclectic array of research epistemologies and methodologies. To use a modernistic metaphor—a toolbox—is appropriate in that it explains how all research knowledge bases and methods can be used in various situations individually and collectively to critically interrogate educational policy and practice.

In addition, the engagement of complexity requires a critical systems view concerning the dynamically interrelated organization and functioning of human activity systems. This systemic perspective provides the foundation for an idealized design of educational systems—an idealism grounded in a concern for social justice, caring, and participatory democracy. Through the design of egalitarian, caring, and democratic educational systems, society can guide their social evolution to achieve these critically idealistic outcomes.

However, in the end, the use of a fundamentally critical postformal inquiry and critical systems approach in the reconceptualization of education is required to attain the critical educational purposes of including all individuals in the process, building egalitarian community, and meeting both the individual and collective needs of those whom education serves.

CHAPTER 55

Postmodern Pedagogy

LOIS SHAWVER

Postmodern pedagogy is about teachers building an educational spaceship. The point of the spaceship is to help students escape the gravitational field of their disinterest, help them find the motivation and inspiration to invent their own futures in a rapidly changing world, the futuristic world of their maturity, a world that their teachers of today will scarcely recognize.

The impulse for such postmodernism seems to begin with the teacher's private and sometimes lonely skepticism toward established methods of teaching in schools. That follows with curiosity and puzzling, an uncertainty. Next comes a surprise, a quite pleasant surprise, and then a flood of new ideas about teaching. Finally, there sometimes develops a productive fascination with postmodern philosophies and, simultaneously, a new hope that the postmodern impulse can promote a pedagogic breakthrough. Somehow, along the way, the early sense of loneliness is lost. In its place is a sense of adventure.

Postmodern ideas shed light on educational psychology as a whole and help in the larger effort to recontextualize all of educational psychology. This is because postmodernism is less a theory unto itself than a point of view, a point of view that fosters a contextually nuanced appreciation of the teaching process. It is a perspective that diminishes the tendency of teachers to overgeneralize and it frees them from needing to make universal pronouncements about such things as child development schemes or cognitive stage theory. After all, no one method works in all contexts for all students, and no two students are exactly alike. What seems most valuable, from the postmodern perspective, is that the teachers develop a contagious sense of inspiration that infuses the classroom. This sense of inspiration is easiest to achieve when the teacher is seen and valued for being an innovator, when teachers place great value on their own practitioner-based knowledge, and also on that of their colleagues. Postmodern teachers work to tailor their ideas to particular students or particular classrooms or situations. And, when it all comes together, postmodern teaching becomes, quite simply, an effective quest for planning and developing situationally based teaching masterpieces, masterpieces that might not work for others, or in other contexts.

The first part of this postmodern teaching adventure can be called "skeptical postmodernism" and the second part, "visionary postmodernism."

SKEPTICAL POSTMODERNISM

Postmodernism begins with a serious skepticism about prevailing practices in a given field. This is not a discarding of everything in a field or a radical rejection of specific theories. It is a skepticism toward highly generalized theories that are applied indiscriminately, theories that are taken for granted, institutionalized, and routinized, and are no longer very available for critique or reexamination. For example, when Einstein was a young physicist, Newtonian physics was typically treated as a metanarrative, that is, taken as proven, taken for granted. But Einstein did not take Newtonian physics as a metanarrative. He rethought it. This does not mean he discarded Newtonian physics and went back to an earlier way of thinking. He moved forward. Einstein simply improved Newton's theories, noted that Newton's formulations did not apply in unusual contexts, such as the context of high-speed particles. It is the questioning of what is largely accepted without totally discarding everything being rethought that is uniquely postmodern.

The notable postmodern, Jean-Francois Lyotard, called these taken-for-granted theories "metanarratives." A metanarrative is a narrative (or theory) that provides an umbrella theory for everything. Every new detail in the theory is first tested to see if it fits in the more general grand theory, that is, the metanarrative. Postmoderns don't accept such grand theories. Lyotard put it succinctly when he said, "Simplifying to the extreme, I define postmodern as incredulity toward metanarratives." Postmodernism, then, is a kind of skepticism that does not try to build itself on assumptions. It uses what seems to work best but only temporarily while it both questions assumptions and looks for new ways to cope with the lack of unquestioned assumptions.

But the questioning of assumptions comes first. For example, postmodern teachers might question the use of standardized tests to categorize and evaluate students. In today's educational world, standardized tests are assumed to be established and scientific, especially to those not trained in test construction, even though the interpretation of the tests is often challenged in the courts and controversial in the wider field of psychology. The postmodern educator is likely to point out how standardized tests can falsely pigeonhole students (creating self-fulfilling failures).

Or it might be noted that standardized tests can affect curriculum in a questionable way. Suppose a teacher expects to have her teaching evaluated on the basis of her students' performance on a standardized test, a test that includes some items that are politically correct but highly controversial. In a modernist environment it would be all too easy for such a teacher to assign homework to students so that they did well on the tests even if what they were learning was questionable. Such teaching practices can inculcate discriminatory thinking in students, imposing implicit racist or sexist values on the student's development. The postmodern teacher, therefore, might develop a skepticism toward such practices.

The established literary canon is another example of an educational metanarrative. A canon, of course, is just a list of what is ostensibly the world's greatest writings, must reading for students of a certain level. Postmoderns are likely to think that unquestioned assumption of the accuracy of such a list can trap the imagination of students and prevent their discovering new kinds of literary merit. It is not that any particular item on the usual canon list is being universally challenged but that postmodern consciousness encourages sensitivity toward new idea writing, or writing authored by women and minorities, writing that students might not study if the traditional canon was taken too literally, as the only correct subject matter for literature students.

Many teachers today are postmodern without knowing it. It would be like being a romantic without knowing it, or like being an idealist without thinking of oneself as one. Postmodernism is not a school of thought. Postmoderns are eclectic, selecting ideas from various schools. People from all persuasions are postmodern if they take their current theories and practices as working drafts, subject always to a revision. The same theories might inspire postmodern teachers that inspire others, so long as the theories are reconceptualized as working drafts and not assumed to be absolutely correct in all their detail. Also, people may be postmodern in some areas and not in others; they might sit in a balance between endorsing metanarratives and moving toward postmodernism.

It is possible to think of postmodern authors prior to current times, but there is much that has happened to foster a postmodern skepticism today, enough to encourage some to speak of this current era as "a postmodern era." Much of this increasing postmodernism results, surely, from the astonishing way the Internet is restructuring our picture of knowledge, and this restructuring is arguably the reason for the current flood of postmodernism.

However, the Internet is not the first restructuring of knowledge. Our concept of knowledge was restructured over a period of a few centuries starting with the invention of the printing press in the late fifteenth century and the subsequent growth of popular literacy in Western culture. Prior to that time, knowledge was generally thought of as something stored in the minds of an elite authority. The common folk could do little more than rely on the wisdom of the authorities to know what to think and do. But, with the increase in books and literacy, knowledge shifted subtly to become something that could be stored in the library of a culture. This made knowledge much more accessible. The knowledgeable people were increasingly seen as the authors of books and, to a lesser extent, those who read these books and remembered what they said. Thus it became possible for common folks to study, go to school, and to become more "knowledgeable." Naturally enough, as knowledge became more widespread and democratic, people referred to the emerging seventeenth century as "The Enlightenment."

And today, the Internet is stimulating another period of "enlightenment," potentially bigger than the first. The Internet and other electronic advances offer the vision of fingertip knowledge. One only needs to know how to do an Internet search to have seamless access to a store of knowledge never dreamed of a century ago. One need only press a few keys for the answer to a math problem, a spelling question, a biography on anyone, and virtually any other tidbit of information one might desire. In a culture of such instant information, it is harder to endorse the exceptionless generality of metanarratives.

At least in the postmodern culture, metanarratives seem to belong to another era, a bygone era when people studied a couple of books in their libraries as if there were no others, a time when readers were more gullible. Such a gullibility was natural enough. With the book, the reader turning each page is being guided by a trail of thought that leads from assumption to conclusion. This gave authors an enormous cultural power to define conclusions.

Things are different with today's electronic texts. Here the reader can run a search through a database of abstracts, or choose which links to follow on a Web page. No longer is the author the unquestioned guide for the passive reader. Instead, each reader cuts a distinctive path through the available writing, leading, potentially, to new and distinctive conclusions, conclusions that no one before has drawn. If a document is published on the Web, leading from assumptions to metanarrative conclusion, another essay will follow with contrary assumptions and conclusions.

Can it be any wonder, then, that many people today are increasingly skeptical of metanarratives? What is being questioned is the magical ability of the author, or any human mind, to wrap truth up in perfectly chosen words, or for the author to arrange a telling of truth so that, when examined in more detail, or from a variety of angles, every conclusion remains exactly the same. For the postmodern, the instructor who teaches a simple metanarrative as if it were a universal truth is hiding the tools that the student might need to find a new path to an unexpected and helpful conclusion.

THE PUZZLING IN POSTMODERN PEDAGOGY

This leads to the puzzling in postmodernity. The puzzling is just the group of postmodern teachers scratching their collective heads and wondering how to proceed, asking themselves things like, "How is a postmodern teacher like myself to teach?" And then adding, "I have no idea how to replace these old practices. Still, too many of my students are simply bored. There must be better ways to do things, ways to energize my classroom. But how?"

In the past, things did not seem so complicated. Before postmodern skepticism, the teacher was the unquestioned authority, the person who knew the right answers, the one who handed out grades. The student, almost by definition, was the one in need of information, the one who wrote and spoke only to be corrected. The good teacher instructed and guided. The good student listened and absorbed.

Then comes postmodernist skepticism with its countless questions. What becomes clearer is that, sometimes postmodernity needs to continue with the old ways until better ones can be developed. Sometimes it is better to keep the old car until a new one can be found, and sometimes it's better to ditch the old one and catch the bus for a while. That is what is most puzzling: how much to accept provisional metanarratives until something better can be imagined.

It is not always easy working with so little guideline. It is easier to repeat the past unquestioned methods. Moreover, supervisors and administrators are often more comfortable with teachers working within a traditional frame—but an educator does not become postmodern because it is easy, or because the postmodern solutions are glaringly apparent—quite the opposite. A teacher becomes postmodern without any decision to do so. It begins with a skepticism and then becomes a puzzling.

Then comes the surprise, and, finally, a flowering of new ideas.

THE POSTMODERN SURPRISE

So, what is the postmodern surprise? It is the unexpected camaraderie that develops around postmodern conversation. Sooner or later a person expresses a postmodern skepticism, or a post-modern puzzling, and is surprised to discover that there are many people who share this skepticism. A surprising dimension of postmodern thinking is the way it breeds social bonding with other postmoderns. Once people discover each other, they have good social times—postmodern discussions, mutual brainstorming and collaborative thinking, and sometimes debates that, usually, do not disintegrate into rage and mutual disgust.

Why does postmodern conversation become cohesive like this? At first glance it might seem that postmodernity would be less cohesive than the conversation in traditional circles. After all, in traditional circles people can identify with each other for sharing faith in a metanarrative while postmodernism lacks such a unifying metanarrative. But sharing a metanarrative can invite divisive controversy over who has the best version of the school they share. Consensus about the correct metanarrative is not, therefore, the end of divisiveness. When it is clear from the start, on the other hand, that there is no common denominator in opinion, then people seem to listen better and tread more gently over other people's beliefs. Dissension increasingly becomes valued and reframed as "diversity of opinion" so that it does not become a threat to the discussion.

So, the postmodern surprise is the delightful discovery that conversations work more agreeably when they become more postmodern. In postmodernity it is easier to consider ideas other than one's own because one is not buying an entire theoretical package. It is easier to find something useful in another's theory when one does not have to buy all its parts.

Or perhaps the surprising postmodern bond results from the blurring of authorship and the continuous reweaving of each other's thoughts in the paralogical conversation. In postmodern circles, so Lyotard tells us, "The self does not amount to much." Minds and personalities exist in a network together. The people in postmodernity are often less desperately engaged in frantic competition. There is enough victory for all to share. Also, in postmodernity there are a few more tools for defusing endless disputes and thus more opportunities for all players to win.

And what could be a bigger surprise than this new kind of conversation that Lyotard has named "paralogy." Paralogy is known for its shunning of authority, for its toleration of a wide range of opinion from people present in a conversation—and for its facilitation of a cohesive bond. It is also a veritable greenhouse for postmodern ideas.

VISIONARY POSTMODERNISM

The New Ideas

Over time, skeptical postmodernism becomes visionary in that it brings forth a flowering of new ideas. These new ideas emerge in the postmodern conversational paralogy. Lyotard calls them "little narratives" and he said that these little narratives are "the quintessential form of postmodern invention." These little narratives facilitate the shift from a skeptical to a visionary form of postmodernism.

Especially prized in visionary postmodern pedagogy are the teaching of ideas that break out of old paradigms, ideas that find breakthrough paths that might ignite the learning process, especially for a specific group of students in a particular moment. Contrast this kind of teaching with teaching students to pass a standardized test.

"Which student wants to have ten minutes to be teacher tomorrow?" asks one postmodern teacher hoping to inspire more motivated study. "Let's create a panel of the American founding fathers tomorrow," says another postmodern teacher. "You choose which founding father to study. Then you can be on a panel with the other founding fathers and have a debate. Oh, yes, girls can play a founding father too." Those students will read their history books tonight, hopes the postmodern educator.

Such little narratives, sketchy plots, mini-theories, local practices, can arise automatically once the teacher is released from the script of traditional metanarratives. All these forms of new ideas are greatly fostered, so it seems, by the conversational brainstorming in which ideas are thrown out without being turned into metanarratives, without anyone claiming, or needing to claim, that they have discovered the final, best answer. Almost as cherished as the invention itself is the spirit of invention and the adventure, the mutual sparking of each other's dreams, the collective sense of possibility. Postmodern pedagogy is about ways to inspire students to identify with their own creativity. And since inspiration between students and teachers is often contagious, it is important that teachers find ways to think about teaching that they also find exciting. It is important for the students as well as the teachers.

THE STUDY OF POSTMODERN PHILOSOPHIES

After enjoying their postmodernism for a while, teachers can become fascinated with the work of certain philosophers—and it's no wonder. Today's postmodern era deconstructs the authority of authors, turning their books into recorded streams of ideas written by thoughtful people communicating across time and place barriers. The philosophers' theory as a unified whole wanes in importance. Instead the text is read for inspiration, for ideas. This reading of philosophers for inspiration might be hard to imagine for many teachers, raised as many are in the culture of books, thinking the study of philosophers means grasping the whole of the philosopher's thought, but postmodern teachers who study these philosophers with their compatriots learn to discuss their work without converting the human author into soothsayers.

Among the most inspiring authors for these purposes are Ludwig Wittgenstein and Jean-Francois Lyotard. Both authors have much to say of value for postmodern teachers. Compare the kind of teaching their work fosters with teaching that is routinized around standardized evaluation, pigeonholing students in preformed categories and the routinization of teaching prescribed information and even values.

PREPARING A PLACE

For example, a concept that Wittgenstein left us is the concept of "preparing a place". Wittgenstein asks us to imagine a child watching a chess game. Suppose a five-year-old boy points to a particular chess piece and asks, "What's that?" An adult replies, "It's a rook." But unless the child knows the names and functions of the chess pieces, such an answer will not be meaningful. Still, in some sense, the boy is educated by the answer. At least, he can now answer his adolescent sister who soon asks him, so we might imagine, "What's that you're holding in your hand?" Picture the boy answering with an air of pride and authority. "It's a rook," he tells his big sister.

Now, suppose this big sister knows how to play a little chess—at least, she knows the names of the pieces and how each piece moves differently on the chessboard. Usually she can recognize a rook. However, this is an odd chess set. The pieces have nonstandard shapes. She has heard there are sets like this, but she has never actually seen one. Yet the moment she heard her brother say "It's a rook!" it all came together for her. She knew immediately quite a bit about that piece, quite a lot more, in fact, than her little brother. She knew how to move the rook and its part in the game. Her brother didn't even know what chess was, and had only the vaguest idea of any kind of a board game. In a sense the little boy taught his big sister something that he himself did not understand. She understood more from the name "rook" because she had some experience with chess, which had, to use Wittgenstein's phrase, "prepared a place" for this new piece of information that her brother gave her.

Do not think of "preparing a place" as a concept merely for the instruction of infants. Normal adults hear information now and then without an adequately prepared place for the hearing. When that happens, any instruction goes over their heads, much like it does with the children. If one knows nothing about modern artists, say, then reading a book comparing several will not be meaningful because a place has not yet been prepared. But if one has studied each of these artists in depth, the comparison could be meaningful. If a philosopher seems obscure, it may not be that the work is poorly written but that the reader has not yet established background hooks on which to hang the material being read. That is, the problem may be that the reader has not prepared a place for understanding the book.

Unless the reader has a place prepared for the new information, that information is likely to seem nonsensical, no matter how well written it appears to the people more prepared for it. Compare the teaching that exploits the background knowledge students bring to their education, building new ideas from old, with teaching that packages all lessons the same and tailors them to performance on a standardized test.

HOW DO TEACHERS PREPARE A PLACE?

Which brings us to another pedagogical question. Not only does the postmodern teacher learn to exploit the teaching opportunities afforded by the student's background training, but also to prepare a place for new knowledge. The question is, How can teachers help students prepare a place that will help them make sense of what they are about to study?

The initial preparation is, according to Wittgenstein, through a certain kind of training he called "primitive language games." Teachers teach primitive language games whenever they teach a child who has little or no background for a subject, and when teaching by explanation is completely useless. How can teachers do this? Or, perhaps the better question is, How is it possible to prepare a place for future learning?

One does it by engaging the student in primitive language games. "Puppy!" says a mother pointing to the dog outside the window, and before long, the child says "puppy!" too. Then, both mother and child laugh with delight. That is an example of what Wittgenstein called "a primitive language game." The child has no way of knowing what exactly the word means, whether it refers to a class of animals or to this single puppy. How would the child know? Or maybe the child thinks "puppy" means "brown" or perhaps that all animals are "puppies." Children do not need to understand what they say in order for such memory work to be preparing a place for more advanced learning. Primitive language games give little more than the most rudimentary kind of exercise and drill, mixed often with a little fun, yet they do not provide understanding. Nevertheless, their role is critical. Primitive memory work lays a foundation for richer understanding to come. Even children in postmodern classrooms need to learn their alphabet and that two plus two equals four.

Here is another kind of primitive language game: A two-year-old skins her knee and cries. Her mother says, "Oh, you've hurt your knee!" It's the child's first introduction to the concept of "hurt"—but what exactly do we imagine the child thinks the mother is referring to by the word *hurt*? Perhaps she is referring to the red stuff dripping down her leg, or the fact that her knee seems to have tiny pebbles stuck in it. In other words, the child does not have a place prepared for these distinctions. If she learns to say that something hurts at this point she is simply replacing "hurt behavior" (such as crying) with a phrase that she does not fully understand —because she does not yet have the language tools for understanding, a place has not yet been prepared for understanding.

Training in primitive language games, all done without in-depth understanding, it seems, is what prepares a place for more mature understandings, independent thought and reflection as well self-directed education.

THE BIGGER PICTURE OF LANGUAGE GAMES

Wittgenstein thought of all language as consisting of language games, subunits of the language, existing like little languages within the language as a whole. He never carved these little languages up into specific language games with enduring names. Instead he wrote saying, almost with a sweep of the hand, that all of language consists of countless language games, some emerging while others withered away. These rich but disorderly language games of older children and adults were all of particular interest to Wittgenstein. It was with these more mature games that people could talk about minds, or philosophize about the universe. Primitive language games were vital because they prepared a place for the more sophisticated games. The more sophisticated games, in their turn, made possible each human form of life. Is the cultural emphasis on religion? Then expect a predominance of prayer and sacred language rites. Is the emphasis on science, or commerce? Then look to these vocabularies and language games to be shaping the form of the culture.

How do primitive language games prepare a place for more sophisticated ones? It is all outside our immediate awareness, and it happens differently in different language areas. However, in many areas the elaboration of primitive games to create more sophisticated ones takes place through a kind of metaphorical extension of the vocabulary. It apparently works like this: The child learns the primitive games and then learns to borrow their meanings to say things that could not otherwise be said.

Imagine a child having learned a primitive language game with the word *sharp*. Picture the toddler copying a parent who is saying, "No, Tommy! That's sharp! Don't touch! Sharp!" Then, picture Tommy standing there with his mother, pointing a little finger at the blade, and staring at her as he says "sharp!" He is captivated by the new term, but he has, as yet, no real idea what *sharp* means. Still, he can read her frown, and make some sense of her hand pushing him away. A deeper understanding of the word *sharp* awaits further training or experience. Gradually, however, the necessary experience and training accumulates.

Finally, as an older child, Tommy might be taught to use the term *sharp* metaphorically. "Is the pain sharp?" the doctor of nine-year-old Tommy asks—but Tommy does not understand the question. Seeing a blank look on the child's face, the doctor explains, "You know, a sharp feeling, like when something sharp sticks you?" Tommy winces. He doesn't remember his original lesson in "sharpness" but he has acquired a number of unpleasant associations to the term. "Do you have a pain like that," the doctor continues, "or is it just uncomfortable like wearing clothes too tight?" Suddenly, a look of comprehension washes across Tommy's face. Tommy understands that a "sharp pain" is like the pain of being stuck by something sharp. The primitive language games of his past prepared a place for the growth of his understanding. The doctor's explanation would have gone over the head of a two-year-old Tommy. Can you imagine trying to explain what a sharp pain is without such a metaphor?

Wittgenstein's philosophy suggests that this kind of metaphorical extension of primitive language is a key means for humans to develop introspective language, philosophical language, and languages for observing nuance and aspect. These higher orders of language are rooted in the places prepared for them by a training in primitive language games.

And while we seldom notice, ordinary adult language contains many metaphors sprinkled through out. (Take the word *contains* and *sprinkled*, for example, in the last sentence.) Part of our sense of understanding things in more depth comes from seeing metaphoric connections that we cannot see without the mastery of the primitive language games. Sophisticated games build one on top of each other, creating lattices of improved and enriched understanding by connecting topics and exposing the wealth of their relationships, permitting us to talk much more meaningfully than we could otherwise do.

Postmodernity has much to learn and to offer in this challenge of enriching the advanced language games through more deliberate teaching. This brings us to the frontier of pedagogy for maturing students, paralogy. And, since we have already talked about paralogy, we are now at full circle.

THE PARALOGY OF POSTMODERN LANGUAGE GAMES

Paralogy is the concept discussed earlier in this chapter when talking about the way skeptical postmodern teachers discover each other in conversation. Paralogy is the kind of conversation they use that creates social bonding. Its parameters are still being discovered, except for the fact that the conversationalists are not reaching for universal metanarratives. They are discussing more specific situations and have tolerance for different points of view, considering ideas, not whole theories.

Paralogy helps postmodern teachers, but is not just for teachers. Teachers can learn to facilitate it in their student groups—once a place for doing paralogy has been prepared. Good seminar leaders, for example, know how to initiate paralogical discussion by seeding the discussion with interesting and meaningful remarks and questions. In such a discussion, new metaphors, new associations, based on a common set of primitive language games, can emerge to enrich everyone's understanding. This is done in part by inventing new language games, language games that the teacher could not have invented independently for the students, language games that grow out of the creative interaction of the students themselves while engaged in their own paralogy.

This is a very advanced form of instruction. Infants have much to learn before they can enter into paralogy. At the same time, the student who is not encouraged to engage in paralogy is infantalized by being taught only through the mastery of primitive language games. That is surely a stultifying form of education for most adolescents and adults, except, perhaps, in the very beginning of a subject being studied. Primitive language games can mesmerize the mature student into the false sense that everything has already been figured out, that there is nothing to do but commit the work of wise teachers to memory.

And, again, shattering that sense of an already understood universe, of course, is what post-modernism is about. It is about building a spaceship that permits the student to escape disinterest in the service of fashioning a future life even before the parameters of that life are known.

TERMS FOR READERS

Language Game —This is Wittgensein's term. In general, *language game* refers to a somewhat bounded rule-governed subsegment of ordinary language. For example, answering the question "How are you?" would differ depending whether the speaker was playing the greeting language game, or the language game of doctor and patient. The term *language game*, however, is used in several related senses. For example, a *primitive* language game is a training tool for the most elementary forms of language. Wittgenstein, however, felt that the whole of language consisted of countless language games, many being invented, and many passing away. Some of the most interesting language games are the ones that require prior training with primitive language games. The term *language game* is also sometimes used for the whole of language.

Meta-narrative—This is Lyotard's term. It means a story or narrative that is presumed to have great generality and represents a final and absolute truth. Lyotard's famous definition of postmodernism is, "Simplifying to the extreme, I define postmodern as incredulity toward metanarratives."

Paralogy—It is a stimulating conversation that generates ideas without necessarily resulting in consensus. These new ideas emerge, in large part, because paralogy encourages speakers to define the rules of language terms locally and provisionally. That is, in a local conversation a person might say, "I am using the word in this sense." Also, in paralogy, the speakers do not strive for consensus but value a diversity of opinion because the point is to create new ideas, and new ideas seem to emerge best when there are varied opinions being expressed and when the listeners are looking for inspiration rather than mastery of complete theories.

REFERENCES

Lyotard, J. F. (1984). *The Postmodern Condition: A Report on Knowledge.* Minneapolis: University of Minnesota Press.
Shawver, L. (2006). *Nostalgic Postmodernism: Postmodern Therapy,* Vol. 1. Oakland, CA: Paralogic Press.
Wittgenstein, L. (1953). *Philosophical Investigations.* New York: The Macmillan Co.